AHEAD _{OF}_{THE} GAME
How to Use Your Mind to Win in Sport

a practical guide for coaches,
athletes & players of all levels

Jeremy Lazarus

AHEAD OF THE GAME

How to Use Your Mind to Win in Sport

© Jeremy Lazarus 2006

Cover photo credits: **iStockPhoto: Grafissimo** (footballer/swimmer) **Jennifer Trenchard** (tennis player) **Dan Brandenburg** (runner)

Set in **Helvetica Neue** 11 on 13pt

Cover Design & Book Typesetting by
Martin Coote: Creative Designer martincoote@googlemail.com

Illustrations produced by
Sarah Patience, Saronyx Design www.saronyxdesign.co.uk

Indexing by
Phyllis Van Reenen pvr@indexology.fsnet.co.uk

First published in 2006 by;

Ecademy Press

6 Woodland Rise, Penryn,
Cornwall, UK TR10 8QD
www.ecademy-press.com

ISBN: 1-905823-09-6
9-781905-823093

Printed and Bound by;
Lightning Source in the UK and USA

Contents

Appendices

Acknowledgements

There are several people who I am indebted to. This is in no order of importance.

- My parents, for having taught me right from wrong, and everything else they did for me, (whether I appreciated it at the time or not!)
- My Uncle Roger, for the countless hours he spent with me as a boy teaching me how to play football and cricket
- A certain sports master at school (who will remain nameless) who told me I'd never be any good as a sportsman – fortunately I channelled the initial disappointment into motivation
- All the founders and subsequent developers of NLP
- The many people who have taught me NLP, especially (in alphabetical order) Shelle Rose Charvet, Robert Dilts, John Grinder, Tad James, Ian McDermott, Tony Robbins, David Shephard, Suzi Smith and Wyatt Woodsmall (apologies for any omissions)
- My students and clients, whose courage is an inspiration to me
- Lisa Wake, my friend and fellow traveller on life's journey, for her love, support and encouragement, and feedback on the book
- Karen Moxom, the courageous head of the Association of NLP and a true inspiration
- Gabriella Goddard, who planted the seeds of this book and encouraged me to write it
- JJ Smith, for his wisdom, knowledge and support
- Sally, Jo and Tom for reading through and commenting on the draft
- Those friends and colleagues who helped and encouraged me in a large or small way to write the book, especially Yvette, Lynda, Sanjay, Dave, Julie, Derian, Ros and Marcia

- Authors of the books referred to in this book
- Wyatt Woodsmall, for providing information about his involvement with the US Olympic Diving team
- Mindy Gibbins-Klein for her wisdom, encouragement and guidance in writing this book
- Andy and Martin Coote of Ecademy Press for their patience!

All references made in this book to 'Jeff Grout & Sarah Perrin, *Mind Games – Inspirational Lessons From The World's Biggest Sports Stars*, © Capstone Publishing Ltd, 2004' have been reproduced with permission of John Wiley & Sons Ltd on behalf of Capstone Publishing Ltd. I thank them for this permission.

All references made in this book to 'Romilla Ready and Kate Burton, *Neuro-linguistic Programming for Dummies*, © John Wiley & Sons, 2004' have been reproduced with permission of John Wiley & Sons Ltd. I thank them for this permission.

All references made in this book to 'Lew Hardy, Graham Jones and Daniel Gould, *Understanding Psychological Preparation for Sport*, © John Wiley & Sons, 1996' have been reproduced with permission of John Wiley & Sons Ltd. I thank them for this permission.

All references made in this book to 'David Hemery, Sporting Excellence. *What Makes a Champion?* CollinsWillow, 1991' have been reprinted by permission of HarperCollins Publisher Ltd © David Hemery 1991. I thank them for this permission.

Preface

Wow! What an honour it has been to be asked to write this opening extract for what is an exciting, thought provoking, and behaviour changing book. I have known Jeremy for only twelve months and within this period my knowledge, understanding, and ability to help athletes make performance changes has grown dramatically.

As a lecturer and researcher of Sport Psychology at Loughborough I have spent almost ten years understanding the impact of the mental side of sport on athletes' performance and as importantly their enjoyment. All of this knowledge and experience I have then used within my work as an Applied Sport Psychologist to both junior and senior elite sportsmen and women including a past National Skeet shooter and Commonwealth Silver medallist, U18 England Rugby Players, and Junior National tennis players. What I have found from my experience is that there is an exceptionally high knowledge within the sport psychology community of the impact of the mind on sport performance and the mental qualities need to be an elite performer, due to the enormous amount of research that has been undertaken. However, what I have always craved to read more about and better understand is the knowledge of the HOW to make the most difference at its most 'nitty gritty' – how do you improve an athlete's confidence who has just lost a match and has to compete again in five minutes? How does an athlete ensure they play well one day, and the same the next, and how can a coach help the athlete stay continually motivated?

Where sport psychology answers the 'Why', Neuro Linguistic Programming answers the 'How'. It allows a coach, sport scientist or sport psychologist to understand how the athlete thinks and how to help the athlete change the way they think, giving them the tools to achieve their aims and goals whether it is to win Gold at the Olympics or win their local squash league – and NLP enables them to make these changes quickly.

What Jeremy does on his training courses and achieves as effectively throughout this book is bring together his expert knowledge of NLP, his personal experiences over many years delivering coaching in business and sport, and his engaging personality, to explain the 'why' and the 'how to' of developing individuals and teams to reach their true potential.

Within the book, Jeremy simplifies the learnings of what at first glance are some complex areas through the activities that he presents, the tips that he supplies and the intriguing personal stories he provides as to how he has worked with athletes to enable them to make huge leaps in their performance - all of which allow the reader to extract the vital information presented quickly and effectively.

I urge anybody who is an athlete wishing to improve their sporting potential, or anybody working within the athlete set-up to read this book and challenge themselves to implement the learnings from it in all aspects of their lives. The implementation of the knowledge I personally gained from completing the NLP Practitioner course with Jeremy and the reading (and re-reading!) of this book has been invaluable whenever I work with an athlete or look to change my own behaviour. *Ahead of the Game – How to Use Your Mind to Win in Sport* is an essential handbook for sport psychologists, coaches and athletes alike.

JJ Smith
Applied Sport Psychologist
Lecturer and Researcher of Sport Psychology
NLP Practitioner

Introduction

Welcome to *Ahead of the Game – How to Use Your Mind to Win in Sport*. It has been written for mental skills coaches, sports coaches, athletes, sportsmen and sportswomen of all levels, whether seasoned professionals or enthusiastic amateurs, or somewhere in between.

The purpose of *Ahead of the Game* is to provide the 'how to' for many of the techniques and concepts that are written about in sports psychology books. Although there will be some theory, I am mindful of a message that one of my many tutors gave to me about books. He said that typically 80% of what is written in a book is written for the author's benefit, and only 20% is actually useful for any particular reader.

Now, whilst this may be somewhat harsh on most writers, I personally have found that many books I have read contain a significant amount of information which is not particularly useful to me, even if some aspects of the book and the topic overall is highly relevant to my needs. So even if we assume that the tutor was being harsh, it's probably not unrealistic to say that around 50% of any book is actually useful.

So to assist your learning and to save you valuable time, **I've omitted the other 50% that isn't useful to you!** *Ahead of the Game* will be full of practical tips on HOW to use your mind more effectively to gain more success in your sport, with diagrams and bullet point summaries. Theory and discussion will be kept to a bare minimum.

The basis of the approaches in this book comes from Neuro Linguistic Programming (NLP). The origins and foundations of NLP will be briefly considered in Chapter 3. Suffice it to say that NLP is commonly considered as 'the new science of success', a series of techniques and processes to help you to use the language of your mind (that's the 'Neuro Linguistic' element) to program yourself for success. At its core, a main aspect of what NLP is about is how to control your mind (and help others to do the same) and therefore influence the results you get.

And if you're in any doubt about the importance of controlling your mind and using it effectively before and during sports events, here are a few quotes for you to consider:

> *'For success, first performers must have talent, then they must work and third they must have control of their mind.'*[1]
> **Valeriy Borzov, Olympic 100m & 200m champion, 1972.**

> *'I think there are so many would-be clones, so many people who have tried to imitate her game. But they've imitated the most obvious thing about her, and that's her (baseline) game. And I don't think that's her strongest point, I think her mind is her strongest point.'*[2]
> **Virginia Wade, Wimbledon Singles Champion 1977...**

...speaking about Chris Evert, winner of at least one 'Grand Slam' tennis tournament for 13 consecutive years.

> *'The mental side of it played the biggest part; that was the difference between silver and gold.'*
> *'...for any athlete who stands on the starting line, as much as 70% of the race outcome is shaped by the mental aspects.'*[3]
> **Sally Gunnell OBE, Olympic 400m hurdles Champion 1992.**

The book will draw on material from sports psychology that is already in the public domain, plus NLP practical tools, together with the author's experience and that of his colleagues in this field of work.

The book will also mention several points which may seem obvious to the reader. There is, however, a difference between 'knowing what to do', and 'doing what you know'.

---

[1]David Hemery, *Sporting Excellence. What Makes a Champion?* CollinsWillow, 1991. p. 163
[2]http://chrisevert.net/CE-FromTheSideline.html
[3]Jeff Grout & Sarah Perrin, *Mind Games – Inspirational Lessons From The World's Biggest Sports Stars*, Capstone Publishing Ltd, 2004, p. 51 and p. 64

Some Terminology Explained

I intend to keep the jargon used in this book to a minimum, and to explain any jargon used. There are a few aspects which are best pointed out here to assist the reader.

Firstly, the term 'mental skills coach' will be used to refer to the person using the techniques referred to in *Ahead of the Game*, be they NLP Practitioners, Master Practitioners, Trainers or simply skilled coaches and 'sports coaches' using what they learn in this book and from other NLP sources. I could equally have chosen the terms 'performance coach' or 'sports performance coach', and you may sometimes see these terms used to describe the mental skills work dealt with in this book. The term 'sports coach' will be used to refer to what is traditionally known in sport as a coach, a trainer or manager. These people will tend to concentrate on the physical skills and tactical skills required in sport.

Secondly, within the NLP world there are three main levels of qualification – Practitioner, Master Practitioner and Trainer. In the academic world this is akin to Bachelors, Masters and Doctorate. Certified Trainers are authorised not just to work with individual clients, but also to train and certify Practitioners and Master Practitioners.

Generally, NLP Practitioners are trained to be able to use NLP techniques effectively with 'clients'. NLP Master Practitioners receive further training and learn additional techniques, and are expected to demonstrate greater flexibility and fluidity with NLP techniques. Trainers take this level of knowledge even further, not just able to do the techniques but also to teach them.

In the section headed 'Further Reference Material', there is some information about how to progress your studies should you choose to extend your NLP knowledge.

The third point is the use of the words *sportsman, sportswoman, sportspeople, player, athlete* and occasionally *client*. Essentially these words will be used interchangeably.

Fourthly, I will abbreviate the term 'personal best' to PB. This is a standard term used by athletes.

Finally, the book will make reference to both the masculine and the feminine, singular and plural interchangeably when referring to athletes and sportspeople.

Background to *Ahead of the Game*

Why another book on sports 'psychology'?

The moment in Spring 2006 when the Sports Science lecturer said to me that what is lacking in the world of Sports Science and Sports Psychology is the 'How To', and that NLP provides this 'How To' to complement the 'What' (i.e. the large amounts of data and information) in traditional Sports Psychology, I could hear this book calling out to me to be written. The lecturer works at a prestigious university and was one of my students on a Fast-Track NLP Practitioner Certification training. He could see the potential for NLP to be incorporated into lectures to provide students with the practical means to support or coach athletes and sportspeople. I could see how the material in this book would hugely benefit players and coaches alike.

It all fell into place.

I had quit the world of finance in 1999, having had what some would say is a very successful career, including having been a management consultant at Ernst & Young, Treasury Manager and then Group Chief Accountant at Unigate PLC and finally Finance Director of YO! Sushi, the restaurant chain founded by famous entrepreneur Simon Woodroffe.

And yet something was missing. Having attended various personal development courses, I realised that a key driver for me was 'making a difference', and I felt unfulfilled as an accountant. At YO! Sushi, I spent much of my time as, in effect, part-time Human Resources Director, dealing with the consequences for staff of being in a rapidly expanding and high paced business, and although I initially wished I wasn't spending so much time on HR issues, I found dealing with people far more enjoyable than dealing with numbers – and I love numbers!

To cut a long story short, I quit as Finance Director to set up my own coaching business, and started studying NLP, initially as a way to improve my coaching results and skills. In 2000 I decided to study to become a Certified Trainer of NLP, in order to be able to train others to do what I do, so that they could make a difference to their clients.

Since then, I have been training and coaching people to improve their results using NLP, and this has mainly been in a business context. Some of my clients had achieved some quite remarkable business and personal results, which was no surprise given the proven effectiveness of NLP and the fact that I have had some superb teachers.

What I failed to notice was that some of my clients and students had also achieved excellent results in a sports context. This lack of focus on the sports results my clients achieved was surprising given how keen I am on sport, having played football semi-professionally, and been reasonably accomplished at cricket and tennis. These students and clients varied in the level of their sports ability from the 'park player' who beat his brother at tennis for the very first time having attended just an NLP evening taster session, to a tri-athlete who came in the top ten out of 650 in an international event and top three in a field of 250.

I remembered seeing Will Carling, the former England Rugby captain, walk into the offices at Ernst & Young for a meeting with the Partners about, as the rumour went, how he could provide management training based on the principles learned in his sporting days. (I also remember the drooling faces of the women in the office when he walked in, but that's a different story!) I had read about and heard people like Sir John Whitmore, the motor-racing champion, talk about him using a similar approach to business and sports coaching, not to mention a conversation in 2005 with the lecturer above referring to several of his lecturer colleagues also being business performance coaches.

It became clear to me: the same principles that I had been applying to my business coaching, heavily based on NLP, could be used in a sporting context. I started concentrating my coaching efforts on athletes and sports people, with some very interesting results, which

I will refer to later in the book.

When Gabriella Goddard, my branding guru and published author, mentioned that at some point I should be writing a book, I put that into the 'yeah, some day, one day' box. Yet the seed had been planted, and the lecturer unwittingly poured water and fertilized the soil in one conversation.

During my research for this book, I have read several books on 'sports psychology'. Several themes recur, and I will refer to these, plus add a few of my own, in order to provide practical, hands-on skills that all coaches and sportspeople can use immediately.

I'd like to say a few words about the term 'sports psychology'. I sometimes use this term to explain what I do, not because I agree with it – in fact what I do is not about psychology. I refer to it sometimes in the book because it is a term most people in this sports industry are familiar with, and it distinguishes the 'mental skills' work we do from the traditional sports coaching work such as how to grip a tennis racquet, or how to improve your VO2 max.

A key distinction between a traditional sports coach and a sports psychologist/mental skills coach is that a sports coach is an expert in the sport and passes on his or her knowledge, acting like a mentor, whereas a mental skills coach believes that the answers are normally inside the athlete or player and the mental skills coach's role is to draw out the resources the athlete already has. A good mental skills coach will bear in mind the old oriental proverb:

> *"if you give a man a fish you feed him for a day; if you teach a man to fish, you feed him for a lifetime".*

So by teaching a player or athlete to come up with their own answers, the mental skills coach will create a resource in the athlete that they can use whenever they wish to. Therefore a true 'mental skills coach' does not need to have more than a relatively superficial knowledge of the sport of the player being coached. Please note that an individual can have the dual roles of traditional sports coach and mental skills coach, although they will be doing both roles at different times, ideally slipping seamlessly between the two.

In the work that I and other NLP Practitioners, Master Practitioners and Trainers do, there is little or no analysis, and as little theory as possible. NLP is simply the study and practice of what works excellently. Often the founders and other early developers of NLP, arguably some of the finest minds around, almost take delight in the fact that they cannot explain why a particular technique works. They just know from the results they get that it does work. And the question they ask, and the question I put to you, the reader, is 'are you more interested in what works or the theory as to why it does work?' As a former accountant and now a business and mental skills coach, my main interest is RESULTS! If you're more interested in the theory than improving your results and/or those of your sports 'clients', I suggest you stop reading this book right now and pass it to someone more results focused!

If you are interested in improving results, you're in the right place!

The Structure Of This Book

The book is separated into four parts:

Part I provides an essential background to the work we will cover in subsequent parts. There is some theory in Part I, but only the minimum required to provide a foundation for the rest of the book.

Part II considers what stops you or other athletes from achieving the desired results and standard of performance.

Part III is the bulk of the book, and considers how to deal with the challenges identified in Part II.

Parts I to III are suitable for players, sports coaches and mental skills coaches.

Part IV covers some more advanced coaching tools and information, and is written particularly for mental skills coaches and sports coaches wanting to learn skills to enable them to do mental skills coaching. It will also be interesting and useful for players, and the Introduction to Part IV will point players and athletes to sections which they may want to look at.

Each of the four parts have their own brief introduction.

Each chapter has some exercises, tips and examples of how the techniques have been used with actual sportspeople. It is recommended that you as the reader do the exercises that are relevant to you.

By the very nature of this topic, some of the techniques will be explained in some detail to enable mental skills coaches, sports coaches and players alike to be able to know how to do the techniques. Wherever appropriate, the detailed techniques have been put in the Appendices for ease of reference and to avoid impacting on the flow of the book.

How To Get The Most From *Ahead of the Game*

As mentioned earlier, *Ahead of the Game* is very much a 'how to' book. There are numerous exercises, and in order to assist you in developing the skill to use the techniques effectively the processes are explained step by step. It may be useful, and even necessary, to re-read some of the processes, or refer to them whilst doing the exercises, in order to develop the necessary competence that you are striving for (the more complex or involved processes and techniques have been put into the Appendices). When I was learning NLP, I found that every time I read through and then practiced a particular process, the better I was able to do it. As a sportsperson, you will already be familiar with the benefits of practice.

I would recommend that you do as many of the exercises as possible, especially those which may initially seem difficult to you but which if you are honest with yourself would benefit you or your athletes. You may want to re-visit sections of this book every few months to refresh your memory – I guarantee you every time you refer to the book you will learn something new because your base knowledge will have increased and therefore you will be reading it through 'new eyes'.

Certain elements of the book are phrased as if the reader were a mental skills coach or sports coach, for example certain exercises are written to assist a coach in taking an athlete through the exercise, and others as if the reader were an athlete. Clearly, it will be useful to you as the reader to interpret and apply what you read to fit your own circumstances.

To assist you in working through this book, there is a glossary with an explanation of the main terminology used in this book

A Quick Word of Caution

NLP coaching techniques are potentially powerful tools. They are not to be abused or misused. Also, they are not a substitute for therapy. If someone needs therapy or counselling, refer them to a therapist or counsellor!

And Finally...

I hope that you enjoy reading the book and using the techniques as much as I have enjoyed learning and using the skills.

Part I

The Building Blocks

This Part provides essential background to NLP-related mental skills coaching for sport.

Chapter 1 considers the concept of communication and covers the key elements of how we communicate (and mis-communicate!). It is hard to imagine any coaching or sporting pursuit taking place without communication, even if the communication is with oneself!

Chapter 2 considers the concept of our 'mind', with particular emphasis on our 'unconscious mind' and how it can work effectively with the 'conscious mind'. Increasingly it is recognised that the unconscious mind provides a powerful and, in the main, untapped source of success potential.

Chapter 3 considers the 'Mindset for Success', the beliefs and attitudes that are commonly found in people who are successful in sport and other walks of life.

Chapter 4 considers the essential skill of goal-setting.

Chapter 1

A Communication Model

Have you ever wondered why people perceive things differently? Why is it that two people can see the same film and have different views, thoughts and feelings about it, or that two 'neutral' football fans will have different opinions about a match? Why is it that two golfers will respond differently to a delay caused by the weather? Why is it that a couple will walk down a road, one will notice and talk about the cars and the other will notice and talk about the clothes people are wearing?

Many of these questions can be answered by the model of communication used in NLP (a brief explanation of NLP was given in the Introduction. The background and principles of NLP will be explored more fully in Chapter 3). It is important to stress that this is just that, a model, not THE model, nor a statement of truth. Diagram 1.1 shows the model.

Overview

For each external event 'information stimuli' happen, which we perceive through our five senses: sight (visual), hearing (auditory), feel (kinaesthetic), smell (olfactory) and taste (gustatory). In NLP these senses are referred to as 'representational systems', in other words how we represent the external world internally.

These 'stimuli' are then filtered internally to produce an 'internal representation' or mental image of what we *think* we have perceived through our representational systems.

Depending on whether the mental image is a pleasant one or otherwise, it will impact on our 'state', in other words how we are feeling emotionally (for example, happy, sad, excited, nervous).

Depending on whether we are in a good state or not, that will be reflected in our 'physiology', such as our posture and breathing.

Mental images/internal representations, state and physiology are inter-related. For example, we can decide to change our physiology as a way to change our state and internal representations. It is not unknown for therapists to prescribe vigorous exercise for people who are depressed. And all sportspeople will know the highs and positivity they feel after a hard training session.

The reason internal representations, state and physiology are important is because they impact on our *behaviours*, and our behaviours impact on our RESULTS.

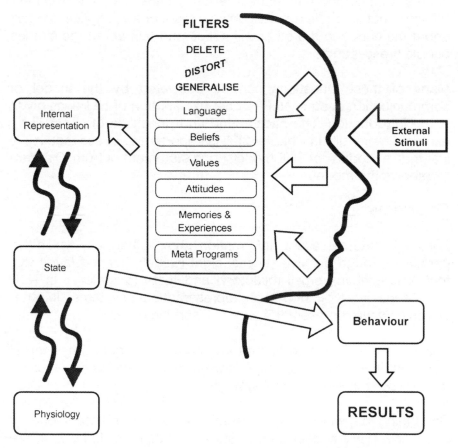

Diagram 1.1: NLP Communication Model

Let's now consider in more detail the key aspects, starting with the three main filters, namely 'deletion', 'distortion' and 'generalisation'. We will then consider some of the determinants of what we delete, distort and generalise.

Deletion

It has been estimated that there are something like two million bits of 'information stimuli' happening to us each second, and that we are only consciously aware of around 126 bits per second. That's a lot of deletion! Even if these numbers are exaggerated, I know you weren't aware of the feeling of your right foot in your shoe until you read this sentence, or of the texture of the pages against your fingers or of the sound of the traffic or people around you, or of the colour of the clothes you're wearing right now.

So we delete a huge amount of infomation (or should that be 'information'!).

Indeed, psychologists have asserted that if we were simultaneously aware of all of the information and stimuli that were happening we'd go insane. When you go into a crowded room, you delete some of the sounds so that you can tune in to the conversation you're having. Sports performers will normally endeavour to delete many of the sounds of the crowd, the antics of opponents and anything else which is not conducive to their own success. It is important to ensure, though, that you do not inadvertently delete the bits which are useful, for example the times when you have performed excellently!

If you're a sports coach, you may want to get curious about what your athletes are deleting, including perhaps some of the things you are saying when giving your team-talk.

According to a study in 1956 by George Miller, a professor of psychology at Princeton University,[4] people are able to handle between five and nine 'chunks' of information at a time before becoming overwhelmed. Miller states:

[4] The Magical Number Seven, Plus or Minus Two: Some Limits on our Capacity for Processing Information,(1956), *The Psychological Review*.
http://www.well.com/~smalin/miller.html

'....the span of absolute judgment and the span of immediate memory impose severe limitations on the amount of information that we are able to receive, process, and remember. By organizing the stimulus input simultaneously into several dimensions and successively into a sequence or chunks, we manage to break (or at least stretch) this informational bottleneck.'

(In plain English, Miller is saying that we can process and deal with a limited amount of information at any one time, and that we can increase this amount if we organise it into appropriate chunks or groupings of information.)

Thus it is important for coaches to be aware of how much information their athletes and players can handle. Giving too much information or detail, especially when the player or team is under stress (for example just before a match or at half-time, or when they are frustrated at not succeeding at a new skill) is probably counter-productive. I am reminded of the phrase used by my first NLP trainer - **'less is more'**.

Tip 1.1

It's probably better that coaches give two or three pieces of information that are fully acted on rather than ten pieces, no matter how valid, which are not acted on, or which serve only to confuse or overwhelm players and athletes.

Distortion

We all distrot (whoops, did it again, 'distort') information in our minds. As with deletions, this is not good or bad, it's just what we do. Examples of commonplace distortions are:

◆   when we shop for clothes, we mentally compare what we are seeing to what we have in our wardrobe to see if it will match.

◆   when we look to buy a property, we imagine the rooms being decorated in a certain way.

- sports players visualising their desired performance before an event, or coaches planning a particular move or tactic.

- thinking that the doorbell or phone has rung when we're in the shower, even though it has not, or that the cricket batsman has 'nicked' the ball when in fact it touched his batting pads.

- imagining that a sports coach doesn't like us just because they didn't say 'hello', or that the referee is 'against us' because he does not give a decision the way we would like.

Distortions can be useful or un-useful. The question I suggest you ask yourself as a player is 'are your distortions useful?' For example,

- Are you blowing the mistake you made last match out of all proportion, putting unnecessary additional pressure on yourself, or are you minimising the mistake so that it informs you yet does not adversely impact on your next performance or match?

- Are you building your opponents up to be something they are not, hence 'psyching yourself out', or are you 'cutting them down to size' in your mind?

- When taking a penalty in football or hockey, or a free shot in basketball, are you making the goal or the basket seem smaller than it is, or the goalkeeper bigger than she is? Conversely, are you making the goal or basket seem bigger, and the goalkeeper smaller?

Generalisations

A generalisation is when we take one piece of data or information and assume that other things within that category are the same or that the pattern will be repeated. Generalisations can be extremely useful when learning – for example if I learn the principles of how to add up 13 plus 24, I can generalise the principles to be able to add up 27 plus 35. If I can kick one football, I can kick another football.

Generalisations can also be either useful or un-useful. They are the basis of all 'isms' such as racism, sexism, ageism, where someone generalises (assumes) that because one or some people in a particular category of people behave in a certain way, all people in that category will do so.

In a sporting context, useful generalisations could be, for example:

- When I train hard I get excellent results in matches, and I have been training hard for this match/event/tournament so I am confident that I will perform at my best.
- Because I/we have won the last three matches against this team/opponent, I/we will win today (but watch for over-confidence!)

Generalisations which may be less than useful could be:

- I find it hard to play against left-handers, and my opponent today is a leftie so it's going to be tough today.
- I froze in my last big match and so I may well do so in today's big match.

You have probably noticed that many of the generalisations expressed above take the form of 'beliefs'. That's because beliefs are little more than generalisations, and the exercise in the following paragraph will give you a very clear experience of that. Beliefs are something that we will refer to at several points during this book, because they are *fundamental* to the results we get, whatever the context. There is also a chapter dedicated to how to change beliefs.

Here's an example of how beliefs are formed. Please do this exercise now.

Imagine that you've set your alarm clock for 7.00 am. You have a big day, say an important sports event or an interview for a coaching role. The alarm goes off, and you switch on the radio and hear the DJ say it's 7.40, and you realise that the batteries on your alarm clock are running low. You start rushing around and stub your foot on the bed-post, hobble to the wardrobe to find that your favourite shirt/blouse that you always wear for interviews has a stain on it. When you get to the kitchen to make the coffee you always have to set you up for the day you notice there is none left.

What do you believe about that day?

The chances are that you think 'it's going to be a bad day', or something similar. Some of you may think 'it can only get better', but generally the former will be the most common response. Now here's the important point – you formed this belief based on up to four selected pieces of information (some of you formed the belief much sooner than that!). You generalised this information and formed a belief.

While the example above is relatively 'harmless', the same principles apply to beliefs that are more damaging and pervasive, such as 'I don't deserve to be successful.' We are not always aware of our beliefs, particularly deep-seated ones – we just automatically operate as if they are true without questioning them. Does a fish believe it's in water? Probably not because it knows no different and takes it for granted!

Exercise 1.1

Make a list of at least three generalisations or beliefs that dis-empower you.

Make a list of beliefs you would like to have but don't yet have.

Make a list of the specific beliefs that dis-empower specific athletes you know or coach. (Make sure it's *their* beliefs, not *your* belief about them!)

So, to summarise, we all delete, distort and generalise the information that comes to us. Let's move on to consider the factors determining what we delete, distort and generalise.

Language

Language is fascinating. The words we use, both externally to other people and internally to ourselves (yes, we all talk to ourselves inside, apart from the reader who just shook his head in disagreement with this statement), can determine and even define our experience. There are examples of cultures that don't have words for certain activities (for example, stealing), and those activities do not exist in that culture.

So if we do not have words for a particular event or feeling, how can we express it? Does that event or feeling actually exist? I have trained several people in NLP who are either bilingual or very proficient in more than one language, and they all say that their world is different depending on which language they are talking.

I have a colleague who is an extremely experienced hypnotherapist, and who has some top sports people as clients. One of the ways in which he helps clients control pain is by using the following process:

Steps:
1. If someone (assume it is female for ease here) is experiencing pain, he asks her to rank it on a scale of 0-100, where 100 is very acute and 0 is no pain at all.
2. Then, he asks her to describe the pain using three words and notes the words.
3. He asks her to describe the pain, using a **different** three words.
4. Repeat step 3, with her not using the six words previously used.
5. Repeat step 3, with her not using the nine words previously used
6. He may repeat the steps once or twice more, and then he asks her to rank the pain on the scale 0-100. The pain level almost always decreases significantly.

The above process is an example of how the language we use not only determines our world, but defines our world.

Tip 1.2

If there is something that you are experiencing and wish you did not, for example 'boredom', banish that word from your vocabulary for a month and notice the difference that makes to you.

Beliefs

Beliefs can be defined in several ways, for example:

- ◆ our best current thinking
- ◆ those convictions we hold to be true

We all have beliefs. When other people have beliefs, especially when they differ from ours, we call them 'opinions', but when we believe something, we often call it 'fact' or 'truth'! Richard Bandler, one of the co-founders on NLP, comments that people are addicted to their beliefs. We only have to look at some of the problems caused by religious beliefs to notice evidence of this – people are willing to kill and die for their beliefs rather than consider the possibility that they may be mistaken.

The whole of Chapter 9 is devoted to beliefs and belief change. From the point of view of the NLP Communication Model and the filters, if we believe something is true, we will often filter out (i.e. delete, distort or generalise) information that contradicts it. You will have heard the saying 'I'll believe it when I see it'. Well, please consider that a more appropriate saying is 'I'll see it when I believe it'.

Let's take a simple example. If someone believes that they have a poor backhand, they will filter out (e.g. delete) any examples of when they did a good backhand, or possibly distort the information by saying 'It was lucky'. It's only when their belief begins to change, or at least they become open to dis-believing that they have a bad backhand, that they can start making useful mental images of themselves doing good backhands and becoming more confident and adopting the appropriate physiology i.e. – the aspects along the left-hand side of the Communication Model.

A more well-known and concrete example is that of Sir Roger Bannister and the four-minute mile. Medical experts 'knew' that it was medically unsafe for anyone to run a mile in less than four minutes (note they didn't 'believe' it, they KNEW it). Once the barrier had been broken, it was broken something like 30 times that year! People's beliefs had changed, leading to a change in their internal representations about the mile, the state and physiology they were in and hence a change in their behaviours and therefore RESULTS.

In summary, 'whether you believe you can or believe you can't, you're right'. In other words, our beliefs determine what can and cannot do.

Values

Values are what is important to us, or what we want or seek, in any particular context. For example, if one of our values in a sporting context is 'self-improvement', we will focus our energy on, ask for advice about, and get to grips with, self-improvement tasks. If one of our values in the context of relationships is 'fun', we will seek people and situations where we can have fun.

Generally, values have two main functions:

◆ they determine how we spend our time and direct our energies; we tend to do things which are important to us, and not do things which aren't important to us.

◆ they determine how we feel about what we have done afterwards. Most of us have probably done things which we regret because they 'go against the grain'.

You have probably realised from this that values are key elements of our motivation – we will generally be motivated to do the things that are important to us, and not motivated to do things which aren't important to us. As with beliefs, values and motivation are an essential topic and will be covered in more detail in a later chapter.

From the Communication Model perspective, if a piece of 'information stimuli' is important to us, we will probably pay attention to it; if it isn't, we probably will not. For example, as a former finance director of a restaurant chain, often when I go to restaurants I will notice the number of people in the restaurant (to make an estimate of whether they are making money – sad but true!). My friends will pay attention to different 'stimuli', for example the clothes people are wearing, the conversations on other tables or the feel of the restaurant, because *that* is what is important to *them*.

From a sporting perspective, it goes without saying that if the coach's words or ideas aren't in line with the players' values, they may switch off during the team talk and become de-motivated.

Attitude

From an NLP perspective, 'attitude' is merely a collection of beliefs and values around a particular topic. Stimuli will be filtered based on our attitude to the stimuli.

Memories and Experiences

Our memories and experiences will impact on how we filter information stimuli. If we have had a positive prior experience or memory from a previous situation that's similar to the one the coach or player is in, it is likely that we will have a positive mental image or internal representation; if we have a negative memory or past experience, then we'll possibly have some negativity about the match or sporting event.

If you are a coach, it is useful to be aware of the player's experiences relevant to the forthcoming competition, so that you can check out if there is any negativity of any kind and take appropriate action.

Meta Programs

This is NLP jargon for filters which in effect sit beyond, or underpin, other filters. For this reason we will refer to them as 'fundamental filters'. They are deeply embedded filters which operate irrespective of the content of what's happening. It is generally accepted in NLP that there are around 15-20 useful fundamental filters.

To illustrate, let me give you an example of one of the fundamental filters, known as the 'direction filter'. People can either be motivated 'towards' what they want or 'away from' what they don't want, or some combination of the two. This is sometimes known as the 'carrot or stick'. The direction filter will be expanded upon in the section on values and motivation, but for the purposes of illustrating fundamental filters all we need to cover is the following.

In any given context, let's say sport, some people will direct their energy towards what they want (presumably 'winning'), having one set of internal representations, whereas others will focus their energy on avoiding what they don't want (presumably 'losing' or 'not winning') and with a different set of internal representations, *regardless* of the specific content of the external situation.

Some other key fundamental filters will be covered in Chapter 15.

Conclusion

So given that we have all had different:

◆ experiences
◆ beliefs
◆ values
◆ attitudes
◆ fundamental filters profiles
◆ levels of proficiency in our own native tongue languages

is it any wonder that there is so much confusion and 'mis-communication' between people? Even between so-called expert communicators there will be mis-understandings and confusion. The lesson I would urge you to take is to be aware that what you think you have communicated may not be what the other person(s) have taken from your communication.

I have deliberately kept and used the term 'internal representation' rather than 'mental image' because the pictures, sounds and feelings that we have inside our head are also internal *re*-presentations of what we *think* we have seen/heard/felt externally. That is why we all notice different things. Normally when I run training courses, I ask attendees to complete a feedback sheet. They have all been subject to the same 'information stimuli' as each other, yet the feedback is always different from anyone else in the room. At its simplest, in a sports match each player in a team will take away different memories and 'truths' about the match. As a mental skills coach or sports coach, it might be useful for you to find out what each player has taken from the match.

On one of my NLP trainings a few years ago a senior police officer, having heard my explanation of the Communication Model, said that even eye-witness accounts given by independent police officers attending a crime (information stimuli) will differ to some degree; and these are people trained to observe! He went on to say that the only time he gets suspicious about eye-witness accounts are when they are identical!

Summary

- We all filter out externally generated information to provide ourselves with an 'internal representation', or rather an internal *re*-presentation of what we think we have experienced through our five senses.

- The key filter processes are deletion, distortion and generalisation, based on our language, beliefs, values, attitudes, memories and experiences and fundamental filters.

- Beliefs can be formed from a relatively small amount of information.

- Given that we all filter differently, it's useful for a sports coach to understand what internal representations his or her player has formed from a particular training session or competition, so that the coach can adjust their approach accordingly, and/ or enlist the help of any relevant specialists such as a mental skills coach.

Chapter 2
Your Mind

Now that we've covered some ground regarding communication in the last chapter, and given that you're probably reading this book to improve the way you and/or other people use their mind to enhance sporting results, it is important that we spend a little time explaining what we mean by the term 'mind'.

In essence, we can consider the mind as having two key aspects – the 'conscious mind' and the 'unconscious mind'. (Some people refer to the latter as the 'sub-conscious mind' or the 'other-than-conscious mind'). This chapter will consider:

◆   An overview of these two
◆   Why it is important to know a little about them
◆   Their main functions and purposes

Overview

Put simply, the conscious mind contains everything you are consciously aware of, and, for simplicity's sake, the unconscious mind contains everything else.

Clearly, within the unconscious mind there are different depths – so, for example, your telephone number is on the surface of the unconscious mind – you don't have to delve far to retrieve it, whereas, for example, all the memories you can't remember are deeper. As you will recall from the last chapter, we are aware 'consciously' of a relatively small amount of 'information stimuli', yet, as we will explain later in this chapter, the unconscious mind stores ALL of our memories.

Why Is This Important?

By having a greater understanding of the way the mind works, both as sportspeople and mental skills coaches, we can better understand how to get the most from ourselves and others, and how to overcome more easily the inevitable challenges that we face in sport.

Given that for many people the unconscious mind is a little-known concept, I will explain its main roles in a separate section later in this chapter. We will refer to this in later chapters since, as you will discover, one of the keys to improved performance is to utilise the powers of the unconscious mind.

Regarding the power of the unconscious mind, it is a commonly-quoted statistic that we only use between three to five percent of our brain power. The extent of the power of the unconscious mind is relatively unknown by the medical profession. Indeed, I had the privilege of training one of Britain's leading neurosurgeons on an NLP Practitioner course in 2002. When we were covering the segment on the mind, he stated that the medical profession is only scratching the surface in terms of what it knows about how the brain works and its full potential.

The Main Functions of the Two Minds

The key functions of the two minds is best described by the following analogy. Let's consider a ship with the captain and senior officers on deck and the crew down below. The captain's job is to think, analyse, plan and set directions. It is the job of the crew down below to make happen the captain's plans, directions and goals.

In this analogy, the *captain* is the *conscious mind,* planning, setting targets and goals and saying where he wants to go. The *crew* is the *unconscious mind*, whose job it is to follow instructions and make the captain's wishes happen by achieving the goals and targets.

To the extent that there is good communication between the captain and the crew, (i.e. the conscious and unconscious minds), then the journey will be relatively smooth, and any turbulence or challenges will be relatively easily overcome, and goals will be more likely to be achieved. If there is poor communication, then the journey will be rough and the target may not be reached.

Also, the more the crew is well-versed in its duties and has had the necessary training and practice, the better it will be able to execute its tasks efficiently and effectively.

So from a sporting point of view, the conscious mind does things such as:

- ◆ setting targets and goals
- ◆ planning tactics
- ◆ deciding what new skills to learn or existing skills to practice
- ◆ deciding which tactic to execute, for example which golf club to select, what type of cricket delivery to bowl, where to place a tennis serve

whereas the unconscious mind executes the plan. For example, a golfer would consciously decide which type of shot to do, based on factors such as the wind direction, the lie of the ball, where the bunkers are, where the hole is etc. Once she has (consciously) decided which shot to do and starts addressing the ball, the unconscious mind takes over. It co-ordinates the bodily movements, the micro-muscle movements etc. The golfer (assuming she has the necessary skill gained from practicing) would probably not think to herself 'make sure the grip is correct, remember to turn your shoulders at the right speed, keep your head still, etc. Performance will be better when the golfer just lets the unconscious mind do its job, just as the ship's crew would do better without the captain bellowing in their ear every single instruction needed to do its job!

If we consider other sports, where there is more interaction and interplay with the opponents such as football, rugby and cricket, it is highly unlikely that, for example, a batsman will consciously be able to act when the ball is being bowled at him at speeds approaching 100 mph. Nor is it likely that a goalkeeper's conscious mind will be involved in making a reflex save.

Let's look at the key roles of the unconscious mind.

The Unconscious Mind's Roles

There are several key roles of the unconscious mind. We will consider the ones that are relevant to sport and coaching here. Before you read this, please do the following exercise:

Exercise 2.1

Remember a time when you were playing sport and everything was just flowing naturally. The ball seemed to go just where you wanted it to, easily. Your body just flowed, and did the dive/jump/run just as you had dreamed. Step into your body, as if you were in that particular event. Notice the lack of 'internal dialogue', the absence of 'instructions' from your conscious mind, notice how you were just in the flow or the 'zone', re-producing what you had practiced.

Take a few moments to relive that event.

My guess is that you were aware of the lack of conscious mind interference. And the next time you perform excellently and effortlessly, when you review the event or match, notice how you just allowed your unconscious mind to do its job.

Please bear this exercise in mind as you read this section on the roles of the unconscious mind.

1. Runs The Body

The unconscious mind runs the body. Are you consciously breathing right now? When you slept last night, who breathed for you – did you do it consciously? Obviously not.

Therefore, given that it's the unconscious mind that runs the body, why not allow it to do so unimpeded? So, using the golfing analogy from the last section, once the conscious mind has done its job in choosing the club to use and the shot to do, LET THE UNCONSCIOUS MIND DO ITS JOB! Resist any temptation to interfere with, for example, the execution of the shots during competition (your unconscious mind will tell you whether your grip on the club is just right or not). The time to work on new techniques and improve specific aspects of the sport is during practice, not in the heat of the battle. Let your body flow! Obviously, if there are some tactical switches to be made during a competition, involving conscious thought processes, then do that.

2. Needs Repetition Until Habit Is Installed

That's why we practice! The unconscious mind, clever and powerful as it is, will struggle to perform a task that it has never practiced, compared to one with a similar level of difficulty that it has practiced. And the more we practice, the better and more automatically we are able to re-produce what we have practiced. Please note that does not mean that performance will improve. It is a common misconception that practice makes perfect.

Tip 2.1

Practice makes *Permanent*.
Only *Perfect Practice* makes *Perfect*.

So make sure you practice perfectly – ensure training is taken as seriously as the competition itself.

3. Enjoys Serving, and Need Clear Orders To Follow

Your unconscious mind is like a young brother or sister. It loves you, wants to please you, yet sometimes only has the ability to understand relatively simple communication. So when you are (consciously) asking your unconscious mind for something, for example to put the serve down the middle, or to kick the penalty into the bottom right hand corner, keep it simple! 'Fast down the middle' is easier for the unconscious mind to grasp than '104.75 miles per hours at angle of 12 degrees compared to my current position, taking into account the wind speed of two knots!'

The importance of keeping instructions simple will be expanded upon in Chapter 4 on Goals, and links to the next point.

4. Responds to Symbols and Symbolic Language

The unconscious mind responds better to its own language, which is one or more of the following:

- pictures
- sounds
- feelings
- smells
- tastes

rather than words, which is the language of the conscious mind. Using the examples from the previous section, once he has (consciously) chosen to hit the serve down the middle, if the tennis player:

- sees the ball in his mind's eye going fast down the middle, and/or
- hears inside their mind the sound the ball will make and/or
- gets the feeling inside of his body serving to make it go fast down the middle,

that will be far more useful in helping the player's unconscious mind do what is necessary to make it happen than if the player uses words and tells himself what he needs to do (bend the knees, throw the ball at a certain angle, take the racquet back etc), as you will have realised from the exercise at the start of this section.

So whether you're a coach or a player, from a motivational point of view,

- a suitable picture in your mind's eye or on your wall (for example, of the medal you want to win) and/or
- hearing the sounds of the crowd roar your name (or other sounds appropriate to your sport) and/or
- imagining the feeling of touching the trophy and even
- the tastes and smells of it happening

will be far more motivating to the unconscious mind of you or your players than just talking about it. We will be exploring this further in later sections.

5. The Domain of the Emotions, Beliefs and Values

Our beliefs, values and emotions are in the domain of the unconscious mind. Rather than explain this, let me give you two examples.

In 1982, an American lady called Angela Cavallo lifted a heavy car a few inches so that neighbours could replace the jack which had moved, leaving her teenage son trapped under the car. Once replaced, the car was lifted by the jack and the boy was pulled out from under the car.[5]

In 2005, the BBC website reported that Kyla Smith, a 23 year-old from Sunderland, lifted a car 20 times her own weight to allow a trapped friend to escape from a car accident.[6]

Essentially, in both cases the women were deeply emotional, and it was imperative to them that they lifted the car i.e. it was totally in line with their values. The power of the unconscious mind enabled the two ladies to access immense physical and psychological power.

So if we bring this back to a sporting context, by creating a situation where a player or a team is exceedingly motivated and much depends on their performance, sporting 'miracles' can happen. Mention was made of the impact of beliefs in the last chapter regarding the impact of Sir Roger Bannister breaking the four-minute mile.

6. Cannot Directly Process a Negative Statement or Command

I was in the gym during the period I was planning this book and I heard a well-meaning fitness instructor say to his client as she was straining every sinew 'don't think about how tired you are'. Let me ask you – how can you think about what you don't want to think about without thinking about it?! The lady in the gym had to think about how tired she was in order not to think about it!

This is a theme we will refer to several times during the book. Essentially, what you focus on increases, so if you think about how tired you are (just by not thinking about it you're thinking about it) you'll get more tired.

---

[5] http://www.nunatsiaq.com/archives/60217/news/nunavut/60217_03.html
[6] http://news.bbc.co.uk/1/hi/england/wear/4746665.stm

Tip 2.2

When talking and thinking about goals or tasks, say and think about what you want as opposed to what you don't want.

Summary of the Roles of The Unconscious Mind

1. Runs The Body
2. Needs Repetition Until Habit Is Installed
3. Enjoys Serving, and Need Clear Orders To Follow
4. Responds to Symbols and Symbolic Language
5. The Domain of the Emotions, Beliefs and Values
6. Cannot Directly Process a Negative Statement or Command

To sum up this section, here is a simple example which you will probably be able to relate to. If you want to drive from your home to a place where you frequently visit (sports club, gym, work, parents, friends), you probably normally find that you arrive at your destination without being able to remember in detail much, if any, of the journey. You simply did it on 'automatic pilot', in other words, you were doing it unconsciously. Your unconscious mind

- was running your body i.e. changing gears, looking in the mirror, steering, indicating, (not to mention breathing for you!)

- was probably only able to do it this way if you were an experienced driver and had driven that journey several times i.e. had generated the habits of driving and driving to that destination,

- had clear instructions to follow e.g. the gym, the tennis club,

- had a picture in mind of the destination i.e. a symbol. Please note that often we are not aware of the pictures we make in our minds because it happens so quickly – more of this in Part III,

- knew what you wanted and where you wanted to go, as opposed to lots of places you didn't want to go i.e. it was stated without negatives.

Summary

- The conscious mind's purpose is to think, plan and set goals.

- The unconscious mind's purpose is to achieve goals and serve the conscious mind, and it has several roles and methods of doing that.

- The unconscious mind is extremely powerful, and does things automatically out of our conscious awareness.

- Get out of your own way when playing competitively, in other words once you have learned a skill, just let your body and unconscious mind do what it does best i.e. let it flow!

- Train and practice as if it were the real thing – the way you practice will determine how you perform. Practice makes *permanent*. Only *perfect* practice makes perfect.

- Use mental imagery (pictures, sounds and feelings) to motivate and perform sporting tasks or manoeuvres. (Much more will be said about this in Chapter 10.

- Keep your language positive – say it how you want it to be, and focus on what you want because what you focus on increases.

Chapter 3

The Mindset

for Success in Sport

This chapter will cover the following topics:

◆ An Overview of NLP, including briefly its history
◆ Why NLP is so useful in a sports context
◆ How does NLP work?
◆ The 'pillars of NLP'
◆ The fundamental beliefs within NLP – 'The Mindset for Success.'

As with all endeavours in life, being successful in sport, at whichever level you are playing, requires some solid foundations, and this chapter contains essential beliefs and attitudes that are found in successful people generally, not just in sport.

An Overview of NLP

NLP, Neuro Linguistic Programming, is rapidly becoming seen as a set of tools and approaches of major benefit to people in all walks of life, including business, sales, management, health, education, coaching, therapy and just about any aspect of human endeavour where there is some form of communication (which covers just about everything!).

It was developed initially by John Grinder (a linguist and university lecturer at UCLA Santa Cruz) and Richard Bandler (one of Grinder's students and a computer programmer) in the mid 1970s, and since then there have been numerous people who have further developed the art and science of NLP. Essentially Grinder and Bandler wondered how it was that successful people became successful. What was the difference that made the difference? They modelled and studied carefully some leading communicators at the time, and developed a series of approaches and techniques which we now call NLP. Those techniques relevant to sport will be covered in this book.

The techniques developed by Grinder and Bandler, and many others subsequently, have been developed due to a willingness to experiment. And whilst the techniques here are tried and tested, there is no substitute for common sense and the ability of the mental skills coach to use his or her observational skills.

Because NLP is an art and a science, there are differing views about certain aspects of NLP within the NLP community. So if you hear or read about certain different points of view, I'd suggest you consider that your toolkit has been enriched so that you can use the technique(s) that seem most appropriate to the situation at the time.

Why Is NLP So Useful?

NLP was developed by modelling excellence and success, so those who now use NLP can benefit and help others to benefit from applying the mindset of successful people. Since the mid 1970s, NLP has been used to help people make rapid and lasting changes to their particular life circumstances, whether it's having more of what they want or less of what they don't want, or both.

Here are some examples of how it has been used. It has helped:

- ◆ business people become keen on making cold calls rather than dreading them
- ◆ people who were nervous about making presentations or attending interviews feel comfortable and resourceful
- ◆ people who are nervous before a sports event feel at their best
- ◆ phobics get rid of the phobia in around five-ten minutes
- ◆ children and adults improve their spelling

- ◆ people change disempowering beliefs
- ◆ people to dislike a particular food, drink or activity (e.g. chocolate, beer, procrastinating)
- ◆ people to like a particular food, drink or activity (e.g. salad, water, exercise)

Given NLP can assist people to make such radical, quick and lasting changes such as those above, the potential to use it to provide the extra resources to win the mental game of sport is immense. And for those readers who are sports coaches, being able to use these techniques as a coaching aid will inevitably enhance your ability to coach.

Moreover, NLP was developed by modelling the work of Milton Erickson, a famous hypnotherapist, and has some of its roots in hypnosis. Given:

- ◆ power of the unconscious mind
- ◆ hypnosis works with the unconscious mind
- ◆ the fact that NLP is based on hypnosis but without actually putting people into a deep trance

this means that the NLP techniques you will learn in this book are compatible with both conscious and unconscious processes, which will give you an edge whether you are playing or coaching.

OK, So How Does NLP Work?

Essentially, there are four key aspects that make NLP work.

First and foremost is the willingness of the 'client' i.e. the sports person, to use the techniques. The athlete has to want to make some changes or do things differently, otherwise the mental skills coach will probably experience the processes as hard work and there is a good chance that they will not be successful. Conversely, when the 'client' does want to make some changes, the NLP work tends to go smoothly and effectively.

Story 3.1

The most obvious case I have experienced of this was when working with a lady who was two days away from giving birth to her third child. The first two births had been extremely difficult, the labour lasting 12-14 hours each. The client was seriously motivated to have things be different in the future!

We used a particular technique, one which I am well-used to using. Having explained the process to her, once we actually started the process the client did the change work faster than I could get the words out of my mouth – and I can speak quickly!

At the end of the session, she was convinced the labour would last no more than six hours. The actual labour lasted less than four hours, with none of the negative side-effects from the previous two labours. Her husband, a leading medical doctor, told me that, given her history, this was most unlikely.

The second key element is the skill of the mental skills coach. If he or she builds sufficient trust and 'rapport' (see later this chapter), and knows how to guide the client/sportsperson through the technique(s), excellent results are likely.

The third element is the underlying beliefs within the NLP framework, the 'Mindset for Success'. These will be covered in more detail later in this chapter. Suffice it to say that the founders of NLP noticed that excellent performers held these beliefs, and that all competent NLP Practitioners, Master Practitioners and Trainers will adopt these beliefs when working with clients to enhance results. Therefore it is important for mental skills coaches to adopt these beliefs.

The final element is the techniques themselves. The numerous NLP techniques that have been developed since the mid 1970s have been proved time and again to be highly effective tools to assist clients' progress. And whilst they are tried and tested, it is essential to bear in mind the points made in the third paragraph of the section earlier in this chapter regarding having a willingness to experiment.

The Principles of Success

There are two aspects to the foundations upon which NLP is built. The first is known as 'the principles of success', and there are six points.

i. Know what you want (know your 'outcome')
ii. Be aware of what is happening and of your progress to get feedback
iii. Be flexible if what you are doing is not working as you would like
iv. Build and maintain 'rapport'
v. Operate from a physiology and psychology of excellence
vi. Take action!

Let's take each in turn.

i. Know What You Want

It is essential to know what you want before beginning any activity. The concept of outcomes and goals is a big one, and the whole of Chapter 4 is devoted to this topic. Suffice it to say at this juncture that a trait of successful people is that they know exactly what they want. I would urge everyone never to begin a task without firstly knowing what they want from it. This includes not just big aspects of the goal (for example, Olympic Champion, run a marathon in less than three hours) but also every single training session, particularly in events like golf, snooker, running, where most aspects of the sport are within your control.

Many of the talented semi-professional and top amateur athletes I have coached did not always set themselves training targets before I started coaching them. Their results always improved once they consistently set training targets.

ii. Be Aware, Take Feedback

Notice what results you're getting. Notice what works, and what doesn't work. Notice the impact on your body of, for example, certain types of training routines and certain foods. Notice the first signs of feeling stressed or pressured. Notice the subtle physiological shifts when you do your particular sport well, and if you do it not so well, for example the level of relaxation in your shoulders when you're serving at your best compared to when you're not serving well, or the feeling in your stomach as you approach the rugby conversion kick that goes between the posts compared to how it feels before you do an unsuccessful kick.

If you're aware of whether you are on track to get the results you want, you can respond accordingly.

iii. Be Flexible

It's simple. If what you're doing is not working, do something different! Remember one of the definitions of insanity – doing the same thing over and over again and expecting a different result!

So if you know what you want (step 1) and are aware enough to take the feedback (step 2), then step 3 is a natural progression. Knowing exactly what to do differently may not be evident, but at least the mental skills coach and/or athlete can direct their attention on finding something that could work, perhaps something that does work for someone else, or some other possible different approach. That's where being flexible comes in. Sometimes it's important to be very flexible, being willing to do something which may seem unusual.

Story 3.2

I was coaching a marathon runner who wanted to achieve the qualification time for the elite ladies championship start at Flora London Marathon, which would have meant her knocking two minutes off her PB. One of her concerns was that she had been unable to complete the 20 mile race that was considered 'essential' training by all marathon runners, and therefore would she have the stamina to complete the race in the necessary time.

We had about 45 minutes of the mental skills coaching session remaining (the final session before the race), and there were several things that I still wanted to cover. So I took a flyer. I asked her to visualise running the 20 miles race as if she was actually doing it, but speeding it up so that she could do it in her mind in five to ten minutes. (The whole of Chapter 10 is dedicated to visualisation). I was watching her as she did it, and she was clearly 'associating' into the event i.e. actually inside herself doing the event as opposed to watching herself doing it. This technique, plus the others we covered during the session, left her feeling as prepared as she could be given the circumstances.

She beat her PB by 10 minutes, and her 'dream race' by five minutes. Who knows how much of it was down to this particular visualisation. She did say however that before and during the race, she felt very calm and prepared, knowing that she had done all she could.

iv. Build and Maintain Rapport

Rapport is a term used in NLP to describe a feeling of mutual trust between two or more people. The deeper the rapport, the more people will unquestioningly follow instructions.

Rapport between a mental skills coach and player is essential. A relatively inexperienced mental skills coach who has built great rapport will almost certainly get better results as a mental skills coach than someone who has years of experience but poor rapport skills.

It is also useful in a team context. Where a team really 'bonds' i.e. builds great rapport, results are normally far superior than for a group of individuals who may be technically better but who haven't bonded.

Appendix 1 gives some information on how to build rapport with people. I would urge you to read this Appendix before using any of the techniques in Part III with other people. There are numerous books and NLP training courses which teach people advanced rapport skills. Please see the 'Further Reference' section at the end of this book.

v. Operate from a Physiology and Psychology of Excellence

Quite simply, think positive thoughts and use body movements and posture that are appropriate for someone seeking excellent results. Our mind and body are linked – you'll probably recognise this from the Communication Model discussed in Chapter 1, and will be explained further later in this chapter in the section on 'Presuppositions of NLP'.

The impact is best illustrated by an example. Tony Robbins, a leading exponent of NLP and world famous NLP coach, talked at one of his seminars about the coaching he gave Andre Agassi, the famous tennis player. In 1992 Agassi won Wimbledon, and was one of the leading players in the world. By the mid 1990s his ranking had slipped significantly, and he sought coaching from Robbins.

Robbins showed Agassi a video of his 1992 5-set victory over Goran Ivanisevic. Robbins drew Agassi's attention to when both players were walking out onto the court. Robbins asked him what he was thinking (noticing Agassi's purposeful stride onto the court). Agassi replied words to the effect of "I'm gonna whoop you, you don't stand a chance!"

Robbins showed Agassi a clip from a match in the mid 1990s, when the same two players played each other. Robbins noticed a different physiology shown by Agassi, and asked him what he was thinking at that point. Agassi replied with words to the effect of 'I'm remembering the last time he beat me and hoping it's not going to be that bad today!' One of the first pieces of coaching that Robbins gave Agassi was to change his posture, in other words adopt a physiology of excellence.

vi. Take Action!

I hesitate to state what seems to be obvious, yet often I am reminded when working with clients, be they sporting or in business, that there is a world of difference between:

- ◆ 'knowing what to do' and
- ◆ 'doing what you know'.

And although most sportsmen and sportswomen, especially top performers, are generally very motivated, there is always scope to improve one's effectiveness, and taking action to do the tasks which may be in some way unpleasant is essential.

Story 3.3

I was doing some business coaching with a man who had been a world champion marksman. He wanted to transfer his sporting success strategies into the work-place, so that he could fulfil his potential in that arena. One of his key success strategies as a sportsman was to:

◆ list each aspect of his sport

◆ rank his level of proficiency in each of the aspects (he drew a ladder in the air as he spoke of this)

◆ work on his least proficient until it became the most proficient, and then repeat the process continually so that he was always ratcheting up the level of performance

He knew what to do. But did he apply this principle in his career? No!

Guess what was the key piece of tasking I gave him. 'Apply the successful sports strategy to your career'.

NLP 'Presuppositions' – Key Underlying Beliefs

The second of the two aspects to the foundations upon which NLP is built are known as the 'NLP presuppositions'. These are not 'truths'. These are a series of convenient beliefs and assumptions which, when people assume and *act as if* they are true, help people to produce better results in whatever field of endeavour they are applied.

As I mentioned earlier in this chapter, there are different 'schools' of NLP, and some have a slightly different 'take' on these 'presuppositions'. I will list those and the interpretation which is most useful in the context of sport.

Please also note that these presuppositions are most useful when taken together, not just in isolation. And remember, apply common sense!

Summary of the Key NLP Presuppositions for Sport

1. Have respect for the other person's point of view.
2. The meaning and outcome of communication is in the response you get.
3. There is no failure, just feedback.
4. Flexibility rules, OK!
5. People have all the resources that they need to make the changes they want.
6. Behaviour is always useful.
7. Modelling excellence leads to improved performance.
8. The mind and body affect each other.
9. The 'map' is not the 'territory'.
10. Change can be quick, easy and lasting.

1. Have Respect for the other person's Point of View

Based on the information in Chapter 1 on the NLP Communication Model, it should be evident that we all have different views on situations. (NLPers will know the phrase 'view on situations' or 'point of view' as 'Model of The World', i.e. we each have our own 'model' of how life is, based on our own totally unique experiences.) In order to coach or create change effectively in a player, you do not have to believe what they believe. It is not your responsibility to change a player's point of view through an attempt to convince them of yours. However, by respecting their 'model of the world', you are more able to effect change rapidly.

I'm sure you will agree that if you feel that someone is respecting your point of view, even if they don't agree with it, you're more likely to want to co-operate with them than if you don't feel they respect it.

2. The meaning and outcome of communication is in the response you get

Conventional wisdom suggests that by clearly communicating our thoughts and feelings through words, that another person should understand our meaning.

However, they will respond to what *they* think you said, not what *you* think you've said (remember the Communication Model). You can determine how effectively you are communicating by the response you get from the person you are communicating with. In addition, when you accept this presupposition you are able to take 100% responsibility for all of your communication rather than adopt a blame approach.

So as a mental skills coach or a sports coach, if you ask a player to play a particular role in the team for tactical purposes and he does not do what you think you have requested, it is your responsibility to change the way you communicate to the player.

Similarly, if you are coaching someone on a new skill, if what they are doing is not what you have requested or demonstrated, that's due to your communication (apply this in conjunction with point 4 below).

3. There is no Failure, just Feedback

If a person does not succeed in something, this does not mean they have failed. They have not succeeded YET, and it could be useful for them to do something differently. They can vary their behaviour and find a different way of achieving their outcome.

Tip 3.1

If what you are doing isn't getting you the results that you want, do something different!

According to tennis legend Billie Jean King, *athletes should look at failure as feedback.*[7] Roger Black MBE, 400m champion at World and European Games, *'...spent much of his career thinking about what would happen if he didn't succeed. He finally worked out that there was no such thing as failure, and when he knew that, he really had the ability to perform under pressure'.*[8]

---

[7] http://www.dailycelebrations.com/failure.htm
[8] Jeff Grout & Sarah Perrin, *Mind Games*, Capstone Publishing Ltd, 2004, p. 73.

4. Flexibility Rules, OK!

The system (person) with the most flexibility (choices) of behaviour will have the most influence on the situation. What this means is that the more options you have in the techniques available to you as a mental skills coach, the more likely it is that you will be able to find an approach that works for your client or player. Similarly, the more options you have as an athlete or a team, the more likely it is that you will get the result you want. The ability of players and teams to adapt to weather conditions, the oppositions tactics, referees' decisions, the crowd atmosphere, the playing surface etc is essential.

As Richard Bandler says, if we have one option we are a robot, two options we have a dilemma, three or more options and we have choice.

If we extend this to communication, the more ways we have to communicate our ideas, the more likely we are to be able to alter a player's perceptions and actions.

5. People have all the resources that they need to make the changes they want

People themselves are not unresourceful. They are experiencing unresourceful states (as mentioned early in Chapter 1, our 'state' is how we are feeling emotionally at any given moment). When athletes change their state, they then have access to all the resources within them to accomplish far more than they can when they are feeling unresourceful states such as anxiety, fear, or overwhelming pressure.

Story 3.4

When I first started running NLP courses I taught 'board breaking' on my Fast-Track Certified NLP Practitioner course (I've subsequently moved this to my Fast-Track Certified NLP Master Practitioner course for logistical reasons). 'Board breaking' is where someone puts their hand through a solid piece of a certain type of wood measuring roughly 30 centimetres (12 inches) square and around 2½ centimetres/1 inch thick.

There is a certain technique required to do it, and when people follow the instructions and get into a positive mental state they can break the board, almost regardless of their size, age or strength. Indeed, I have seen it done by people over 70 years old, and by pregnant women, and by tiny women.

On one particular NLP course was a man who said to me before the course that he was really anxious about doing the board break. This man is well over 6 feet tall and solidly built. Moreover, he had done karate for many years, reaching brown belt, yet whenever he had previously attempted to do a board break he had been unsuccessful.

In the early part of the course I happened to ask him how he was feeling about the board break, and he said he felt really confident about it and knew he would do it. So in an anxious state, he could not do it, yet when he changed his state, he knew he would do it, and when the time came he broke the board easily.

6. Behaviour is always Useful

Stay with me on this one (yes, of course behaviour is useful). There are three key aspects to this presupposition.

People Are Doing the Best They Can

People are making the best choices they can given their 'point of view' or 'model of the world'. Now, I can hear you saying words to the effect of 'this is nonsense because people make ridiculous decisions and do inappropriate behaviours'. Yes, people may behave in ways which seem ridiculous to on-lookers and even to themselves in the cold light of day, yet if we can bear in mind that all behaviours have a positive intention for that person, it helps us to have compassion for people when they appear to be acting in ways that are annoying to others – they're just doing the best they know how. Please consider that their present behaviour is the best choice they believe is available, and has a positive intent for them. Why would anyone do anything that wasn't the best choice they believed they had available at the time?

It follows then that a person's behaviour is not who they are. Accept the person. Support and assist them to change their behaviour. Equally, if the person you are thinking about is yourself, you can be a bit more patient and understanding with this approach.

Positive Intention

Following on from the above points, all behaviours have a positive intention for the person doing the behaviour.

From the point of view of changing behaviours, if we find out the intention of that behaviour, and the intention of that intention and go to a sufficiently high level of abstraction, then we can ask 'so how else could you get <that intention>?', which helps the client provide more options for themselves to achieve the outcome they want. I find with all clients (yes, ALL clients) regardless of whether this is in the context of sport, business or others, that at some point they make choices because they are unaware of other options available to them. This approach helps overcome that.

Tip 3.2

Honour the intention, change the behaviour

Let's take an example – let's assume an amateur athlete wants to give up smoking because, in their words, "I want to improve my health and set a good example to my children."

Step 1 (See Diagram 3.1)
Find out the 'positive intention' of the behaviour and the positive intention of that, and get to an abstract level of intention ('to be myself' in the example shown in Diagram 3.1). You can do this by asking questions such as:

Diagram 3.1

◆ What's the purpose of <behaviour/ intention>? (note we do **not** ask 'Why do you smoke /want space?')

- ◆ What does <behaviour/intention> do for you?
- ◆ What does <behaviour/intention> get for you?
- ◆ For what purpose do you do/want <behaviour/intention>?

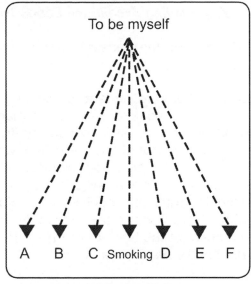

To be myself

A   B   C Smoking   D   E   F

Diagram 3.2

Step 2 (See Diagram 3.2) Then ask the athlete 'how else could you be more yourself, in a way that will improve your health and which will set a good example for your children?' Please note that the words used in the question are the same as those used by the athlete – we will cover the importance of using the athlete's own words several times in this book.

List the words in the suggestions that the athlete comes up with (shown as A-F in Diagram 3.2).

Step 3
Explore with the athlete which of these new options would be most appropriate for him, and what new actions he will actually take.

Pay Attention to Behaviour

Behaviour is the best quality information that people will give you. People may say one thing yet do another. Actions speak louder than words. So if a golfer says that he wants to improve his putting, yet does not spend much time practicing, the coach could complain, moan, cajole, shout or use whatever approaches a coach may traditionally use. An additional approach would be for the mental skills coach to get curious about the lack of practice, and to ask about the positive intention of not practicing putting.

7. Modelling Excellence Leads to Improved Performance

'Modelling' is the process used by Bandler and Grinder in developing NLP.

Clearly there are limits to someone's capability. But by modelling excellence, improvements can be made by taking the best from the best. As a mental skills coach, by finding sports people who do a particular aspect of sport excellently, modelling them and teaching others to do the behaviour, significant improvements in performance can be made. Dr Wyatt Woodsmall, a leading NLP Trainer, was among a small group of modellers who did this extremely successfully with the US Olympic diving team in the 1980's and 1990's to assist members of the team to win medals, including gold medals in the 1992 and 1996 Olympic Games.

8. The Mind and Body Affect Each Other

The mind and the body are one unit, interconnected. It is not possible to make a change in one without the other being affected. There are numerous examples, including from the worlds of medicine and sport, where changes in one's mental approach yield changes in physical results and vice versa. We have probably all heard of the term 'psychosomatic illness', (where illnesses are brought on by stress or other psychological factors) and the 'placebo effect' is well-documented. (A placebo is a neutral substance given to a patient under the pretence that they are receiving a proven or active drug. Often patients' health will improve because they believe the 'drug' will work.)

9. The 'Map' is not the 'Territory'

You will have already realised from the Communication Model that the words we use to describe an event or situation are not the event or the item they represent. They are simply the way we have filtered the information stimuli.

We create our own reality based on, amongst other things, our past experiences, beliefs and memories. One way of looking at NLP is that it is the art of changing our 'map' to create more choices.

From a coaching perspective, we can use this presupposition to help our athletes and players to consider things in a new way. So if someone loses badly, their initial response could be something like 'that was crap' (or some other similar technical term that sports people often use!). Unlike the sports coach, they may not have noticed some of the good aspects of their game that they can use as a platform for the future.

10. Change can be quick, easy and lasting

It's the build-up to change that may take a while or be difficult. The moment of changing a belief or attitude is rapid.

Of all the many NLP change techniques, probably the one which best highlights this presupposition is the 'fast phobia cure'. Even if people have debilitating phobias, providing it is not a symptom of a much deeper psychological issue the phobia is permanently gone in between five and ten minutes, and the actual moment of change takes seconds.

Exercise 3.1

Make a list of at least five sporting situations, plus some non-sporting ones if you would like, where you were 'successful' and got the results you wanted. Which of these 'presuppositions' were you operating from (even if you didn't realise it at the time)?

Make a list of at least five sporting situations, plus some non-sporting ones if you would like, where you did not operate as if these 'presuppositions' are true (even if you didn't realise it at the time). How were your results in these situations?

Notice how your results were better when you operated as if the 'presuppositions' were true.

Cause and Effect, Results and Reasons

The above can be usefully summed up by the concept of 'cause and effect'. In essence, we can either be 'at effect' of some 'cause' over which we have no control and which 'makes' us respond in some negative way, or we can be 'at cause'.

Being 'at effect' is not comfortable – we make excuses, have lots of really good 'reasons' for not getting the results we want in sport or life and generally don't get enough of what we want. When we are 'at cause', we take full responsibility for what happens in our life and the way we respond to it; we make no excuses, and tend to get better results than if we are 'at effect'.

Yes, maybe performances have been under our normal standards lately, maybe the referee has always seemed to favour our opponents, maybe the other team has more money to spend, maybe it is really windy. And? Who is in charge of our mind and how we respond to situations? WE ARE! As a mental skills coach, are you 'at cause?' Do you make excuses? And what about your players? Are they 'at cause?'

Clearly even with an 'at cause' attitude we may not always get the results we want in the short term. However, competitors who are 'at cause' will usually get better results over the long term than those who are 'at effect'.

Exercise 3.2

Make a list of the excuses that you use as a player. If you are a mental skills coach or a sports coach, make a list of the excuses you use and those that you hear others use.

The purpose of this exercise is for you to become acutely aware of when you and/or other people are making excuses, so that you can change what you are saying to yourself (if you are a player) and make appropriate 'comments' to players if you are a mental skills coach or a sports coach.

Summary

- ◆ Whether you are a player or a coach, operate from the principles of success.
- ◆ Always start with the goal in mind.
- ◆ Notice whether you're on track to get the results you want.
- ◆ Be flexible enough to change if you are not on track.
- ◆ Take action!
- ◆ Learn and operate from the NLP presuppositions – they work!
- ◆ Notice when you are 'at cause' and 'at effect'. Whenever you are 'at effect', ask yourself how you can move to being 'at cause'.

Chapter 4
Winning Goals

There are many compelling reasons to set goals, and even more reasons to set them appropriately. NLP has an approach to setting goals that will help you, your team or your athletes to achieve their goals. Some of the aspects of goal-setting are well-documented in 'sports psychology' books and dovetail with the NLP approach. However, there are some essential aspects which are fairly unique to NLP.

Why Set Goals Properly?

The three main reasons for setting goals are:

1. Sense of Direction

The key reason to set goals is simply this:
If you don't know exactly where you're going, how will you know whether you're on track or not, and whether you've arrived or not?

Remembering back to the principles for success in Chapter 3, if you

- ◆ know what you want, and
- ◆ are aware enough to know whether or not you're on track and
- ◆ are able to be flexible to make changes if you're not on track

then you have a far better chance of achieving your desired outcome. So having a clear goal or goals will help give you a sense of direction and avoid you going down the wrong approach for too long.

2. Focus our Energy and Attention

Having clear goals helps us to focus our energy and attention. There is an element within our brain called the 'reticular activating system' (RAS), '....which influence wakefulness, overall degree of arousal and consciousness'.[9] 'The RAS works like an antenna, noticing stimuli and alerting your brain to pay attention.'[10] As you'll remember from the Communication Model, we delete a lot of information, and the RAS is a significant part of the mind's mechanism to make that happen.

The key point about the RAS is that by having clear goals, and also focussing on what you want, your mind will unconsciously seek out 'resources' (people, articles in magazines, adverts etc) and opportunities to help you to achieve it. Have you ever noticed your eyes drawn to an advert or an article which just 'coincidentally' happened to contain just the information you wanted? Or you just 'happened' to overhear a conversation or a news item on the radio which helped you towards your goal? These things aren't coincidences – they are examples of your unconscious mind, through the mechanism of the RAS, helping you to achieve your goal.

3. Avoid Wasting Time and Effort on a 'Wrong' Goal

Just as a player's sense of motivation will rise if they have a goal or series of goals which are truly appropriate for them, by having a goal or series of goals which are not right for that person, they could spend many hours, weeks or even years, not to mention money and energy chasing after something they don't really want, or which for some other reason is not right for them.

Types Of Goals

Within the sporting world it is generally accepted that there are three types of goals:

♦   Outcome goals

---

[9] http://www.brainexplorer.org/brain_atlas/Brainatlas_index.shtml
[10] Romilla Ready and Kate Burton. *Neuro-linguistic Programming for Dummies*, John Wiley & Sons, 2004, p. 54.

- ◆ Performance goals
- ◆ Process goals

In NLP, we often use the terms 'goals' and 'outcomes' interchangeably.

Outcome goals are the 'big picture', the 'ultimate goal', for example, to win the Olympic Gold medal. With the best will in the world, to achieve such an outcome is something which is often outside our control. We could run the best race of our lives, yet if there is someone better, stronger, faster, then we may not achieve our goal, especially where the sport is non-contact such as athletics or golf. That's why we need performance goals.

Performance goals are, as the name suggests, goals which are about our performance, not the result, and these goals are normally within our control. A performance goal could, for example, be to run the 100 meters in 9.75 seconds. So, assuming an athlete has the talent, right training and the dedication, he could achieve that level of performance, which may or may not result in him winning the Olympic Gold. Performance goals are more under the control of the athlete than outcome goals. In order to achieve the performance goal of 9.75 seconds, he would need to have some 'process' goals to keep in mind.

Process goals are the more day-to-day goals that the athlete would need to work towards in order to be able to do the performance goal, and also the actual process required to perform the particular task or skill effectively. Examples of process goals could be:

- ◆ bench-press 50 kg 20 times per session, four sessions per week
- ◆ run 100 meters in less than 10.1 seconds five times in training at least three sessions per week
- ◆ run 50 meters in less than 5.5 seconds at least 10 times per week
- ◆ keep my hands out in front of me (when skiing)
- ◆ watch the ball all the way onto the racquet or bat (tennis, squash, cricket or baseball)

- ◆   lift off four feet from the hurdle and keep my lead leg straight as it goes over the hurdle

With sports such as golf or snooker, a process goal could be to hone a particular aspect of a putt or cue shot, so that the player can re-produce it at least, say, 28 times out of 30 in training.

I stress that these are examples – clearly the athlete and his sports coach (as opposed to mental skills coach) would need to agree on specific process goals.

One of the key reasons why it is important to have process goals is that, in the heat of the battle, by focussing on the process of the task at hand you can shut out external factors, and if the performance is not going as you would like you can focus on the specific aspects of the process (e.g. the aspect of the putt that you have been practicing).

Howard Wilkinson, the former technical director at the Football Association, is referred to as saying that

> *'aspiring champions need to concentrate on the process of their particular sport – their performance – rather than the outcome.'*

> *'There's still too much emphasis on outcome. More people can become winners if they focus on the process.'*[11]

Dr Stephanie Cook, Olympic Gold medallist in modern pentathlon, says:

> *'You have to focus on the process, not the result. If you focus on the process, the results take care of themselves.'*[12]

Exercise 4.1

Make a list of your sporting goals, with at least one outcome goal, and as many performance and process goals as are relevant to the achievement of that outcome.

We will come back to these goals later in this chapter.

I find with my clients when they first see me that, in general, they don't know how to set goals in a way that will give them the best chance of success. Fortunately, one of the pillars of NLP is setting goals and outcomes, and there is an extremely useful approach to goal setting, which we'll move onto next.

How To Set Goals

In NLP there is a concept of having a 'well-formed outcome' (WFO). Setting WFOs are extremely useful if an athlete wants to give herself the best chance of success. That is **not** to say that people **must** follow the principles that will be outlined in this chapter in order to succeed, only that when they do follow these principles they improve their chances of success.

Here are the main factors and considerations that make goals and outcomes 'well-formed'. You will probably have heard of SMART goals – Specific, Measurable, Achievable, Realistic and Timed. The factors and considerations below add some essential points to the tried and trusted SMART goal process.

1. Is the goal stated in the positive (towards what you want)?
2. Is the goal stated simply?
3. Is it stated specifically and measurably? Does it describe the evidence procedure that would let you know UNDENIABLY that you have achieved your desired outcome? At the very least, even if the goal does not describe it, would you know UNDENIABLY when it is achieved?
4. Is there a target date? Is it timed?
5. Is it self-initiated, self-maintained and within your control?
6. Is the context clearly defined?
7. Is it ecological and responsible for you and the people in your life? Is it in keeping with your sense of self, and worth the time, effort and energy?
8. Is there a purpose beyond the goal?
9. Is the goal achievable and realistic? Is there more than one way

---

[11] Jeff Grout & Sarah Perrin, *Mind Games – Inspirational Lessons From The World's Biggest Sports Stars*, Capstone Publishing Ltd, 2004, p. 304
[12] Ibid p. 305

to achieve the goal? Do you know the first step to achieve the goal?

10. Do you have the resources to achieve the goal, or do you know other people who have those resources and who either could help you or who you could 'model'?

11. Is the goal stated in the 'now'?

Let's take each briefly in turn. As we go through each point, I will give examples for the point being covered. At the end of this section, I will give examples of well-formed outcomes.

1. Stated in the Positive

You will recall from earlier chapters that:

- ◆ it is our unconscious mind that actually achieves the goals for us
- ◆ our unconscious mind cannot process a negative directly (don't think of a blue tree!)
- ◆ what we focus on increases

Therefore, if the goal is stated in the negative in some way, or with some comparatives, then to some degree or another we are thinking about what we don't want. How many fitness instructors have heard clients say 'I want to lose weight', or 'I want to be fitter'. 'Lose weight' is saying that the client doesn't want to be where they are without saying where they want to get to. 'Fitter' than what? Presumably where they are right now.

So, state the goal in the positive, for example 'to weigh 50 kilos', or 'to run 5 miles in less than 45 minutes'.

Tip 4.1

Say it how you want it to be!

2. State the Goal Simply

Remember that your unconscious mind is like a five year old in some respects. If the goal is stated in a complex way, the unconscious mind may get confused. State your goal simply.

'To run a mile in 4 minutes 10 seconds unless it's windy, in which case in 4 minutes 20 seconds, as long as it's not too windy or too hilly and as long as I'm feeling quite fit...........' **Too complicated!**

'To run a mile in less than 4 minutes 15 seconds.'

3. Specific, Measurable and Undeniable

The more specific and measurable you can make the goal, the more you will know whether or not you're on target, and when you've achieved it. Make it so specific and measurable that you can see, hear and feel (and possibly taste and smell) what is happening as you imagine yourself having achieved that very last step that will let you know UNDENIABLY that you have achieved your desired outcome.

Sports people may say things like 'I want to knock 5 seconds off my personal best this season.' My questions would be:

- ◆ 'What is the time you want to run/swim, and for what distance?'
- ◆ 'How will you know undeniably when you've achieved your goal? What will you be seeing, hearing, feeling, saying to yourself and possibly even tasting and smelling when you do it?'
- ◆ 'Is it possible that the event referred to in the previous bullet-point above could happen and you not achieve your outcome?'

I had been taught during my NLP studies of the importance of the last question, and it was demonstrated with a colleague of mine (not sports-related, but the principle still applies). He set a goal to do a training course in Hawaii on a specific date. In answer to the second question, he saw himself stepping out of an aeroplane into a hot sunny airport, with blue skies on that specific date. The final step

happened just as he imagined it, but it was in **Corfu**, not Hawaii
– his wife had booked a holiday for them!

4. Target Date

Some people let this one slip through the net. They either aren't
specific with a date, or they say things like 'within three months', or
on '25th June' (WHICH YEAR?!). **Be specific with the date** and if
necessary, the exact time of day.

Story 4.1

I ran a course in 2001, where attendees set some goals after
removing any limiting beliefs. One particular delegate set
a goal to swim a certain distance in a certain time by June.
He emailed me in 2003, saying that he achieved it just as he
expected, but that it happened in 2003 rather than 2002, and
he had ignored my strong advice to state the exact date when
writing his goal.

Story 4.2

A business client had set a goal to be the most profitable
company in their sector within five years. The problem for them
was that they had been trying to achieve that goal for three
years and were not very close to it.

The first thing I asked them to do was to set an actual date.
They made more progress in the following six months than in
the previous three years.

5. Self-Initiated and Self-Maintained

'My goal is for you to achieve your goals.' This is a laudable sentiment,
but it is not a goal. I cannot make you or anyone else do something.
Goals are best set for ourselves and our team, providing we all want
exactly the same thing (see later in this section). Can I initiate or

maintain you or others achieving your or their goals? Clearly not. I can only initiate and maintain the momentum for my goals, just as you can only do the same for yours.

This does not mean that there are no other people involved – often we need the help or support of others to achieve our goals. The key is to ensure that the goals are self-initiated and self-maintained, and in a team situation that the team all want exactly the same thing and can initiate and maintain the tasks themselves.

6. Clearly Defined Context

Being clear when, where, how and with whom we want something may help us to clarify our thinking around our goal, for example by helping us be aware of when we don't want something. Knowing that you want to be part of a winning team is different from knowing that you want to be part of a winning team in, say, London. Being aware of this will help you focus your attention on what you want and seek ways to find that team.

7. Ecological and Responsible

This will be covered more fully a little later this chapter. Suffice it to say at this point that is essential for goals to be:

- ◆ right for you in ALL aspects of your life
- ◆ right for those around you, or at least having no negative impact, so that people in your life will support you (and not sabotage you) in achieving the results you want
- ◆ in keeping with your sense of self
- ◆ worth the time, effort and energy inevitably required to achieve it.

8. A Purpose Beyond the Goal

John Grinder, one of the co-developers of NLP, says that, in his experience (which is quite considerable!), the single most important reason for people not achieving their desired goals is because they don't have a goal beyond the goal.

From an intuitive point of view, this makes sense, because if there is nothing to strive for beyond the goal, the goal could lose its meaning and, at an extreme, could become almost pointless. Therefore people could 'unconsciously' sabotage themselves to prevent them from getting to a dead-end, preferring the excitement of chasing a goal rather than the actual achievement with nothing afterwards.

Also, a goal becomes even more motivating if, by achieving it, other possibilities become available, or there is a new sense of direction. By being even more motivating, it becomes more likely that the goal will be achieved.

9. Achievable and Realistic

At first glance this seems obvious. Of course a goal must be achievable and realistic for it to be achieved!

Yet in sport, as in other walks of life, there are always exceptional feats and ground-breakers. Well-known ones in sport are the four-minute mile that doctors thought was impossible, and Bob Beamon's mammoth long jump in the 1968 Olympics in Mexico City. He beat the World Record by 21¾ inches when in the previous 33 years it had increased a mere 8½ inches. His World Record stood for almost 23 years.[13]

Ultimately, only the player and possibly the sports coach are the best judges of whether the goal is achievable and realistic. I have known of people in both a sports and business context who want to set goals but feel the goal is not achievable for them, yet they believe that someone similar to them could achieve it. This is an indication of a 'limiting belief' – we will cover some ways to address those beliefs which limit us and/or others in Chapter 9. It is worth sports coaches being aware of potential limiting beliefs that their athletes may hold – these beliefs are easier to change than you might think!

I would urge sportspeople to set goals which are challenging yet achievable. Research done has suggested that goals which are specific and difficult provide the best performance in sport.[14]

---

[13] http://www.infoplease.com/spot/mm-beamon.html
[14] Lew Hardy, Graham Jones and Daniel Gould, *Understanding Psychological Preparation for Sport*, John Wiley & Sons, 1996, p. 20

I would like to add two additional pointers under the 'achievable and realistic' banner. Firstly, is the first step specified? If not, it's a recipe for procrastination. As the ancient oriental proverb goes, 'A journey of a thousand miles begins with a single step.'

Secondly, is there more than one way to achieve the goal? If there is only one way, then should that way become impossible there are no options. From a sporting viewpoint, there will almost certainly be several ways to achieve a goal; there are numerous training routines, types of exercise and ways to improve skills.

Tip 4.2

If you are a coach and you do not believe that the goal is realistic and achievable for your athlete, you have three choices:

- have a discussion with the athlete

- change your beliefs

- resign!

It is inappropriate to coach someone towards a goal if you do not believe they can achieve it. The athlete will pick up on your beliefs, which could limit their ability to achieve their potential.

10. Resources

It is useful to consider what 'resources' and skills would be needed to achieve the goal, and the extent to which we have them or could get them. 'Resources' can be anything from specific tools of trade (for example, the right goalkeeping gloves, golf clubs or running shoes) through to more personal attributes such as confidence, focus or ability to relax.

Acting 'as if' you had the resources, particularly the personal resources, may assist you in actually performing in a way you would like to.

11. In The Now

Most people when they set goals say things like 'I want to be the champion....' Or 'I will be the champion .....' What champions tend to do is already see it as if it were actually happening, or had just happened. In other words, they are stating (or at least thinking about) the goal in the 'Now'.

By saying 'I want' when setting a goal, some people often find that they are just left wanting; by saying 'I will', the achievement of the goal is always somewhere out in the future, never actually realised! Stating it in the present or past tense means you actually get to experience it in the 'Now'.

Remember, **say it how you want it to be!**

Ecology and Goals

We touched on 'ecology' in point 7 earlier in the chapter. From an NLP perspective, 'ecology' is the study of consequences of our actions on others and ourselves. In order to ensure that we have a well-formed outcome and to give us the best chance of success, we need to fully consider the impact of achieving our goals. Here are some invaluable questions to assist you in doing this.

>   i. What will you gain if you achieve this goal?
>   ii. What will you lose if you achieve this goal?
>   iii. What will happen if you achieve it?
>   iv. What will happen if you don't achieve it?
>   v. What won't happen if you achieve it?
>   vi. What won't happen if you don't achieve it? (a brain-twister, but a very useful question)

I strongly recommend that you answer all six questions, and take into account the impact on:

- ◆ you personally
- ◆ other areas of your life, for example health, relationships, money
- ◆ other people in your life, particularly those close to you

Ideally, a goal is ecological if:

- there are ultimately no negative consequences of achieving the goal.

- any short-term negative consequences are more than compensated by positive ones. For example it may take time and money to achieve the goal in the short-term, but it's something you really want and will give you a great sense of achievement and hence it is worth the 'sacrifice'.

- the answers to all six questions i) to vi) above point to it being appropriate for you to achieve the goal.

If there are any negative consequences, these need to be considered and addressed **before** beginning the drive towards the goal. This will assist you in making the goal ecological. As an example, if in order to achieve the goal you will need to spend time away from your partner, it would be useful to discuss it with him or her so that you can agree mutually acceptable ways to 'compensate' the partner, such as going on a holiday that your partner wants to go on. It is extremely important that those close to you are supportive of you achieving the goal - having a sulking partner will not help you!

If the goals are not ecological for you, then it is possible that your 'unconscious mind' may 'gently' sabotage your (conscious) attempts to reach the goal, given that the 'unconscious mind' runs the body and that there is a mind-body link.

Examples of Well-Formed Goals

Here are some examples of well-formed goals for a tri-athlete. There is an outcome goal, some supporting performance goals and supporting process goals. It is assumed that

- the goal is ecological, achievable and realistic
- there is a purpose to the goal i.e. a goal beyond the goal
- the athlete would know undeniably when she had achieved the goal
- the athlete can initiate and maintain the goal herself, and that the other conditions for well-formed goals are met

Clearly the athlete would have to consider these four points immediately above for herself.

Please note that the dates in the goals below are notionally a long way in the future (the book was written in 2006).

◆ **Outcome goal** – 'It is the 30 September 2020 and I have won a medal in the triathlon in the World Amateur Games.'

◆ **Performance goal** - 'It is the 31 May 2020 and I have run a World Amateur Games length triathlon in less than two hours ten minutes.' (Let's say this is the qualifying time.)

◆ **Performance goal** – 'It is 31 July 2020 and I have run a World Amateur Games length triathlon in less than two hours eight minutes.' (Let's say that this is within 30 seconds of the personal best of the race favourite.)

◆ **Performance goal** – 'It is 31 August 2020 and this month I have run a 10 km race in less than 40 minutes.' (Let's assume that the running element of the triathlon is the athlete's perceived weakness, and that by running a 10 km race in this time will mean that the athlete has progressed significantly.)

◆ **Process goal** – 'It is 30 June 2020 and I have:

– bench-pressed 50 kg five times a session, four sessions a week for the past four weeks
– swum one mile each day in less than 25 minutes each day for the past four weeks
– cycled 100 miles each week for the past four weeks, including one session of 10 miles in less than 30 minutes each week
– cycled the final mile of each session in less than 2½ minutes in the past four weeks.'

With the Process goals, the athlete can set goals for specific technical processes, such as:

◆ ensuring they breathe every three swim strokes,
◆ just before the end of each swim and cycle practice they have mentally rehearsed a perfect transition to the next leg of the event. (Although there are three types of sport in a triathlon, tri-athletes consider that the two transitions are also very important aspects to a race and hence worthy of practice.)

Summary of the Questions To Ask When Setting Goals

Here are a series of questions which can act as a summary of how to set goals. Whenever you set a goal, ask yourself, or better still get your sports coach or mental skills coach to ask you, these questions:

1.   *Stated in the positive.*
     What specifically do you want?

2.   *Specify present situation.*
     Where are you now?

3.   *Specify outcome.*
     What will you see, hear, feel, etc., when you have it?

4.   *Specify evidence procedure.*
     How will you know when you have it?

5.   *Is it congruently desirable?*
     What will this outcome get for you or allow you to do?

6.   *Is it self-initiated and self-maintained?*
     Is it only for you?

7.   *Is it appropriately contextualised?*
     Where, when, how, and with whom do you want it?

8.   *What resources are needed?*
     What do you have now, and what do you need to get your outcome?
     ◆   Have you ever had or done this before?
     ◆   Do you know anyone who has?
     ◆   Can you act as if you have it?

9.   *Is it ecological?*
     ◆   For what purpose do you want this?
     ◆   What will you gain or lose if you have it?
     and
     ◆   What will happen if you get it?
     ◆   What won't happen if you get it?
     ◆   What will happen if you don't get it?
     ◆   What won't happen if you don't get it?

In NLP, these questions are known as the 'keys to an achievable outcome.'

Exercise 4.2

Re-visit the goals you set for the exercise at the start of this chapter. Consider them in light of what you have read in this chapter, and re-write them and/or re-set them as appropriate.

Summary

- Set goals – outcome, performance and process goals.
- Set goals using the principles outlined in this chapter, whether you are a player, a sports coach or a mental skills coach.
- Pay particular attention to whether the goal is ecological, and whether by achieving it you will have more choice, options and subsequent benefits just from achieving this one goal.

Part II
What Stops You?

Now we're beginning to get to the 'juicy' bits! We've covered the basics:

- how we communicate
- how our mind(s) work and the role of the unconscious mind
- the mindset for success
- how to set goals

In this Part we are moving on to what stops us from achieving our potential, from performing at the levels we are capable of. It is important to understand what it is that stops us from performing to our true potential so that we can address each of these issues, which we will do in Part III. For many sportspeople, operating at or near their true potential is extremely rewarding and one of the reasons why people participate. For others, winning is the key motivator, and they are more likely to win if the get to grips with what stops them from winning!

In essence, there can only be two types of factors which stop us:

1. Those relating to ourselves, or 'internal factors'.
2. Those relating to others or external causes, or 'external factors.'

When considering factors relating to others or external causes, in many cases those really are about ourselves anyway. Ultimately we choose how to react or respond to situations, and this will be highlighted during the next two chapters.

For the time being, let's stick to these two types of factors and deal with each in turn in the next two chapters. The topics of 'What Stops Us?' will be discussed only to the extent that it raises your awareness of these factors. The real 'juice' is in Part III, where you will discover numerous ways to deal with the points raised in the next two chapters.

Chapter 5
What Stops You?
Internal Factors

Before we get into the meat of this chapter, please do the following exercise.

Introductory Comments

Let's consider probably the four key factors which determine how well we perform in sport:

1. Our motivation
2. Our beliefs
3. Our ability
4. Our fear

Some people may want to add a fifth category, namely the ability to play well under pressure. From an NLP point of view, this is covered by beliefs and fears.

The quote mentioned in the Introduction from Valeriy Borzov sums this up. 'For success, first performers must have talent **(ability)** then they must work **(motivation)** and third they must have control of their mind **(managing their beliefs, fears and ability to perform under pressure).'**[15]

There is an extremely useful model from NLP which is helpful in putting these points into a context – it is shown in Diagram 5.1.

In sport, as in life, we get a set of results, which are dependent to some extent on

- ◆ the environment (for example, we probably perform better in conducive weather conditions than poor conditions)
- ◆ our behaviours
- ◆ our skills and abilities

However, we could have the skills, abilities and behaviours to perform effectively, and it could be the right time and place, yet if we don't BELIEVE we can do it, will we be able to 'activate' the behaviours, skills and abilities? Probably not.

And even if we believe we can do something, if it is not important to us (i.e. it doesn't fit with our values and are we not motivated to do it), will we do it? Again, probably not.

And even if all these factors point to us being able to get the results we want, if it does not fit with our sense of identity (which is simply one or more BELIEFS about ourself), will we do it? Again, probably not.

Diagram 5.1

---

[15] David Hemery, *Sporting Excellence - What Makes a Champion?* CollinsWillow, 1991. p.163

Therefore of the four factors mentioned above, our motivation, beliefs and abilities fall directly within this model. Fear, as we will discuss later in this chapter, is strongly linked to the three points just mentioned.

Let's take each of these four key factors in turn.

1. Motivation

I could devote a whole chapter or more to this topic alone. Much research has been done on motivation. I'll stick to the essential aspects here.

As you know from earlier chapters, our 'values', those things which are important to us, are keys to our motivation or lack of it. Tony Robbins, a leading NLP personality and coach, has said that if someone has enough reasons they will do anything! And if we remember the examples mentioned in Chapter 2 regarding the two incidents of ladies lifting a car to save people close to them, they certainly had motivation!

As well as being what is important to us, values also normally determine what we spend our time, effort and energy doing. So examples of sport values could be:

+ Winning
+ Improving
+ Being part of a team
+ Doing your best
+ Standing out from the crowd
+ Creativity
+ Hard work
+ Being the hero
+ Being the unsung hero
+ Fun
+ Challenge

Many times I coach and train people who, for some reason, say that they 'cannot' do something or don't have the 'willpower' to do it. If

I ask them, as I sometimes do, whether they would do it if the lives of someone they love would be adversely affected if they didn't do it and positively affected if they did, without exception people say that they would do it.

So for many people a key factor in their 'non-success' is a lack of motivation, or as we will see later, the wrong type of motivation. It is worth adding here the importance of having goals that are well-formed (see previous chapter), and which are in alignment with our values (in other words, achieving the goals will give us more of what is really important to us).

Is it possible to change one's level of motivation? YES! Some approaches are discussed in Chapter 15. (There are ways to make more profound changes to motivation which require training to at least NLP Practitioner level, and hence are outside the scope of this book.)

For the purposes of this chapter, I would like to distinguish two key types of motivation that all sports people at whatever level need to be aware of. These are 'towards' and 'away from' motivation, or as some people call it, carrot and stick motivation. We briefly touched on this in Chapter 1 in the 'meta program' section – this is called the 'motivation direction filter'.

Why Distinguish Between the Types of Motivation?

As a general rule of thumb, 'if it ain't broke don't fix it'. So if you are performing to absolutely the best you can, are getting the results you want and are happy with those results, just keep doing it! However, if you are not getting the results you want, or if your results are inconsistent, then looking at and possibly changing your motivation direction could help you to improve results.

What is 'Towards' and 'Away From'?

'Towards' motivation is where people are motivated to achieve something or fulfill a 'value' because of the things they will get, gain or benefit from when they have achieved it.

On the other hand, 'away from' motivation is where someone is motivated by the thought of avoiding NOT having it. A classic example in sport is that some people are motivated by winning because of all the things that winning will bring to them, whereas others are motivated by the desire not to lose and to avoid the negative consequences or feelings that losing brings.

Whilst neither is inherently good or bad, and most people will have some degree of both types of motivation, I and other people who do similar work to me often find is that where someone is not getting the results they want in a particular areas of life (for example sport) they have a significant amount of 'away from' motivation.

How Can 'Away From' Motivation Cause Sub-Optimal Results?

There are two main ways. Firstly, as we discussed earlier, what we focus on increases. So if the reason you want something is because you want to avoid the negative consequences of not having it, you'll be thinking about not having it, which paradoxically makes it more likely that you won't have it!

Secondly, if a sports person is primarily 'away from' motivated, once they have moved away from what they don't want, they can lose interest and motivation. Many fitness trainers have clients who do a 'yo-yo diet'? Many sports coaches find that players seem to lose that edge and get 'complacent'? This is best illustrated by a diagram.

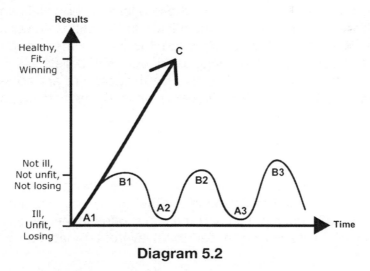

Diagram 5.2

At point A1 on Diagram 5.2, the person is really motivated. They are at a place where they don't want to be and not where they want to be. They are ill, and/or unfit and/or losing. If the person is 'away from' motivated, they will want to move away from where they are and will be extremely motivated.

However, once they get to point B1, they will lose motivation because they are not ill, not unfit, not losing. Consequently they may take their foot off the accelerator or generally ease up in training, which will probably lead to results deteriorating until they move toward point A2, at which point they begin to get really motivated again because they are where they don't want to be, and so the cycle continues.

On the other hand, if someone is 'towards' motivated, they will want to be fit, healthy and winning, AND STAY THAT WAY! So when they get to point B1, they keep going towards point C, and because once we have stayed at a particular point we get used to it, they redefine their level of fitness upwards and so enhance performance – they just get better and better, always looking to improve.

How Is 'Away From' Motivation Formed, and Can It be Changed?

The answer to the second question is simple – YES! 'Away from' motivation is formed generally by decisions we make and beliefs we form, often as children during or as a result of a negative event, without necessarily being aware of why we made those decisions. By using some NLP techniques, these decisions or beliefs and any negativity can be removed quite quickly. In Chapter 9 we will look at some ways change beliefs, although it is outside the scope of this book to discuss ways to change the deeply held beliefs which often form our 'away from' motivation. For this, players are advised to consult an NLP Master Practitioner or an NLP Certified Trainer.

Story 5.1 – 'Joan'

In 2005 I ran a training course which was attended by a lady called Joan who had attended another of my courses in 2002. At the 2002 course, she and the other participants dealt with many of the issues which lead to 'away from' motivation.

At the 2005 course, Joan announced to the whole group just what had happened to her in the previous three years (I had no idea what she was about to say). In her words, in 2002 her relationships with men had not been great, she hated her job and was unfit and not getting the sports results she wanted. By 2005, she was getting married in a month's time, was in a job she loved and from a sports point of view, did competitive tri-athlons and had recently come in the top 10 out of 650 in an international competition (winning her age group) and in the top three out of 250 in a major UK competition.

Joan stressed to the others on the course how her whole motivation had changed as a result of the work she did on the 2002 course, and hence it impacted on her results.

Exercise 5.2 – Values and Towards/Away From

In the context of your particular sport, write down what's important to you. You can do this as follows:

1. Ask yourself the question 'what's important to me in the context of sport / football / golf / my career (if you are a professional athlete)?' Make a full list, when you think you've come to the end ask yourself the question again! Often there are more answers than you think!

2. Think of a specific time when you were really motivated in that same context. What was it about that situation that really motivated you? Some of the answers will already be on the list. Add new points to the list. These are your 'values'.

3. Hierarchy/rank the list – do the top six values.

4. For each of the top six values, take each in turn and ask yourself 'why is that important to me?' Whatever the answer, ask yourself 'and why is that (i.e. the previous answer) important to me?' The purpose is to get a sense of whether your energy and attention for each value is more on what you want ('towards') or what you don't want ('away from'). Each value can be either 100% towards/0% away from, 0% towards/100% away from, or some combination of the two (e.g. 80/20 or 30/70).

5. Notice to what extent you are getting the results you
   want, and to what extent you are towards or away from
   motivated.

As a tip, it may be easier for someone else, for example your
sports coach or mental skills coach, to take you through the
exercise. Please make sure if someone guides you through
the exercise, that they

- follow the process above,
- write down your words and
- resist any temptation to suggest answers to you.

They should be getting YOUR values, not THEIRS!

Please Note: There is an additional aspect of eliciting values
that is covered in the section containing Exercise 15.3 in
Chapter 15.

2. Beliefs

You will remember from earlier chapters and earlier in this chapter the
importance of beliefs, and that beliefs are our best current thinking
around a particular topic. They tend to be generalisations, in other
words how we have generalised certain events and assumed they
are truths. There are a few points that are important to make at this
juncture.

Firstly, we have all heard of sports commentators and knowledgeable
'experts' saying that someone has lots of 'self-belief' or a strong
'self-belief', and that someone else lacks 'self-belief'. This is missing
the point. **We all have self-belief.** The question is, are the beliefs
we have about ourselves helpful to us?

Secondly, clearly in this book we are only interested in addressing
those beliefs which dis-empower people, so I will not dwell on
empowering beliefs.

Thirdly, even though the impact of a dis-empowering belief may
appear huge, often it is relatively simple to deal with. The NLP
approach is to look at HOW people do things, so HOW does someone

create and operate from a dis-empowering belief? Often we do not need to deal with the content or specifics of WHY someone believes what they do; we merely need to consider the structure of how someone believes what they believe. And the structure of a belief which has a big impact is normally the same as one which has a small impact. This will become clearer in the next part of this book, which deals with how to change whatever is not working, but for now let's consider an analogy.

In the early 1990s I was employed as a management consultant by a leading consultancy firm. One of the assignments I had was in the foreign exchange trading room of a bank in The City of London. The trading room was always a hive of activity, and the dealers were heavily reliant on their computers. Occasionally some or part of the computer system would crash, which caused chaos in the trading room. If it was related to the computer programs, the computer programmers and experts would sometimes need to go through the program code line by line, and normally it would be as trivial as a 'comma' instead of a 'full stop' in a particular sub-routine of a sub-routine.

In other words, the systems worked excellently except under a certain set of circumstances, at which times a relatively minor programming error would have a major impact on results. Given that experts liken our brain to a computer, this is a useful analogy, because often a sportsman's limiting belief only 'activates' under certain specific circumstances, such being under pressure in

- a penalty shoot-out
- crucial putt on the 18th green
- a tie break
- having to pot the black to win the snooker event
- needing to get double 20 to win the darts trophy etc

Many people assume that someone 'can't take the heat' and by implication will never be able to do so. But behind a sportsman's negative response to pressure (which is a behaviour) will be a belief, for example:

- 'people won't like me if I lose'

- ◆ 'I'm not good at coping with pressure'
- ◆ 'my coach will drop me if I lose/don't win'
- ◆ 'I'm a failure if I don't win'

Finding that belief and helping the athlete to change it will have a major impact on the athlete's results.

Categories of Beliefs

There are different ways to categorise beliefs. One way which I find particularly useful is to categorise them into beliefs about:

i.   ourselves as people

ii. our abilities

iii. external aspects, such as other people, events, results or 'life' generally

Regardless of which category, it is up to the person holding the limiting belief to deal with it, possibly by asking for assistance from someone such as a mental skills coach. Remember some of the NLP presuppositions – 'we are in charge of our mind and therefore our results', 'there is no failure, just feedback', to list just two; and remember also the concept of being 'at cause'.

i. Beliefs About Self

It has been said that we can't out-perform our own self-image. These are beliefs we have about ourselves as people or sportspeople, as opposed to what we believe about our abilities. Examples of the kinds of beliefs that fall into this category (remember we're only concerning ourselves with dis-empowering beliefs) are:

- ◆ I don't deserve/am not worthy to succeed
- ◆ I'm a bad/stupid/lazy (or similarly unhelpful adjective) person
- ◆ If I succeed then people won't like/love/want to know me
- ◆ If I fail then people won't like/love/want to know me
- ◆ I'm not a lucky person

With some people, we are not aware consciously that we have this belief – we just carry it around with us like a piece of excess luggage, and because we've carried it for so long we have forgotten that it's there! So we just assume something like 'that's the way I am', without questioning it.

Other people are aware of an 'inner voice' or 'inner critic', which just nags away at them with jibes such as:

- ♦ 'you're not good enough'
- ♦ 'you don't deserve to be here'
- ♦ 'you stupid idiot for missing that simple 20 foot putt'

We will get to grips with some ways to handle these types of beliefs in Chapter 9.

ii. Beliefs About Our Abilities

We will consider the concept of 'ability' later in this chapter. At this point, I'd like you to draw a distinction about your confidence and your competence. Ideally, these two should be broadly equal – if someone has significantly more **competence** than **confidence,** the chances are that they will not reach their potential unless they address their confidence level.

If someone has significantly more confidence than competence, then people consider them to be a 'jerk'!

So having a fairly realistic view of one's ability is probably a useful thing in the long term for any athlete, bearing in mind that ability and skills can normally be improved through practice.

iii. Beliefs About Others and External Factors.

We can have beliefs about other people and outside factors generally, such as:

- ♦ life's purely a game of chance
- ♦ the referee is against us/for the other team
- ♦ I never play well in these conditions
- ♦ the home crowd are worth a goal to the other team

Again, we will consider how to address beliefs such as these in Part III.

How to Spot Limiting Beliefs

Here are some tips to help you spot when you or someone else has a limiting belief. They fall into four key categories:

i.   Statements with negative connotations where people use the word 'feel' about something you can't actually 'feel'
ii. Negations
iii. Comparatives
iv. Others limiting thoughts

i. Things you can't feel – some people say things like 'I feel I have to worry', 'I feel I can't win'. These aren't feelings or emotions, these are beliefs.

ii. When people make statements describing something with a negation like 'I can't serve well today', 'I'm not clever', these are indications of limiting beliefs.

iii. When people compare themselves to something or someone, for example 'I'm not good enough', 'I won't be able to make enough money'.

iv. See Appendix 5 for a list of examples of limiting beliefs.

Please note that there is an important distinction between a limiting belief and a statement of fact. Limiting beliefs limit us in the future; statements of truth are valid for the past and present only. Here are some examples:

POSSIBLE TRUTH/FACT	LIMITING BELIEF
I don't have any money.	I can't make any money.
I am not a good athlete.	I cannot become a good athlete.
I don't have any qualifications.	I need qualifications to succeed.
I don't trust people.	People are not trustworthy.

Exercise 5.3

Make a list of five situations where, for some reason, you did not perform well when it mattered.

Have a guess as to what belief(s) you had which caused you to perform not to the best of your ability. We will return to this belief in Part III of the book.

Exercise 5.4 – Belief Assessment

(The purpose of this exercise is to assess the strength of a belief about a goal and provide insight as to next steps and what type of sports or coaching mental skills coaching may be required.)

1. Write down (or ask a player to do so if you are a sports coach or mental skills coach) a brief, one sentence description of the goal or outcome.

2. Rank your degree of belief in the outcome in relation to each of the statements on a scale of 1 to 5, with 1 being the lowest and 5 being the highest level of belief.

i) 'The goal is desirable and worth it.'

| 1 | 2 | 3 | 4 | 5 |

ii) 'It is possible to achieve the goal.'

| 1 | 2 | 3 | 4 | 5 |

iii) 'What has to be done to achieve the goal is appropriate and ecological.'

| 1 | 2 | 3 | 4 | 5 |

iv) 'I have the capabilities needed to achieve the goal.'

| 1 | 2 | 3 | 4 | 5 |

v) 'I have the responsibility to achieve the goal.'

| 1 | 2 | 3 | 4 | 5 |

vi) 'I deserve to achieve the goal.'

| 1 | 2 | 3 | 4 | 5 |

The scores from Exercise 5.4 will highlight areas where further mental skills coaching may be required. For example, if the score for question ii) (possible to achieve) is 2 or 3 out of 5, perhaps the goal may need to be amended slightly, or there may be a belief which the player has that needs to change.

3. Our Ability

It almost goes without saying that ability is a pre-requisite for success in sport. No amount of mental skills coaching will be able to turn someone who has very limited basic natural ability (and/or who has not put in the required effort and training) into a good player. However, there are a couple of basic points to keep in mind.

Firstly, especially for amateur players or players of a low professional standard, please be realistic about the level of ability you have in respect to your sporting ambitions. Whilst I absolutely believe that it is possible for people to improve and reach targets and standards that seemed unattainable to them, there are certain aspects of reality which dictate how far someone can progress within sport. For example, it is very unlikely (not impossible, just very unlikely) that a 5' 8" man will play in goal for the England football team, when most professional goalkeepers are between 6' and 6' 4".

This is not to say that we can't reach our maximum potential and get a huge amount of satisfaction and personal development through our chosen sport, or coach others to do the same. We just need to bear in mind that ability counts.

Secondly, put simply, good practice and training will improve our ability.

4. Our Fear

One of the major aspects of people not fulfilling their potential is 'fear'. People can be scared of many things, such as:

i.   Fear of success/winning
ii. Fear of failure, be it losing or making some form of basic error

iii. Fear of the unknown, perhaps reaching an advanced stage of a tournament for the first time, or competing in a new stadium that you have not visited.

Fear is a natural emotion that we all have. When man lived in the wild, without fear man would not have survived the many natural hazards and threat to life, so the purpose of fear is to let us know to take appropriate action. However, in most sporting competition, there is no threat to our lives, yet the fear is still there. Interesting! We'll cover how to deal with fear in Part III, but for now let's just consider briefly the three key aspects of fear in a sporting context mentioned above.

i. Fear of Success

You and many other readers may be thinking 'how could anyone be scared of winning? That's why we compete, isn't it?' However, we humans are extremely interesting characters. There is a psychological principal called 'cognitive dissonance', which essentially describes the uncomfortable state that people experience when there is a conflict between how they see themselves and what is actually happening. In such situations, people often revert to their comfort zone, even if it means sabotaging their success – many of us have heard of people who have done that.

Let me quote three examples of this.

I have read that Sweden's Annika Sorenstam, the LPGA (Ladies Professional Golf Association) champion, said in an interview that early in her career she was so afraid of having to speak in public and being the centre of attraction that she would deliberately miss putts just so that she could finish second. Fortunately for her she was able to overcome that, and win numerous tournaments – she earned over US$ 2.8 million in 2002 alone.[16]

In 1999, golfer Jean Van De Velde, a 150-1 outsider at the start of the tournament who had only won one tournament on the European Tour, led the field by three shots at the start of the final round of the British Open and stood at the 18th tee needing to score six or less (the par was four) to win the tournament. He could have played it

---

[16] http://www.pgatour.com/u/ce/feature/0,1977,837190,00.html

relatively safe and easily won, but instead he 'went for it', scored a seven (three over par) on the final hole and lost the play-off. Who actually knows what went through Van de Velde's mind. It's likely that, faced with the prospect of changing from someone who won very little to someone who beats the world's top golfers, he made sure that he retreated back into his comfort zone.

I did some mental skills coaching work with a client who, as a teenager had a very promising sporting career. He had represented Britain at the highest level for his age-group. However, on seeing a particular photograph of himself in a newspaper, he became extremely self-conscious and preferred the relative anonymity of being a good athlete rather than striving to fulfil the potential he had to be an excellent one. Who knows what could have happened had he been able to overcome this at an early age the way one presumes Annika Sorenstam did.

Part of my intention in writing this book is to raise the awareness of athletes and sports coaches both that this kind of issues exist, and that there are ways to deal with such issues relatively quickly (when I say 'quickly', I mean minutes or perhaps a couple of hours, not months or years!)

ii. Fear of Failure

Research done by various sports psychologists have found that one of the key sources of stress is fear of failure.[17] And remembering the Law of Dominant Thought (i.e. what you focus on increases), the more we think about failure or not performing well, the more it is likely to happen. John Newcombe, who won numerous tennis Grand Slam tournaments, is quoted as saying: 'If doubt or fear that they might lose enters someone's mind, and if the other person does not have any fear of losing,......then that person will win.'[18]

Often with fear of failure, there will be some belief that the person holds which in some way dis-empowers them, and so finding that belief and helping the sportsman to change it is invaluable. Part III will cover this more.

---

[17] Lew Hardy, Graham Jones and Daniel Gould, *Understanding Psychological Preparation for Sport,* John Wiley & Sons, 1996, p.143

[18] David Hemery, *Sporting Excellence - What Makes a Champion?* CollinsWillow, 1991, p.208

iii. Fear of The Unknown

It is not unknown for competitors at all levels to have some apprehension, or even fear, of being in a new situation, whilst some competitors thrive on it. For example, some competitors 'freeze' when playing in front of crowd larger than they are used to. Others freeze when playing against opposition of a much higher or lower standard.

As a mental skills coach, I would be curious about the belief(s) that a competitor who had a fear of the 'unknown' held.

Summary

◆ Negative beliefs about ourselves and our abilities underpin much of our inability to perform to the levels that we can.

◆ If you or the people you coach produce inconsistent results, elicit their values and towards/away from motivation.

◆ When our sense of identity, beliefs, values, skills and abilities and behaviours are focused and in alignment, we have a powerful force within us that can focus on getting the results we desire. Any out-of-alignment could lead to a dissipation of focus and energy.

◆ Fear is a natural response to threatening situations. Most sports situations are not threatening, so any fear is misplaced.

Chapter 6
What Stops You?
External Factors

One of the learnings I have gained over the years since I began as a student of personal development, is that it's not what happens to us that counts – it's how we deal with it.

So in writing this chapter, I am aware that it should be entitled 'What Stops You? **Seemingly** External Factors!' As I am sure you have realised, by operating from the Mindset for Success, we can deal with almost any situation that sporting competition can present us with. Does that mean we will always win? Of course not, but it does mean that we will produce more consistently good performances and hence results and gain more enjoyment than if we allow external factors to adversely impact our game or performance.

Before we look at the types of issues that we might otherwise consider as being 'external factors', I am mindful of hearing of the experiences of Victor Frankl. Frankl was an Austrian Jew imprisoned in a concentration camp by the Nazis for many years. He was also a medical doctor and a psychotherapist. He wrote about the experiences he endured. These experiences and his thoughts on them had a profound impact on me, and are relevant to anyone interested in the concept of being able to deal with unpleasant or difficult circumstances (they don't come much more unpleasant than those he endured). One of the key points he makes, and certainly the one most relevant to this chapter, is that no matter what someone does to us or what happens to us, as humans we are free to retain the ability to choose our attitude to any set of circumstances.

So when we (and I include myself here) think that the referee, the conditions, our preparation, our team-mates etc are against us and it is negatively impacting our state of mind, or we're in a bad run of form, or we keep missing simple shots/passes/putts, before we feel too sorry for ourselves and believe our own hard luck stories, it may be helpful to let the thought of Frankl's attitude gently rise to the surface.

Let's move on to a more 'grounded' approach, and look at the main types of external factors. Broadly, they can be split into two groups:

- ◆ people, such as coaches, team-mates, opponents and possibly family
- ◆ circumstances, such as playing conditions, the importance of the match

People

Competitors can get put off or negatively impacted by all sorts of other people, be they opponents, coaches, other team-members, officials or spectators.

I have known footballers noticeably wither in football matches due to comments made by their team-mates or manager, tennis players intimidated by the thought of playing with their partner and athletes go to pieces at the sight of someone who made a disparaging remark about them years previously. Here are two examples of this.

Story 6.1

I coached a young tennis player who was extremely nervous before a mixed doubles final. I asked what she was anxious about, and she said 'my partner!'. He was the club coach, and the young lady felt intimidated at the thought of playing with him.

Within a few minutes she was feeling fine about playing with him, and went on to win and play well. We will cover the techniques used in Chapter 11.

Story 6.2

I coached a very promising athlete who almost went to pieces whenever he saw a particular female competitor, because she had made a disparaging remark about him several years previously.

Within ten minutes when he thought about her he just burst into laughter, and couldn't get back his previous nervous feelings when he thought of her. Again, we will cover the techniques used in Chapter 11.

There are numerous examples, some of them high-profile in sports such as football, where a new manager can either bring the best out of players or reduce their effectiveness. Some competitors get put off by comments made by spectators, and there have even been examples of professional sportsmen blatantly remonstrating (and even fighting) with spectators.

With the possible exception of managers and sports coaches, it is unlikely that any of these other groups of people can actually physically impact on your performance. Coaches and managers may not select you, and I suppose in theory team-mates may avoid including you during competition and training, but situations like

- ◆ negative comments made by people (for example, the crowd, managers, team-mates and opponents, who may attempt to distract you as part of 'the game')
- ◆ being paired with a top player
- ◆ a bad referee decision

do not need to impact more than momentarily, if at all, on performance.

Playing Circumstances

Yes, in some matches there is more at stake in the context of the sport. But when taken down to its basics, apart from the players' attitudes, there is no difference between match point and any other point in a tennis match. Someone serves, the other person attempts to return, and eventually the point ends.

What is the difference between sinking a 10 foot putt on the 18th in the first round and doing the same putt on the final round?

The only difference is the attitude of the player, which is about their mental approach and skills.

Exercise 6.1

From Exercise 5.1, look at the 'external' factors which stop you from performing at the level you would like and from getting the kind of results you would like from your sport.

In the light of this chapter, what do you notice about these 'external' factors?

How much of your own 'power' are you giving away by being 'at effect'?

How could you change your response to the external factors, and what impact would changing your response have on your performances and results?

Summary

♦ This chapter is deliberately short. For almost all of the factors which sportsmen and women assume are external to them, whilst what has happened has happened, in reality they can learn how to deal with the mental aspects of the event. It is often said that 'it isn't what happens that counts, it's how you deal with it', which of course is all down to players' mental skills.

Part III
The 'HOW TO'

So up to this point, we have laid the foundations of how we communicate, how our mind works and some key beliefs and approaches that successful sportspeople have. We have also considered some of the key things which stop sportspeople from reaching their potential and desired level of performance.

In this Part, we will be considering the 'meat' of the subject, namely some specific techniques and approaches that will help you to help yourself and/or other people to enhance sporting results. This Part is split into eight chapters, covering the following topics:

◆ How to be in 'THE right state', as opposed to 'A right state'!

◆ How to use the language of your mind

◆ How to deal with some limiting beliefs

◆ Mental rehearsal techniques

◆ Dealing with mistakes, disappointments and setbacks

◆ Gaining insight through other perspectives

◆ Preparation and other miscellaneous topics

◆ A brief chapter on finding a mental skills coach.

Because this book, and in particular this Part, is about giving you the information and ability to know HOW TO improve mental skills in yourself and/or others, there will be a sufficient amount of necessary detail so that you will know how to use these techniques.

Please note that as you go through the exercises in this section it would be worthwhile to remember that the developers of NLP knew little of this – they were willing to experiment and had a curiosity that meant that if the results weren't as they expected, they would take it as feedback and do something different!

Also, as you practice and learn the techniques, it is important to remember that there is usually more than one way to deal with an 'issue' that a sportsman may have. So if one technique doesn't work, either change the way you are doing that technique or use a different one! When I was learning NLP, I used techniques with a lot of success, and sometimes when mentioning to fellow students what I had done and my approach to particular client situations, they said that they would have done something different. Initially I used to feel that I had done something 'wrong' or not been as 'effective' as possible, until it dawned on me that with NLP there is normally more than one approach we could use to address our own challenges or to coach someone through one that they are facing. Please bear this in mind.

The exercises and techniques referred to in this section are focussed on sport. You will no doubt notice that they can be applied to other aspects of your life. **Please feel free to do that if that would be useful to you!**

There are some key steps to all the NLP techniques we will cover in Part III. I will explain them here, rather than repeating them in detail for each technique. Some of these are for the benefit of mental skills coaches, sports coaches and managers reading this book and planning to guide others through the processes. For athletes and players doing certain exercises by themselves, the principles still apply.

Steps
1. Explain the process to the athlete.

2. Ascertain where they are and where they want to get to. Sometimes it's useful to rank 'problems' or 'challenges' on a scale out of 10, for example currently 9 out of 10 anxious on the 'anxiety scale', and I'd like to be 2 out of 10 on that scale. Check whether and how they would know they were where they wanted to be (2 out of 10 in this example). Doing this helps the athlete have a goal to aim at, and lets you both know when you have achieved it.

3. Check that it is absolutely OK for the athlete to change their thinking. Make sure there are no negative consequences, and only positive consequences, of making the change.

    Useful questions here are:

- ◆ For what purpose do you want this?
- ◆ What will you gain or lose if you have it?
- ◆ What will happen if you get it?
- ◆ What won't happen if you get it?
- ◆ What will happen if you don't get it?
- ◆ What won't happen if you don't get it?

Make sure you are paying attention to their 'non-verbal' communication. Does their voice tonality and body language match the verbal responses they are giving?

4. Do the technique.

5. Test that your work has been effective, and that they have changed. (It is useful to refer back to what they said at step 2.)

6. 'Future Pace'. This means asking the athlete to consider the future situation(s) that previously would have given them a problem, and notice how it is now. Repeat this as often as you need to for the athlete to be convinced they have changed – normally three times over different future time periods will suffice (i.e. think of a situation in one month, another situation in six months and another in one year). This particular part is covered in some detail in the chapter on mental rehearsal and visualisation.

Tip

It is common for many people when starting to do this kind of work to be eager to demonstrate to the athlete how great these techniques are. This eagerness can lead to us almost 'coercing' the athlete to tell us she/he has changed and what a wonderful experience it was.

The most effective way, rather than us to convince the athlete they have changed, is to let *them* convince *us* they have changed. So when doing the testing and future pacing, please be neutral in your questions – it is better to say something like 'how are you feeling about running in the 400 meters?' rather than 'this has worked really well for your confidence, hasn't it?'

Remember:

- ◆ Work within an ecological and ethical framework when doing any kind of 'change work'.
- ◆ Operate from the presuppositions of NLP. NLP and mental skills coaching is a process we do **WITH** someone, not **TO** someone.
- ◆ Make sure you have an agreement to do this sort of work before beginning.
- ◆ We are all different, and so even if someone does not respond to a technique the way others do or the way you would expect, resist any temptation to make any remark that could infer they are 'strange' or 'doing it wrong!'
- ◆ When working with others, build and maintain rapport. If you intend to use this material with other people, I would urge you to read Appendix 1 before going any further.

A Word Of Caution

Some NLP techniques are powerful. When working with athletes (and non athletes for that matter), occasionally as a mental skills coach you may find that it becomes apparent that athletes have 'issues' which are outside your scope of competence and may even be best dealt with by someone who is a qualified therapist. (I am a qualified NLP Master Practitioner and Trainer, and have been working with people using NLP since 1999, and I will sometimes refer prospective clients to a therapist). The kinds of issues referred to above could be where the athlete indicates that, for example:

- ◆ they have deeply repressed or traumatic events in their past
- ◆ they could be harmful to themselves or others, outside the context of the sport they compete in
- ◆ they have a history of mental illness or depression
- ◆ They have Obsessive Compulsive Disorder (OCD)
- ◆ they are seeing a counsellor, therapist or are being treated by their GP for a psychological disorder
- ◆ they have a history of epilepsy

When in doubt, do not work with them using NLP-related change techniques – **REFER THEM TO SOMEONE SUITABLY QUALIFIED.**

Chapter 7

Being In THE Right State

Sports people can often get themselves into 'A right state' before or during a big match or event. It is far more useful to be in 'THE right state'. State can be defined as our emotional mindset at any given point.

Why Is State Management So Useful?

We probably all know intuitively why this is so important. Many of us can think of situations when we were overly uptight and hence unable to perform at our best, and times when we were in the right state and our performance just flowed easily and effortlessly.

Additionally, research has been done on very experienced and elite performers, which suggests that 'they are more likely to interpret their anxiety symptoms positively than their non-elite counterparts', and that 'mood enhancement strategies may well be a valuable tool for sport psychologists to possess.'[19]

Personally I think the latter point is an understatement – it **definitely** is a valuable tool for sports psychologists and mental skills coaches to possess. And as you will see in this chapter, there are some powerful yet very simple techniques that we can use ourselves or that coaches can help their players and athletes to use.

Another key reason why state management is so important is that there is the 'inverted U' graph shown in Diagram 7.1 that is known so well in the sports psychology field. Essentially, it suggests that there is a correlation between 'arousal' and 'performance', so as

---

[19] Lew Hardy, Graham Jones and Daniel Gould, *Understanding Psychological Preparation for Sport,* John Wiley & Sons, 1996, p.166

we get more aroused, initially our performance improves, but there reaches a point where we become too aroused or 'psyched up', and performance deteriorates. Hence it is useful to be able to manage our arousal levels, especially before either big events or ones that are too routine. How many times have teams unexpectedly beaten far superior opposition because the 'favourites' weren't ready for the level of intensity that the 'weaker' team produced (in football's FA Cup there have been numerous examples of so-called 'giant-killings'). The ideal is to be in 'the zone', represented by the two vertical dotted lines.

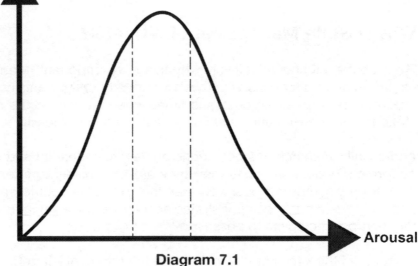

Diagram 7.1

In this chapter we will cover four approaches and techniques for state management:

1. **Anchoring**
2. **Peripheral vision**
3. **Event management**
4. **Breathing**

1. Anchoring

Introduction

In terms of the mental aspects of sport, there is probably only one equation to be aware of:

'Present State plus Resources equals Desired State.'

For example, if we are feeling anxious about a tennis match and we add resources such as

◆ confidence
◆ being energised
◆ being relaxed
◆ feeling anticipation

we will be in the sort of state that we want to be about the match. We gain access to resources such as these by a process of 'anchoring'.

An 'anchor' is a term used in NLP to describe a stimulus that leads to a response. One of the early exponents of anchoring was Ivan Pavlov, a Russian doctor, who did the well-known experiments with dogs early in the 20th century. Essentially, he showed them some meat, rang a bell and the dogs salivated. He repeated this a few times, and then rang the bell without showing the dogs any meat and the dogs, responding to the stimulus that had been created, duly salivated.

Anchors exist everywhere in our lives. Hearing the first few bars from our favourite up-beat dance song will probably make us feel energised. The first few bars from a relaxing song, however, will probably have a mellowing effect. Seeing the face of a loved one or of our best friend will make us feel good in some way. Seeing the face of someone we don't like will have the opposite effect. Similarly, holding a small baby will change our emotional state, as will smelling certain aftershaves or perfumes that remind us of past lovers.

The simple theory of anchoring is that if we can consistently link the state that we require to be in to a particular picture, sound, feeling, taste or smell, of some combination of these, we can replicate this stimulus and get into the desired state when we need to, for example before or during a sports competition.

Story 7.1

In 2002 I ran an NLP taster evening, where the attendees learned anchoring. One of the delegates used the process during a tennis match with his brother the following weekend, and won 6-4 7-6, the first time he had ever beaten him.

So whatever level you play at, this stuff works!

Some Useful States to be Anchored

Here is a suggested list of states that could be useful to be anchored:

- confidence
- motivated
- powerful
- strong
- excited
- curious
- anticipation
- feeling extremely happy
- feeling totally loved
- energised
- relaxed
- calm

The list is by no means exhaustive.

Exercise 7.1

Make a list of the 'resources' or states that you would like to have access to.

Make a list of events in your life, be they in a sporting context or not, when you experienced one or more of those states.

Add to the list any other great experiences you have had, even if you can't put into words the strong positive feelings from those events.

How Do We Do Anchoring?

We will go through the overview of the process and then I will explain the points in more detail and provide a 'script' for how to actually use this process. The basic process of anchoring can take just a minute or two.

There are seven steps to setting an anchor.

1. **Explain** the process (only relevant if you are a mental skills coach guiding an athlete through the process) and agree on the desired states to be anchored.
2. **Recall** a vivid past experience of an event where you felt the way you would like to feel in the future e.g. confident, motivated, powerful. Pick one feeling/emotion at a time, and then one past experience at a time that relates to that emotion.
3. Make sure you are really **'associated'** into that event, in other words you are reliving it as if you were there right now, not merely thinking about it.
4. **Anchor.** i.e. apply the stimulus (for example pressing your thumb and middle finger together) at the peak of the experience. The stimulus can also be a sound, for example the roar of the crowd, or the saying of a certain phrase to yourself, or seeing a mental image of, for example, the crowd as you collect your medal, or a combination of all 'representational systems'. This will be explained in more detail shortly.
5. **Change state,** think about something neutral.

6. **Repeat** steps 2 to 5 three to six times as necessary.
7. **Test** by 'firing' the anchor. 'Firing' in this context means triggering the response, e.g. pressing your thumb and middle finger together.

Tip 7.1

It is important to stress that 'anchoring' is about STATES and EMOTIONS. If the 'state' that an athlete wants (step 1) doesn't seem like a state, as a mental skills coach it is important to question it. See Story 7.2 below.

Story 7.2

I was coaching someone who wanted to feel 'efficient'. I questioned whether this was really a state, and asked her how she would feel if she felt 'efficient'. She replied "energised and confident" – these latter two are states!

Tip 7.2

If the states that the competitor wants seem 'contradictory' or mutually exclusive, for example being 'relaxed' and being 'energised' or 'motivated', then ask the competitor whether she can be in both states at the same time. If she congruently says YES, then fine. If not, then create two sets of anchors – one an 'up-time' anchor and the other a 'chill-out' anchor. Both must be done in the same way, but separately and using different physical anchors (for example different hands, or different fingers on the same hand).

There are five keys to anchoring successfully:

1. **Intensity** – if we create an anchor from really powerful intense experiences when we felt, for example, confident, we will be

able to replicate this level of confidence. If we use an example of when we felt just a little confident, that's all we'll be able to re-create when we 'fire' the anchor.

2. **Timing** – we need to capture the peak of the experience. See Diagram 7.2 below.

3. **Uniqueness** of the anchor - to ensure that the anchor is not fired accidentally. Anchors on the palm of the hand, for example, will be constantly triggered when shaking hands and will probably lose their impact.

4. **Replicability** of the anchor - to ensure that you can fire the anchor when you need to. Holding you left big toe is probably unique but not replicable before or during a sports event!

5. **Number of times** the anchoring is done. When doing the anchoring process, typically doing it between three to six times will be more powerful and effective than doing it once or twice.

A useful mnemonic is '**ITURN**'.

Let us look at Diagram 7.2 consider the concept of 'timing', which relates to step 4 in the seven steps to anchoring.

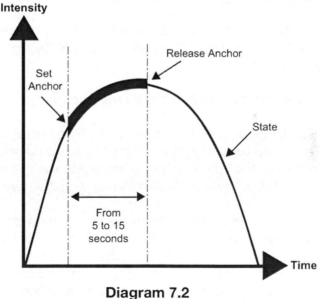

Diagram 7.2

The graph shows that when we relive a given event the intensity of the emotion/state will rise and then fall. If we capture the peak of the state (between the two vertical lines by setting or applying the anchor as the state nears its peak and then releasing the anchor just after the peak) by following the seven steps to anchoring, we can create a very powerful anchor for ourselves and/or guide others to do the same. The diagram suggests that the period where someone is 'in state' lasts between 5 and 15 seconds. This is a guideline – we are all unique individuals – for some people this peak lasts two seconds, for others up to a minute or even longer.

Athletes will show physiological signs of being 'in state', which an alert mental skills coach will notice. Examples of such signs are changes in:

◆ Breathing rate (e.g. fast, slow)
◆ Breathing location (e.g. high in the chest, from the stomach)
◆ Pupil dilation
◆ Pupil focus
◆ Skin colour (dark, light)
◆ Lower lip size (more full, less full)
◆ Posture (standing more/less upright, tilt of head)

Please note that different people will show different signs. For one person, their breathing may speed up when 'in state'. For someone else it may slow down.

The Process and Guideline Script for Anchoring

The process I will be describing is known in NLP as setting a 'resource anchor'. This means creating an anchor with several different desired states linked to it. The whole process, (including the explanation up front), typically takes around 15-20 minutes, possibly even less.

Please note that while much of the remaining section on anchoring is written as if the reader is an athlete or player, it is just as relevant for mental skills coaches wishing to use the processes with athletes. Simply adapt the processes accordingly so that you are guiding the athlete through the process. There are some additional notes and tips for mental skills coaches below.

As an athlete doing anchoring for yourself, it will be important to be aware of the process you will be following and to have it clear in your head. This includes checking that you use an appropriate anchor, one that meets the 'ITURN' criteria outlined above, for example the physical movement you will do to create the anchor was unique and replicable (e.g. press your thumb and middle finger together). For this reason, I suggest that you read this segment once or twice so that you are familiar with it.

You would then decide what sort of 'resources' would you need in order to be able to perform to your best. Let's say the resources are 'confidence, powerful and relaxed', and that it is possible for you to be relaxed and powerful at the same time (see Tip 7.2 above).

Tip 7.3

If you are a mental skills coach, you must get into the same state as the athlete wants to be in. It is no use asking the athlete to get into a confident state when you're feeling and or sounding lethargic or nervous!

Tip 7.4

When guiding someone through the process, it is best to have the athlete stand up (unless it's for a 'chill-out' state), and for you to be standing next to them or at an angle to the side, NOT directly in front of them. Allow them to visualise freely without getting in their eye-line.

Taking the resource of 'confidence' first, you would then use, as a basis, the following script:

◆ *"think of time when you were really <confident>, a specific time. Have you got a time?"* "YES"

◆ *"Go back to that time, relive that experience, see what you saw, hear what your heard, feel what you felt, say what you* *said to yourself, notice what you notice. Really **feel** those feelings of feeling really <confident>."* (mental skills coach observes athlete)

◆ *"As you feel that <confidence> getting stronger and stronger, set your anchor, and as you do really feel that <confidence> surging through you. Hold on to that anchor, feel the <confidence> getting stronger, ...(pause)..... and when you feel the <confidence> beginning to wane, release your anchor."*

NB. – please see the section headed 'Being Flexible With Anchors' below regarding using auditory and visual anchors in addition to kinaesthetic anchors.

Where you would like a combination of anchors, I would recommend doing the anchoring process around six times, typically once or twice for each state to be anchored. (The words <confident> or <confidence> in brackets above would be replaced by the specific state you are anchoring. Apart from that, the 'script' would be repeated each time.) After the second or third time, I suggest you test by changing state (think of something neutral like your mobile phone, your coffee table) and then fire your anchor and notice what impact that has. Typically there will be some impact, which will be strengthened as the process of anchoring is repeated. If you feel no change whatsoever, follow some of the points mentioned in the section *'What To Do if Anchoring Does Not Appear to Work'* below.

Once you have done five or six anchors, test again, and this time you would expect to experience a strong response. (If you are a mental skills coach, when the athlete fired her anchor ideally you would be noticing the physiological signs similar to those when she was anchoring the states earlier in the process.)

Tip 7.5

You can 'top up' your anchor whenever there is a naturally-occurring great event, regardless of whether it is within a sporting context. So when something great happens, ANCHOR IT!

There is one more step I would follow after the anchor has been tested. This involves visualisation of the future situation when the anchor will be used, at the same time as you fire your anchor ('future pacing'). We will cover that more fully in Chapter 10.

Being Flexible With Anchors

In NLP the standard way to do a resource anchor is by using the kinaesthetic system, for example, an athlete pressing a thumb and finger together or clenching their fist while holding a golf club in the other hand. Using other representational systems can enhance the strength and effectiveness of anchoring. So just as athletes can have a unique and replicable feeling, they can also have a unique and replicable sound and/or picture they bring to mind before or as they perform their task.

So you can use sounds and pictures when taking yourself through the anchoring process. Using the golf example in the previous paragraph, the golfer could say to himself "you've got this" and see his first trophy in his mind as he holds the club and makes a fist. It is essential that the golfer chooses the word/phrase and voice tone that is right for him, giving the most appropriate internal feeling.

Also, there are anchoring techniques called 'The Circle of Excellence' and 'The Ring of Power'. Essentially, this involves stepping forward into an imaginary circle (of excellence) or ring (of power) as you set each anchor and then stepping back out, so that the circle or ring contain all your resources. Once this is complete, you imagine having that 'Circle of Excellence' available to you, or shrinking the 'Ring' so that it becomes a ring on your finger that you can 'take off' and lay down. In either case, you would use this when you were 'stepping up to the plate' for example in golf, cricket, baseball, basketball shoot-outs, penalty kicks, snooker, darts etc. Once the shot, kick or throw has been executed, the 'Circle' or 'Ring' are shrunk and taken with you to the next time you need it.

The 'trigger' or stimulus when anchoring can be a specific or unique element related to the sport. Here are some examples:

- ◆ in football it could be touching the touch-line with your hand as you walk onto the pitch before the match starts

- ◆ in cricket, taking guard and marking the spot on the batting crease with your foot or bat
- ◆ in baseball, tapping your bat on the ground as you prepare to face the pitcher
- ◆ in golf, putting the tee into the ground for a tee shot
- ◆ in tennis, zipping your tennis bag up after taking the racket out of it
- ◆ in sprinting, putting your feet into the starting blocks

What To Do if Anchoring Does Not Appear to Work

On the few occasions that anchoring does not appear to work, here are some tips about what to do. Again, this segment is phrased as if the reader is an athlete, and if you are a mental skills coach adapt the following accordingly.

i. Check that you are actually reliving the experience when you felt, say, confident, rather than thinking **about** the experience. Thinking about it implies dissociation, whereas to really feel the emotions you must be fully associated, re-living it.

ii. Ensure you have just one specific event where you felt strongly, say, confident, as opposed to a few in your mind at the same time. PICK ONE AT A TIME!

iii. Check that you understand and feel comfortable with the process, (maybe re-read the segments above headed *The Process and Guideline Script for Anchoring* and *Being Flexible With Anchors*) and feel comfortable with the environment. (If you are a mental skills coach, make sure you are projecting an assurance that this is a great technique which works.)

iv. Make sure that you really want to do the exercise. Is there any 'secondary gain', in other words a benefit (possibly a covert benefit) of you not doing well in the competition and therefore not wanting the exercise to work? (remember Swedish golfer Annika Sorenstam, who deliberately missed putts because she didn't want to win).

v. If you can't think of a time when you felt, say, confident, there are a couple of things you could do. Firstly, give yourself some time to search through your memory banks. The event does not have to be in a sports context, so you could think of events outside sport if that helps. Often, people can't readily think of a strongly positive event, but once they think of one the memories start flowing!

Secondly, if the first approach doesn't work, vividly imagine being, say, confident. Our unconscious mind does not know the difference between an actual event and a vividly imagined event.

vi. This is a little cheeky! If you can't seem to get in touch with feelings, you might want to think of the BEST experience you have EVER had, and notice your reaction. (Mental skills coaches, if you do this please make sure you ask this in an appropriate way!)

vii. If none of the above works, which is highly unlikely, relax, knowing that you can use the second process we will go through in this chapter.

Exercise 7.2

Set a 'resource anchor' for yourself.

1. Decide on the resources/states
2. Re-read the section on anchoring, especially the sections on the process of anchoring
3. Once you know the process, just do it!
4. If you are a mental skills coach, see Exercise 7.3 below.

Exercise 7.3

Help others to set their own resource anchor. If you are a mental skills coach, find at least three athletes or sports people with whom you can guide them through the anchoring process. Each time notice what has worked and incorporate those learnings into the next anchoring session.

Even if you are not a mental skills coach and you simply want to help a team-mate, just guide him/her through the process.

Dealing with 'Negative Anchors'

So far we have covered how to set a resource anchor, in other words how to set a positive stimulus. Unfortunately, just as there are positive anchors, sometimes negative anchors are created. Just as there are sounds, pictures and feelings which make us feel confident and powerful, so there are others which make us feel negative and even powerless.

One example which comes to my mind is the anecdote regarding Liverpool Football Club, one of the most successful British football clubs since the 1960s. Their home ground is called 'Anfield', and there is a sign saying *'This is Anfield'* staring the players in the eye just as they enter the pitch. Many respected and experienced footballers reported that when playing an away match at Liverpool they experienced a sense of trepidation as they walked on to the field as a result of that sign. This is an example of a negative anchor. (Of course Liverpool players experienced a sense of power and confidence when seeing this sign!)

There are ways to remove the negativity associated with the anchor, the most well-used one in NLP is a process called 'collapse anchor'.

The process essentially involves creating a very strong resource anchor and then 'firing' simultaneously the very strong resource anchor and the negative anchor. The formal use of the technique is explained in detail in Appendix 6.

Using the example above to explain the principle, if a footballer who normally felt 'intimidated' when he saw the *'This is Anfield'* sign, happened to have his 2 year old son or daughter in his arms, hugging him and saying "I love you Daddy", for many people the strong positive feeling that would be evoked would collapse the negative anchor of the sign.

A similar approach would be to play, for example, your favourite song loudly a few times when faced with something that causes you to feel negative. After doing this a few times, you would associate the song and the good feelings to the stimulus that previously caused you to feel negative.

Another way to use this would be to link the negative anchor to something ridiculous or comical, such as circus music or Donald Duck's voice.

Story 7.3

I was coaching an athlete who felt anxious at big stadiums. I asked her to think about the stadium and at the same time play her favourite music loudly. After a minute or two when she thought of the stadium there were no negative thoughts. I suggested to her that she have her portable music player with her the next time she went in case she needed to play the song, but she told me she was already convinced she didn't need it.

Story 7.4

I was coaching an athlete who used to feel intimidated by a particular competitor, particularly when the competitor said certain phrases to him. I asked what those phrases were.

I asked him to think of the competitor, and then I said those words but in a really childish, squeaky voice. At first the athlete was shocked, but once I had repeated it a few times he started laughing. I then said (in the same squeaky voice), "Don't laugh at me, don't you know how important I am? Don't laugh." (It is important to note that I had already built good rapport with him.)

This caused my athlete to laugh even more! I carried on for a few more moments, using other similar phrases to "don't you know how important I am?"

After a few moments, I changed the subject (a break state) and then asked him how he felt about the competitor. The athlete just smiled and laughed.

2. Peripheral Vision

Introduction and Benefits of 'Peripheral Vision'

The next technique to cover is useful for helping you to get into a calm state, regardless of the 'pressure' that may be associated with the event. This approach is used by martial artists, and is increasingly taught by NLP trainers as a method to get into a centred state.

Another advantage of the technique is that you are able to be aware of what is happening all around you, which in sports where there is lots of movement such as football, rugby and hockey, is a major benefit.

I will refer to the technique as 'peripheral vision' for reasons that will become apparent in a few moments.

What is Peripheral Vision?

We have two aspects of our vision – 'focussed' vision (sometimes referred to as 'foveal' vision) and 'peripheral' vision. Focussed vision is the vision we use when concentrating our gaze on a particular object. Peripheral vision is the vision that allows us to see what is happening around us and either side of the object of our focussed vision. This is shown in Diagram 7.3 below.

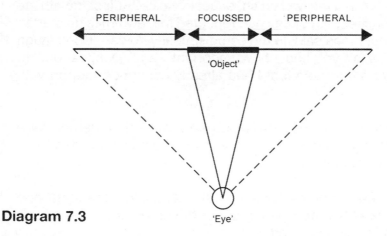

Diagram 7.3

There are two explanations why getting into peripheral vision works.

1. Focussed vision is about detail, whereas peripheral vision takes in 'the big picture'. Any apparent problem such (as a 'pressure match' or a 'pressure shot') when viewed in the context of the big picture of, say, someone's career, their life, the lives of those around them, the whole of the country etc. becomes tiny if not irrelevant. By going into peripheral vision and staying that way for a few moments changes the meaning that we place on such events.

2. Focussed vision arouses the 'sympathetic' nervous system, which is the part of the nervous system that accelerates the heart rate, constricts blood vessels, and raises blood pressure (the 'stress' response), whereas peripheral vision arouses the 'parasympathetic' nervous system. The parasympathetic nervous system is the part of nervous system that serves to slow the heart rate, increase the intestinal and gland activity, and to relax the sphincter muscles (in other words, the 'relaxed' response).[20]

How Do We Get Into Peripheral Vision?

Broadly, the steps are as follows:

1. We pick a spot on a wall a little above eye level that we can focus on.
2. As we focus on that spot, allow ourselves to notice that even though we are focussing our eyes on that spot, we can allow our awareness to spread either side of that spot, so that we can see the whole of the wall ahead of us.
3. We then allow our attention to spread along both adjacent walls at the same time, so that even though we are looking at the object we are aware of everything either side of us (180 degrees). (Some people are able to go beyond 180 degrees, sometimes to as much as 360 degrees.)
4. Once we are able to do this, we can notice how relaxed we feel. (It helps to relax the jaw muscles, possibly by opening the mouth very slightly.)
5. Once we feel relaxed and that our mind is still, lower our eyes so that we can address the situation at hand.

---

[20] http://www.medterms.com/script/main/art.asp?articlekey=4770

Appendix 12 contains a comprehensive example and guideline script of how I have used this.

How Can You Use This In Sport?

By going into peripheral vision, before or sometimes during a competition, you can calm your nerves and remain focussed on the task at hand without distraction. A colleague of mine is an expert in several martial arts and hand to hand combat. He goes into this state before and during competitions, to allow him to feel alert, focussed yet appropriately relaxed. Moreover, our peripheral vision allows us to detect slight movements around us, which in combat sports and probably certain other sports is extremely useful.

When in peripheral vision, it is almost impossible to feel negative emotions like fear or anxiety or to perceive of something as a 'real problem'.

Here's my approach to this when coaching sports clients (if you are an athlete doing this for yourself, the principles still apply).

1. I teach them to go into peripheral vision during a coaching session with me, having explained the process and the benefits.
2. I have them repeat the process several times so that they can go into that state at will almost instantly.
3. I ask them to consider a sporting situation that they are concerned about.
4. I ask them to go into peripheral vision (180 degrees and possibly beyond that) and then to consider that 'problem' whilst in that state.
5. When I can see they are in that state and have considered the problem for a few moments, I ask them how they feel about the event.
6. If they still feel some anxiety, I remind them to make sure their awareness is 180 degrees, and then to re-consider the problem and to take their time to allow the emotions to go easily over the next minute or so.
7. Once they say they feel calm, I keep them there for a minute or so.
8. I then repeat the process two or three times until the athlete is

clearly not concerned about the event. I would probably ask the athlete how they feel about the event that they thought they were anxious about.

9. To round off, I would probably do some mental rehearsal or visualisation techniques (see Chapter 10).

I have used this several times with my clients with great success.

Please note that, as with anchoring, I stand next to the player (or sit next to them if they are seated). It may seem obvious that you would not want to be in front of them, yet I have seen people do it and wonder why the athlete found it hard to do the process!

Guideline Script

Appendix 12 contains a guideline to doing the peripheral vision process outlined in the segment headed *How Do We Get Into Peripheral Vision?*

Having taken an athlete through the process, I would then ask her to do the process as often as she would need to in the room without my input, so that she is totally comfortable and capable with the process and can replicate it by herself at will. Ideally, she should be able to get into that state in no more than two or three seconds – even quicker is better.

Exercise 7.4

Do the peripheral vision process so that you experience going into, and being in, that state.

If you are doing this by yourself for the first time, make sure that you are fully aware of the process first rather than breaking the flow by having to think or refer to the book. Ideally, find a willing partner who can guide you through the process.

Firstly be able to get into that state. Then, once you can do that, do it and consider a sporting 'problem/situation' and notice how it changes.

The aim is to be able to get into that state instantaneously.

> ## Exercise 7.5
>
> If you are a mental skills coach, find at least three sportspeople and guide them through the process. Ideally find people who would benefit from this exercise (so they have a vested interest in making it work!).
>
> A tip – before you do this, have someone else guide you through the process so that you can congruently tell them how good it is.

3. Event Management

The third approach to cover regarding being in the right state relates to stress about a particular event. The stress that competitors feel about an event can be boiled down to two elements:

- those events which are directly controllable by the athlete
- those events which are not directly controllable by the athlete

For the latter, situations where the athlete has done all he can to prepare, then anchoring and peripheral vision are superb techniques. In addition, some of the visualisation techniques we'll cover in Chapter 10 will provide additional tools.

Let's concentrate now on the first category, situations which are directly controllable by the competitor.

I have coached some athletes and competitors who, although not professional, are highly experienced. Yet when I ask them about what blocks them from fulfilling their potential or feeling confident about a situation the issues seem to revolve around how the competitor manages themselves in relation to the event.

The key factors here are to be organised and to prepare. Yes, I know it sounds basic. Sally Gunnell referred to being fully prepared before she won the Olympic 400 meters Gold medal in Barcelona in 1992, including eating well.[21]

---

[21] Jeff Grout & Sarah Perrin, *Mind Games – Inspirational Lessons From The World's Biggest Sports Stars*, Capstone Publishing Ltd, 2004, p.256

Story 7.5

I was coaching a highly successful (and extremely bright) female amateur athlete. One of her concerns before events was 'Do I have all the right equipment with me?' She also sometimes did not train as effectively as she could because she sometimes forgot certain pieces of her training kit. She also at times did not have the right food at home during the week.

So, the coaching was simple:
1. Make a list of training kit to take.
2. Make a list of equipment for the events.
3. Make a shopping list.
4. Keep the lists somewhere where you can access it easily when needed.
5. Pack for events the night before, using the list.
6. Pack for training sessions using the list.

In short, PREPARE!

Tip 7.7

Remember the 6 Ps.

Proper Prior Planning Prevents Poor Performance!

Competitive sports have the potential to lead to stress among competitors. Minimise the chances of adding to the potential stress by planning!

4. Breathing

The final approach to cover regarding being in the right state relates to our breathing. It probably goes without saying that breathing is essential to good performance. It is, however, not just about breathing, but breathing appropriately.

Experienced practitioners of martial arts and yoga, for example, are aware of the importance of the correct breathing, and able to shift their breathing to change their states as required. From the NLP Communication stance, breathing is an aspect of physiology, and if you review Diagram 1.1 you will remember that changing physiology will change our state and internal representations, which lead to our behaviour and results. (This book is skimming the surface of the ways to breathe appropriately. The reader is invited to explore this further by finding specialist books and/or courses on the subject, such as a suitable Yoga class.)

In simple terms, there are three main aspects to our breathing

◆   the rate (fast or slow)
◆   the location (high up in the chest, from the stomach or mid-way)
◆   whether we are inhaling and exhaling through our nose or mouth

Normally when we are anxious in some way, our breathing will change – for example it my speed up, come from high in the chest and be through the mouth. It is outside the scope of this book to say which is the 'right' way to breathe. However, as a simple guide, find out what works for you and do more of it!

Exercise 7.6

1.   Notice how you are breathing when you feel relaxed (the rate, location and mouth/nose/inhale/exhale). If you find it easier to remember by making notes then do so. Pay enough attention to the detail so that you can replicate it.

     Practice replicating the breathing at times when it is appropriate for you to feel this relaxed.

2.   Notice how you are breathing before and during practice, particularly when you are practicing well. (These may differ, depending on the level of physical exertion.) Again, pay enough attention to the detail so that you can replicate it.

Practice replicating the breathing before and during practice. Notice the results.

3. Notice your breathing before and during competition. If you are finding yourself feeling inappropriately anxious, adjust your breathing so that you are in (or at least closer to) the appropriate state. For example, it may not be appropriate to feel the way you did in point 1 above just before a match.

Summary

- ◆ Remember the NLP presupposition 'we have all the resources we need. There are no unresourceful people, just unresourceful states'. In this chapter you have learned techniques and approaches to helping yourself and/or other people get into THE right state whenever required.

- ◆ As with any new set of skills, including sports skills or coaching skills, practice is essential. So the techniques you have learned in this chapter (and the ones you will learn in subsequent chapters) require some practice.

Chapter 8

Using The Language

of Your Mind

One of the key benefits that Richard Bandler and John Grinder, the co-creators of NLP, plus some of those who followed in their footsteps, brought to the field of human knowledge was a greater understanding of how the mind works, and more importantly, how to make changes that are:

- quick
- simple
- easy to use with oneself and/or other people (around 5-10 minutes)
- powerful
- long-lasting

This chapter will cover the techniques that are most useful to players and mental skills coaches. By the end of this chapter, you will have some extremely powerful techniques to help you to change your experience of a sporting (and non-sporting) situation, and if you are a mental skills coach to help others to do the same.

Have you ever had a negative picture of something, perhaps a big challenge hanging over you or staring you in the face? Have you ever talked to your self in a negative tone, or heard someone else's voice in your mind which caused you to feel negatively? Have you ever had an uncomfortable feeling about doing something? Assuming you're alive, you probably have!

We will look at ways in this chapter to change these pictures, sounds and feelings so that the event is less challenging or threatening.

Some Essential Background

You will remember from earlier chapters that we have five 'representational systems', namely:

- visual/seeing
- auditory/hearing
- kinaesthetic/feel
- olfactory/smell
- gustatory/taste

These five systems (our senses), plus 'auditory digital' (our self-talk – "do you ever talk to yourself without speaking? Oh, you do!"), are the ways we represent (or re-present) the external world internally and then how we externalise this. In NLP, we sometimes call these five representational systems 'modalities'.

Bandler and Grinder were curious about these modalities. Given that the only way we can take in external information and process it internally is through these modalities, how do we use these modalities to let us know that:

- we like or don't like something or someone
- we are pleased or not pleased
- we understand something or are confused
- we are motivated or indifferent
- we believe something or don't believe it

and in a sporting context

- it is time to be calm or stressed
- it is time to hit the snooker or golf ball
- we have bounced the ball enough times before hitting the serve

What they noticed and discovered was that it wasn't just the modalities that were important, but that the finer distinctions of those modalities played a **crucial** role in determining our experience. In NLP, these finer distinctions are known as 'submodalities'.

Why Are Submodalities So Useful?

You would use submodalities to change the way someone perceives a situation or an 'object', for example:

- ◆ they are intimidated by the thought of playing against (or with) a particular person or team
- ◆ they don't like playing at a particular ground or venue
- ◆ they had an unpleasant experience which they would like to make less of an issue
- ◆ they have a food or drink which they like and wish they did not (for health or fitness reasons)
- ◆ increase or decrease motivation

Submodalities can also be used with any negative internal dialogue.

Once we have an understanding of how submodalities work, we can use them for ourselves for relatively simple issues. Submodalities are ideal for sports coaches and managers to use with players.

What Are Submodalities?

Submodalities are the finer distinctions of the modalities that provide meaning to events and situations. They are the mind's internal language. Let's take the three key modalities (visual, auditory and kinaesthetic) and consider the finer distinctions.

Visual

A picture that you have in your head when you think of something can have the following distinctions:

- ◆ size (big, small)
- ◆ distance (near or far)
- ◆ brightness (bright or dim)
- ◆ black & white or colour
- ◆ focus (focussed or de-focussed)
- ◆ located in different parts of your visual field (e.g. top left, bottom right, directly in front of you)

◆ still or moving
◆ if moving, what speed (fast or slow)
◆ contrast (yes/no, lots/none)
◆ 3-dimensional or flat
◆ looking through your own eyes (associated) or seeing yourself in the picture (dissociated)
◆ framed or panoramic
◆ viewed from different angles (e.g. straight on, looking up, looking to the side)
◆ 1 picture or a number of pictures

These are the main visual submodalities.

Auditory

Sounds that you have in your head can have the following distinctions:

◆ location - where is the sound
◆ which direction is it coming from/going to/moving
◆ loud or soft
◆ fast or slow
◆ high or low pitch
◆ the timbre (sound quality – clear/raspy)
◆ pauses
◆ a certain rhythm
◆ a uniqueness to the sound

These are the main auditory submodalities.

Kinaesthetic

Feelings (normally in the body) can have the following distinctions:

◆ a location (chest, throat etc)
◆ size
◆ shape
◆ intensity

- steadiness of the intensity
- still or moving
- if moving, fast or slow
- humidity (dry/wet)
- vibration
- temperature (hot/cold)
- pressure (high/low)
- texture (rough/smooth)
- weight (heavy/light)

These are the main kinaesthetic submodalities.

You will notice that some submodalities are a spectrum, such as size (very big, very small or anything in between), whereas others are 'either/or', for example a picture is *either* 'black & white' *or* 'colour'.

The **key points** to bear in mind is that the combination of submodalities gives meaning to our experience (e.g. 'this is something I like/don't like', 'this is something I'm motivated/not motivated about'). **By changing the submodalities of an event or situation or object, we change the meaning it holds for us.** Remember that many NLP techniques deal with the structure or 'how' we do our problem, challenge or limitation. It could be that when we think of an intimidating sports situation we have a big, bright picture right in front of us, with loud noises coming towards us from the left and having a sharp feeling in our throat that vibrates quickly. These are some of the submodalities of that experience, in other words part of our internal 'structure' of the 'problem'. By changing some or all of these submodalities, we can change the experience of the event.

Exercise 8.1

Think of a food you really like. When you think of that food, notice as many submodalities of the pictures, sounds and feelings as you can. Make a note of the key ones.

Now think of a food that you really dislike. Notice the submodalities of this food. Make a note of the key ones.

Notice that there are some differences in the submodalities of the two foods.

This exercise can be done with other things such as drinks, people, places, activities.

NB. The essential thing is to pick the same type for both e.g. two drinks – one you like, one you dislike.

How To Use Submodalities

There are three main methods to do this. We will cover two in this chapter. The third, known as 'mapping across', is slightly more involved, and is particularly useful with changing the way we perceive foods, drinks and situations, and is covered in Appendix 4.

Although much of the remainder of this chapter is written as if the reader is a mental skills coach, if you are a player or athlete you can adapt the steps accordingly. If you are an athlete and wish to use submodalities yourself rather than have someone else guide you through the process, I would suggest that you start with very simple and unimportant examples until you get the hang of it, and that you do not experiment or work with issues or situations which are significant for you!

Method 1

This involves the elicitation of submodalities and then changing them until the player feels the way they would like to feel about the situation.

Steps:
1. Have a copy of the submodality checklist to hand (see Appendix 2).

2. Explain what you will be doing. (You may need to give the player some 'reference experiences' to reassure him that having pictures, sounds and feelings is a natural way for humans to think, and to demonstrate to him that he does get pictures and have sounds in his head, and has feelings in his

body. For example, ask him to remember a really pleasant experience and notice what he is seeing and/or hearing and/or feeling.)

3. Identify the situation to be addressed, and how the player would like to feel instead. As mentioned in the Introduction to Part III, it is helpful to put numbers on these, so for example the player may feel 8 out of 10 on the 'anxiety scale', and would like to feel 3 out of 10.

4. Check that it OK for the player to feel the desired way. Make sure there are no negative consequences of making the change. For example, check that the player would not be overly–minimising a situation which does need some attention, or that she would not lose the 'edge'.

5. Ask the player to think of the situation and elicit the visual, auditory and kinaesthetic submodalities of that situation (see Appendix 3 for information about eliciting submodalities). This step should take about 1-3 minutes.

6. Ask the player to change one submodality at a time, ideally starting with the visual submodalities, and ask whether it improves the situation (in this case does it lower the score?), makes it worse or has no impact.

   For example, if the picture is 'black & white' you would ask the player to make it 'colour' – does that improve it, make it worse or no change?

   Bear in mind that some submodalities are 'either/or', such as the 'colour or black & white'. Other submodalities are a spectrum, such as distance, size and location.

   When asking the player to change a 'spectrum' submodality, make sure you ask for relatively small amount of changes initially. If we take 'distance' as an example, if the picture is 'far', it is better to say 'bring it (a little) closer – better, worse or no change?' than 'bring it right up close', which might be a little too 'in their face', literally and metaphorically! If bringing it a little closer improves the situation, you can always say 'bring it a little more close – does that make it better, worse or no change?' and keep going until it's just the right distance for the player.

7. If it improves the situation, ask the player to keep the picture that new way, for example 'in colour' and 'mid-distance'. If it has no impact or makes it worse, ask the player to move it back to how it was.

8. Repeat steps 6 and 7 until the situation is at the right point (3 out of 10 in this example). Normally I check in with the player after around 3 or 4 changes that have improved the situation rather than go through the whole list. For reasons that will be explained shortly, often by changing certain submodalities, others will change.

9. Once the player has said that it is at the desired level, ask the player to 'lock in the pictures, sounds and feelings to how they now are'.

10. Test by asking the player to consider the situation now – how is it?

11. Future pace. Ask the player to think situations in the future where if it had happened in the past he would have felt anxious (or whatever he was feeling). What is he doing and how is he behaving in this future event?

Tip 8.1

There are ten top tips to bear in mind when working with submodalities.

1. You will find that there are some submodalities which, when they change, all the others tend to change. These are called 'drivers'. If you change the drivers, the person's experience will change more than if you change non-drivers.

2. Generally, working just with visual submodalities will provide the results you need. For some people and in some situations it may be useful to work with auditory and/or kinesthetic submodalities as well.

3. The visual submodalities which tend to be drivers are location, size, brightness, distance and association/dissociation. This may not always be the case, as everyone is different. Kinaesthetic drivers can be the location of the feeling and the way or direction in which it is moving. Auditory drivers tend to be volume, location and direction of the sound.

4. Generally, the impact of an event will be lessened by making pictures smaller, dimmer and further away, lower down, plus making sure you have stepped out of the event and are watching yourself in the picture. The reverse is true to increase the impact of an event.

5. Turning the volume down or even completely off can lessen the impact, as can making the feeling small and moving it into, say, your little finger.

6. When eliciting submodalities, do it QUICKLY, and offer the range of options ('is it near or far?' is better than 'is it near?'). As a guide, to elicit visual submodalities takes less than one minute. This is because the unconscious mind thinks quickly. Pictures come and go quickly, and if you do it too slowly the conscious mind will 'interfere' and may 'play' with the internal representation. It's helpful to go slightly quicker than the athlete would normally like.

7. Please sit at an angle to the athlete, not directly in front of him/her. Allow him/her to visualise without you being in their face!

8. Use the checklist and make abbreviations – for example write 'b' rather than 'bright'.

9. Get familiar with the list of submodalities, so that you can pay attention to the athlete as you elicit the submodalities. It

will help you maintain a 'connection' and be in rapport with them so that they are more likely to remain comfortable with you during the process.

10. Be in charge of the process. Offer clear and polite instructions to make a change. It is far more effective to say, "Now, make the picture smaller please. Does that make it better worse or no change?" than to (meekly) ask, "Can you possibly try to make the picture smaller at some point...(long pause) ...is that better?"

Exercise 8.2

Either:
find two other mental skills coaches or team-mates and do this exercise in groups of three, with one person being the observer each time.

Or:
find three people and separately elicit their submodalities.

In both cases, if this is the first time you have used submodalities, elicit submodalities about something which is not important, for example a food or place they like.

Refer to the guidelines in Appendix 3 and the checklist in Appendix 2.

Exercise 8.3

Once you as the mental skills coach feel comfortable with the elicitation process, work with a player (or another mental skills coach) who wants to make a change to the way they perceive a situation, using the process detailed in 'Method 1' above.

If they do not want to make any lasting changes to the way they perceive the situation, and are willing to help you practice, do the process referred to in 'Method 1' with something of little importance (such as a food or place they like) and ENSURE that after they have told you the impact of the change of each submodality that you ask them to change it back to how it was. This respects the person's wish not to make any lasting changes.

Ideally have an experience of this yourself, with someone taking you through the process. If that is not practical, think of an event, situation or person, elicit your own submodalities as best you can and then change one at a time, noticing the impact. Repeat this with two different situations.

Method 2

Now that you have a good understanding and grasp of submodalities, we can move onto an even simpler method. This method is excellent where for some reason there is not enough time, or it is not appropriate, to do Method 1.

And remember the point in the Introduction to Part III - before you start any NLP change work, make sure you have an agreement to do this – NLP is something we do WITH someone, not TO them.

Let's quickly go through the process and then I will explain how and when you can use it. It works simply by asking the athlete to change certain of the submodalities, the ones which are likely to be drivers and the impact of changing the drivers (see Tip 8.1, points 3, 4 and 5), and asking them whether it makes it better or worse or no change. You can get an idea about which submodalities could be the drivers by listening to the language, although this is not essential.

For example, if they say 'I've got this big problem staring me in the face,' you have a pretty good idea of the location, distance and size of the picture! In this instance, I would ask 'when you think of this problem, do you have a picture?' When they say 'Yes' I would either ask them to tell me 4-6 aspects which are likely to be driver submodalities ('is it big or small, bright or dim' etc), and then either ask them to make specific changes rather like *Method 1*, or I would be more direct and ask them to notice what happens when they make the picture:

- ◆ Smaller – 'better, worse or no change?'
- ◆ Darker - 'better, worse or no change?'
- ◆ Further away - 'better, worse or no change?'
- ◆ Lower down - 'better, worse or no change?'

I would also be prepared to ask them to:

- ◆ step out of the picture so that they see themselves (dissociate)
- ◆ turn the volume down
- ◆ slow the speed of the words down
- ◆ add some circus music in the background
- ◆ hear the person speaking in Donald Duck's or Mickey Mouse's voice
- ◆ move the feeling to a different part of their body
- ◆ stop any vibration of the feeling
- ◆ reverse the direction it is moving
- ◆ or other change to submodalities that might be useful

As a mental skills coach using this approach, to an extent it is trial and error, and also there is some 'common sense' that can be applied. For example, if they are referring to a person who intimidated them, I would guess the key submodalities would be:

- ◆ size of picture (probably big)
- ◆ location of picture (probably above us)
- ◆ distance of picture (probably near)
- ◆ 3-dimensional
- ◆ volume of sound (probably loud)
- ◆ tonality (probably harsh)

So in this case I would ask them to tell me these six submodalities, plus anything else they notice about the picture, sounds or feelings, and then I would ask them to change each one in turn, asking whether it makes it better, worse or no impact.

If someone is struggling to be motivated by a goal or feel confident in achieving a goal, my guess would be that they didn't have a clear picture of the goal, so I would guess the key submodalities would be:

- ◆ focus /clarity of the picture (probably de-focussed)
- ◆ brightness of the picture (probably dim)
- ◆ distance of the picture (probably far away)
- ◆ colour of the picture (probably black & white)
- ◆ size of the picture (probably small)
- ◆ still or moving picture (probably still or moving very slowly)

Remember, because everyone is different, even if it is likely that particular submodalities are important, be prepared to be curious about how the athlete herself actually does the 'problem'. Please under **NO CIRCUMSTANCES** say anything like 'that's unusual' or 'you're strange doing it this way!' to a fellow team-mate or athlete.

Story 8.1

As mentioned in an earlier chapter, a 19 year old from a local tennis club was due to be playing in a mixed doubles tennis tournament final with the club coach. She and I happened to meet as she was waiting for him to meet her. She mentioned that she was really anxious about playing with him, as she always feels intimidated by the thought of partnering him (she stressed that it was nothing he did or said) and never plays at her best, and that she would need to play at her best to win the tournament.

She knew a little of the work I do with clients. I confirmed with her that she was willing to do some quick work about this.

Clearly she was intimidated by the thought of playing with him, and so I asked her to think of him and notice the picture she had. I asked whether the picture was big/small, it's location in her visual field, its brightness, distance from her and whether it was 3-D or flat.

The specifics of the submodalities are irrelevant here, as they relate only to her. I asked to her to change one at a time, checking whether that improved things. With one exception, making the changes had a positive impact on her. For the one exception, I asked her to change it back to how it was.

I then asked how she was feeling about the match, and she said much better, although still a little inappropriately anxious. I asked about whether there were any sounds or feelings that were important, and she said she could hear him in her (right) ear. I asked a little about the sound – it's volume and direction. She said as it approached her, it got louder.

Clearly there was some work to be done with auditory submodalities. Three possibilities came to mind immediately – change to location and/or change the volume and/or change the direction. I asked her to 'experiment' – what happens if the sound got quieter or stayed at the same volume as it approached her? What happens if the sound stayed where it was or even disappeared into the distance? What happened if it transferred to her left ear? For her, keeping the sound at the same volume and not approaching her made the difference.

I asked her how she was feeling now – she said fine – keyed up for the match and looking forward to partnering the tennis coach. I asked her to lock in the changes to the pictures and sounds. I future paced this, asking her to turn the clock forward an hour or two – how is it on court? What happens if she makes a bad shot, or if things aren't going well? She congruently said she felt fine and was able to handle whatever would happen on court.

I saw her a few days later – they won and she played as she would have liked.

Quietening the Noise

By now you have a sense of how you can use submodalities either by yourself or with others. One other way in which they can be used is to quieten noise, either internal or external.

1. Internal noise

Often, people will have a negative internal dialogue such as 'you'll never succeed', 'you should have done more training' etc. Some people would say that it's just a matter of turning your internal dialogue off. That's virtually impossible!

So the other two options you have are:

- change the submodalities
- 'jam' the internal dialogue i.e. replace it with something else

The tonality of our internal dialogue gives it meaning.

Exercise 8.4

1. Say your name inside your mind say it in a soft, sweet tone. Notice the impact.

   Now say your name in the tone of voice you use when you're not happy with yourself. Notice the impact.

   Repeat it in the first tone.

2. Say the phrase you use to 'beat yourself up' when you've done something wrong.

   Now say the same words in a slow, deep, seductive voice. Can you take the words seriously?

So, if we want to adjust our internal dialogue, one way is to adjust the tonality using submodalities.

Another way is to replace the internal dialogue with something else. People who do firewalks (walking across burning coals) are encouraged to say to themselves 'cool moss, cool moss, cool moss' to 'jam' the words which might otherwise be there. If the negative internal dialogue is loud, it may be necessary to use an even louder internal replacement!

> ## Story 8.2
>
> When I run board-breaking seminars (teaching people to put their hands through a piece of wood), if someone is having negative internal dialogue I suggest they say 'YES YES YES' inside very loudly as part of the preparation.

If we consider sports where there is a lot of time to consider and think, it is important to have strategies in place in case negativity creeps in. For example in golf, where the golfer is addressing the ball for around 25 minutes over a round lasting four hours, it is essential that the golfer can keep his mind usefully distracted when not involved with thinking about the job at hand. For example, Lee Trevino used to joke with the crowd. In tennis, particularly between games, there is time for players to think, which obviously leaves time for negative thinking. Pete Sampras used to use a gadget to make sure his strings were evenly spaced after having been moved by the spin of the ball. Apart from helping his racquet, it was a useful distraction.

2. External Noise

One final point to consider – how can we reduce the impact of partisan crowds? If I were to coach a sportsman or a team who were playing an away match in front of a 'hostile' crowd, I would do some work to link the sounds of the crowd to something amusing or meaningless, like someone blowing a raspberry. I would also suggest they imagine that the crowd is cheering them on, not their opponents.

Summary

- ◆ Submodalities are an extremely useful way of changing our and others' internal representations of some situation.
- ◆ There are several different ways to use submodalities, depending on the circumstances.
- ◆ Remember the unconscious mind works quickly, so be quick when using submodalities.
- ◆ Where possible, find the drivers when working with submodalities.

Chapter 9
Changing Beliefs

Introduction

By now you will have realised the important role that our beliefs play in the results we achieve. To recap briefly, amongst other things beliefs:

- are our best current thinking about something
- can and do change naturally over the course of time
- are often generalisations we have made from events in our past
- can be 'given to us' by parents, siblings and other significant people in our life, often when we are young
- may be known to us consciously, or not
- can be empowering or disempowering
- are one of the main filters we have (see Part I) and can determine what we perceive from events
- have different strengths
- define the 'model of reality' that we operate from
- impact on the behaviours and skills and abilities that we have (if we believe we can do something, we will find a way to get the skills to do it even if we don't have those skills yet)

We considered in Chapters 5 and 6 some of the internal and external blocks to success. In Appendix 5 there is a list of some of the limiting beliefs that sports people can have. Readers are reminded of the section on how to spot limiting beliefs in Chapter 5.

NLP has numerous techniques to help people change beliefs. I will cover only those which can be effectively used by those without formal NLP training. Some of these techniques will be possible to do by yourself as an athlete; others are best done with someone guiding you through the process. If you are a mental skills coach yourself, you will be able to use these techniques with other people.

As with any type of 'change' work, it is important to operate from the presuppositions of NLP. In particular, remember that change can be quick and lasting. When assisting others to change limiting beliefs, it is useful to remember that if someone is 100% convinced of a belief which holds them back and they leave the session being only 90% convinced, you have done a good job. Before beliefs change, there is a spell of doubt or being open to not believing. In some situations this spell lasts moments, in other situations it can last a longer period.

Why Change Beliefs?

Exercise 9.1

Make a list of beliefs you hold which do or may hold you back from achieving your potential. It may be useful to look at some of the examples in Appendix 5 or to refer to Exercise 5.3 when doing this.

Write down what impact it would make in your life and sporting results if you no longer had those beliefs.

Exercise 9.2

If you are a mental skills coach, ask some of the people you coach to do Exercise 9.1.

Knowing the impact of limiting beliefs and the benefits of changing them should give you and/or the people you coach the motivation to make some changes to beliefs! **Whilst a positive attitude doesn't always mean you will win, a negative one will almost certainly mean you won't win. A positive attitude puts you in the frame to win.**

We will cover the following four belief-change techniques in this chapter:

1. **Counter examples**
2. **Reframing**
3. **Perceptual Positions**
4. **Provide the 'Why To' and 'How To'**

As I am sure you will appreciate, some approaches will work better than others with certain situations and types of beliefs. Whilst I will offer some tips, ultimately there is an element of using common sense and experimentation, as Bandler and Grinder did.

1. Counter Examples

Bearing in mind that beliefs are generalisations of some previous experience(s), if someone has a limiting belief it may be useful to provide some counter-examples of the belief, or better still, ask them to come up with some counter-examples of their own. A counter-example in this context is an event whose outcome shows that the belief cannot be true.

For example, if someone has a belief that they cannot win races, find examples of races that they have won. If they have never won a race, ask them to find examples of when they did something for the first time when they weren't sure they could, or even when they were sure they couldn't.

Tip 9.1

It is better if the athlete finds their own counter-examples – they find it harder to argue with themselves than with you!

Sometimes just one example will be enough to 'blow out' the limiting belief. Other times a few examples will be needed. Ask the athlete to keep giving you examples until they complain or start laughing, realising that their belief isn't true.

2. Reframing

In NLP the term 'reframe' means to consider something in a different light so that it has a different meaning, or as one of my clients put it, **turning a negative into a positive.** One of the keys to having a successful and happy life and career (sports career or otherwise) is to consistently be able to see the positive in situations which may otherwise be seen as negative. This will help us in our own lives and careers, and help us to help others in theirs if that is appropriate.

With limiting beliefs, a reframe can help someone or ourselves see something less negatively, or even see it positively. It may or may not completely change the belief, and remember that if someone is 100% sure there is a 'problem' and leaves the meeting less than 100% sure, you have achieved something worthwhile.

If we go back to earlier points about beliefs and generalisations, we all make meaning about events and situations numerous times per day, for example:

◆ Someone smiles at you in a shop – you make it mean something about you and/or them and/or the day (for example, "it's going to be a good day").

◆ Someone doesn't smile at you – you make that mean something about you and/or them and/or the day too, (for example "that person is miserable").

All meaning is dependent on the context in which it happens. For example, if you saw someone looking at you and whispering to someone else, what does that whisper mean? It would have a different meaning if it were at a quiz night compared to, say, at a nightclub or party, or at work, to name but three situations. So the whisper in and of itself means nothing, yet we will probably place some meaning on it or the people involved or ourselves. In a more sporting scenario, if we saw two men punching each other we would probably stay well clear, or try to break it up or call the police, but if they are doing it in a boxing ring, that's OK!

So by changing the scenario, we can change the meaning, either for ourselves or others or both.

Some people are natural 'reframers' – they see most things in a positive light, putting a positive spin on events. In effect, they are noticing things that, if the person with the 'problem' noticed they wouldn't have the problem.

The two main types of reframe that we will be covering are known as 'context' reframes and 'content' (or 'meaning') reframes.

As a mental skills coach, the three key questions to ask yourself in order to do a reframe are:

1. What is it that this athlete hasn't noticed about the situation, such that if they did notice it the problem would be reduced or even disappear?

2. What is a different context when this behaviour, situation or experience would be useful or at least not a problem? (context reframe)

3. What else could this situation or behaviour or experience mean (in a positive way)? (content/meaning reframe)

The same principle applies if you are an athlete looking to do your own reframe.

Context Reframes

Bearing in mind the above, it is fairly obvious that by changing the context of a situation, behaviour or experience it will change the meaning of the situation, behaviour or experience. So a context reframe is when someone is asked (directly or indirectly) to consider a different context when the situation, behaviour or experience would be useful.

Examples of different contexts are:

♦ time
♦ age
♦ location
♦ circumstances
♦ family/work

A classic story told on some NLP courses of a context reframe is when a father dragged his 15 year old daughter into a therapist's office. "She's too headstrong – she always argues with me and never does what she is told!" complained the angry father. The therapist paused for a moment (probably asking himself what the father hadn't noticed, and when would the daughter's behaviour be useful). He then said, "Isn't it great that when she is older and goes out with boys, or when she is at work, she'll be able to stand up for herself?" With that comment, the father, who held the belief that what his daughter was doing was 'wrong' in some way, stopped in his tracks and saw the benefits of his daughter's strength of character.

The therapist had delivered a classic context reframe. He changed the time scale (in years to come), the age (when the daughter is older) and the circumstances ('out with boys' and 'at work' compared to 'with family').

Story 9.1

I was doing some mental skills coaching with a very promising young tennis player who was struggling with a particular aspect of his game. He said despondently, "I've had some lessons and I can't do a topspin second serve". The implication was that not only can he not do it at the moment (possibly a statement of truth), he wouldn't be able to do it in the future (a limiting belief).

So I said, "Yes, you probably can't do a topspin second serve, YET".

This was a context reframe, taking him into the future to a time when he would be able to do it, something which he wasn't able to notice before I mentioned it.

From an NLP coaching perspective, I paced his belief by agreeing with it, although I used the word "probably" which subtly introduced some doubt, and by adding the word YET it implied that he could or even would be able to in the future, which had the effect of shaking the firmness of his belief.

Within a few weeks he told me that he was able to do the topspin second serve, and that his tennis coach was delighted with the progress he had made.

Tip 9.2

The great aspect of reframes is that sometimes they work brilliantly like the example with the father and daughter above, and other times they make no difference at all, and other times they are partially effective.

So, there is no pressure on you when delivering the reframe (as the mental skills coach working with athletes or an athlete chatting with team-mates) – after all, it's just a thought you're running past someone, isn't it!

Tip 9.3

The keys to delivering a successful reframe are:
1. It is plausible (it doesn't have to be 'true', just plausible). After all, what is the 'true' meaning of anything!
2. It is delivered in a congruent way, in other words in a manner that lets the person know that you believe it.
3. You have rapport with the athlete or team-mate – sometimes the reframe can appear a little 'cheeky', so if there is not enough rapport and trust, it could serve to further annoy the athlete.
4. Pick your moment to deliver the reframe.
5. If it doesn't have the desired effect, bide your time and, if appropriate, deliver another reframe later.

Tip 9.4

Changing the context of 'time' is normally an effective reframe. If someone says 'I can't do X', as well as adding the word 'yet' as I did in Story 9.1, you could also draw their attention to times in the past 'when they were sure they couldn't do something but now they know they can'. And therefore could they imagine a time in the future when they can do this skill and look back at today's old belief, it being just another example of 'when they were sure they couldn't do something but now they know they can'.

It is important to note that the reframe question can be direct or indirect, or in the form of a statement, or some combination. For example, the therapist above asked, "Isn't it great that........." Although it implies a question, it was said almost in the tonality of a statement and is indirectly asking the father to reconsider. Another useful 'statement' would have been, "At least she'll be able to stand up to boys and bosses when she is older".

Equally, he could have asked a direct question such as, "how will you feel knowing she will be able to stand up to boys and bosses when she is older?"

Content/Meaning Reframes

Content (or meaning) reframes are when the athlete is asked (directly or indirectly) to consider what else a particular behaviour could mean. For example, I'm sure we all know of sportspeople who get upset (angry, frustrated or sad) if their sports coach, manager or a team-mate shouts at them to do better. There could be a limiting belief such as 'my coach/team-mate is shouting at me, he doesn't like (or value or respect or rate) me', or 'my coach/team-mate is nasty and obnoxious'.

By:

♦ asking directly or indirectly 'what else could this behaviour (shouting) mean?', or
♦ by stating directly what this behaviour could mean,

we could find a different meaning to this behaviour. By challenging, directly or indirectly, the implication that 'shouting' means (for example) 'nasty' or 'dislike' or 'disrespect', we break the 'meaning' link that the athlete has made in their minds.

So, for example, we could say things like:

♦ "At least your coach/team-mate is passionate/enthusiastic /fired up/motivated." (Being 'passionate/enthusiastic/fired up/motivated' is an implication of someone 'shouting'. Remember, it doesn't have to be true, just plausible.)
♦ "I wish my coach/team-mate showed as much enthusiasm."

- ◆ "Aren't you lucky to have a coach/team-mate who wants you to win so much that he's willing to push you further than you think you can go?"
- ◆ "Would you rather he didn't show any enthusiasm/passion/ fire in his belly?"
- ◆ "He must think you've got the ability (or skill or potential) to do even better – perhaps he sees talent in you that you can't see."
- ◆ "He must like/respect you enough to want you to do well."

The above approaches are fairly direct, making statements or asking questions that relate to the athlete. Using a more indirect approach would make statements about you or someone else, not the athlete in question, and could then involve statements like:

- ◆ "When my coach/team-mate shouts at me I know he really cares about my success."
- ◆ "If my coach/team-mate **doesn't** shout at me to encourage me I find **that** really disrespectful."

Again, the points in tips 9.2 and 9.3 are relevant here.

Exercise 9.3

Take each of the limiting beliefs you identified in Exercise 9.1. Do context or content reframes on each of them. Look for the advantages of the situations as they currently are. Notice how many of them you can see in a less negative (or more positive) light, or which don't feel as 'heavy' as they previously did.

Tip 9.5

Remember that Richard Bandler said, "people are addicted to their beliefs". Beware of taking your beliefs too seriously - they are just your best current thinking!

If it helps, for a moment, just pretend the belief belonged to someone else. Notice how much easier it is to reframe it now!

Exercise 9.4

Team up with two other willing partners, possibly other mental skills coaches or athletes. Decide who is person A, B and C.

Person A states a problem that they currently have. Make it an actual problem.

Person B makes sure they understand how it is a problem for Person A. (Often, people state problems and assume that other people know how it is a problem for them. Also, often people assume that they know how something is a problem for someone else. So Person B, switch off your 'mind-reads' and 'assumptions'!)

If Person B is in any way unsure how it is a problem, ask 'How is that a problem?' Person B may need to ask the same question to A's reply. The more Person B understands the problem, the better the reframe. You don't need to know the details, just how it is a problem. Ideally this would continue until Person A expresses the problem in the form of a limiting belief, or a statement such as 'X means Y' ('my coach shouting at me means he's nasty/doesn't care') or even 'X causes/ makes Y' ('my coach makes me angry when he shouts').

Persons B and C move so that they are out of Person A's earshot and come up with at least two reframes. Resist the temptation to over-analyse – often the best reframes are the ones that come to mind immediately – trust your unconscious mind!

Go back to Person A, ask him or her to repeat the problem, and then Person B delivers one of the reframe statements/ questions. Watch Person A's response. If appropriate, Person C deliver the other reframe. Remember – stay in rapport, keep it plausible and deliver it congruently.

Person B asks Person A how is that now, and what impact, if any, the reframe had.

The above process should typically take only between five and ten minutes, with a maximum of one minute for B and

C to come up with the reframes. If it takes any longer either B and C are getting into the detail of the problem or they are thinking too hard about the reframe.

Swap round and do the exercise twice more so that each person takes the role of person A, B and C.

Keep going and deal with as many 'problems' and/or limiting beliefs as you would like to deal with.

It helps if you all come to the session with some 'problems' to address. Exercise 9.1 could be useful here!

3. Perceptual Positions

The 'perceptual positions' technique is one of my favourite NLP techniques, one which I probably use more than any other, apart from reframing, which is a more 'conversational' rather than a formal technique.

Essentially, it is an approach to gain insight, wisdom and other perspectives on situations, and we will be covering its uses in Chapter 12.

One of the uses of the perceptual positions technique is to help people change beliefs, and so I'd like to take you through how to do that in this chapter.

What Are 'Perceptual Positions'?

Literally, it involves considering a situation from another view-point. By now I hope you will have the sense that very little is truly 'real', merely our 'take' or perspective on an event or situation due to the way we have deleted, distorted and generalised information throughout our life, leading to our unique 'model of the world'. It has been said that 'wisdom comes from multiple perspectives'.

In its purest sense, there are three perceptual positions – known as:
 ◆ position 1, or 'first position'
 ◆ position 2, or 'second position'

◆   position 3, or 'third position'

Position 1 is 'us', looking at a situation from our own point of view, feeling what we feel and speaking our thoughts.

Position 2 is the other person, parties, or in this case, the concept of the belief. In this position, we literally look at the situation from the perspective of the other person(s) involved, feel how they feel and speak as if we were them.

Position 3 is the neutral, impartial, objective observer, noticing what 'those people' in positions 1 and 2 haven't noticed because they are too involved in the situation.

More will be said in Chapter 12 about the other uses of perceptual positions within sport. The rest of this segment will deal with its use as a belief change tool.

How to Change Beliefs Using the Perceptual Positions Technique

Essentially, the mental skills coach will guide the player through the process of considering the belief from the three positions, allowing the player to see the situation from these three perspectives, listening to what the player says, and being aware if there are any particularly strong emotions in position 2. The process has 12 steps – let's go through them, firstly in summary, and then in more detail.

Please note that the following is written as if the reader is a mental skills coach. If you are a player or athlete it is possible to use this technique for yourself, although I would suggest you only do the process by yourself with a relatively minor belief (players and athletes reading this will of course adapt accordingly the following steps if they are doing this for themselves).

Also, I advise you to read this process at least twice to be able to grasp the process more fully.

Steps: (let's assume the player is a man called Steve, and the mental skills coach guiding Steve through the process is called Jenny. Let's also assume that the limiting belief is *"I'll never be able to perform at my best in pressure situations".)*

1. Ascertain the limiting belief
2. Do the 'groundwork'
3. Set up the technique
4. Position 1
5. Break state
6. Position 3
7. Break state
8. Position 2 (optional)
9. Break state
10. Position 1
11. Repeat steps 4, 5, 6, 7 and 8 as and if necessary
12. Test, future pace, agree next steps

Let's go through this in more detail now.

Steps:

1. Ascertain the limiting belief, check that it is appropriate for the mental skills coach and player to work on this together. (The mental skills coach is reminded that it is essential to build and maintain rapport during the process, as it is not unusual for some players to feel 'challenged' by the questioning.)

2. Assuming it is appropriate to work together, the mental skills coach would check the current strength of the belief (marks out of 10?) and the desired situation, and how the player would know the belief had changed. Check the ecology of changing the belief (see the six questions in the Introduction to Part III).

3. Set three chairs or mark out three spaces, as shown in Diagram 9.1.

    Jenny explains to Steve the process, and that position 1 is Steve, position 2 is the limiting belief or the concept of the limiting belief (i.e *I'll never be able to perform at my best in pressure situations*) and position 3 is a neutral observer.

Third Position

First Position   **Second Position**
                        Diagram 9.1

4. Steve sits or stands in position 1 as 'himself', and Jenny would
    sit or stand next to him (if he sits, Jenny is best seated, if he
    stands the Jenny is best standing. This aids the maintaining of
    rapport).

    Jenny asks:

    *"Steve, as you look at that belief (that "I'll never be able to
    perform at my best in pressure situations") over there, what
    are you thinking, what are you feeling?" (Jenny may or may not
    actually state the belief).*

    Steve describes the situation as briefly as possible. Jenny would
    allow Steve to stay in position 1 for no more than one minute.
    This is because he is already stuck in position 1 (he wouldn't still
    hold the belief if he were able to use perceptual positions!). Jenny
    would make a mental note of Steve's physiology in position 1 for
    comparison to when he returns to position 1 a little later.

5. Jenny asks Steve to move from position 1, and as he does so she
    would discuss a completely unrelated topic. This is known as a
    'break state', the purpose being to get Steve out of the mindset
    of himself (getting players to talk about their kids, their favourite
    holiday spot, their best sporting performance are normally good
    break states). This normally takes only a few moments.

6. When Jenny is satisfied that he is out of the mindset of position 1 (by ensuring his voice and general posture is different from that in position 1), she would ask him to move to position 3 and stand next to him there. In position 3, Jenny would say to Steve something like:

"Here you are as a neutral observer, a 'wise sage', taking a birds-eye view of 'a guy called Steve down there' (pointing to position 1) *and the (concept of the) belief of "Steve will never be able to perform at his best in pressure situations" down there* (pointing to position 2). *What do you notice about the situation from up here/this viewpoint that Steve over there and that belief aren't able to notice from where they are?"*

Please note the importance of the language – Jenny is using third person language such as 'they' and 'he'. If Jenny notices that Steve is using language which suggests he a slipping back into position 1 (eg "the things I do"), Jenny would point this out ("you mean the things Steve/he does"). If Steve is finding it hard to dissociate, move the chairs further away, or possibly stand on them to gain even more dissociation (make sure the chairs are steady and that the player is OK to do this!).

There is no defined set of questions that Jenny can ask from here. The key thing is to avoid giving advice, and to ask the kind of questions that lead Steve to realise that the belief isn't real, it's just a belief. Here are some other possible questions:

"What do you think the belief's positive intention for Steve is? And what is the positive intention of that? etc"

"Has there been a time when Steve has done something that demonstrates that the belief is not actually true?"

Jenny would keep asking questions and guide Steve until it was obvious that he had seen and realised things about the situation that he hadn't realised before and which were 'shaking the foundations of the belief'.

7. Break state – perhaps continue the previous break state story.

8. Then Jenny would guide Steve across to position 2, to take on the role of the 'belief' or the 'concept of the belief'. (NB. This step is optional. Occasionally it is not appropriate to take someone into the position of being a negative belief, although assuming position 3 has been done effectively, the belief is already 'shaking and crumbling'). Here, she would ask questions like:

"As you look across at Steve over there, what do you notice about Steve?"

"What is your purpose for Steve?"

"What do you feel about Steve?"

"What else?"

(There is an infinite number of possible responses that 'Steve' may have to these questions when in position 2. Generally, it is not unusual to find that the belief serves a purpose of, for example, helping Steve to try even harder, to be the best he can, to prevent him from being arrogant, to stop him from being disliked if he wins, to avoid disappointment, and so the answers will often reflect this.)

Jenny would keep going until it was clear that the belief was not 'true', or had lost its 'charge', and was weakening or even had disappeared!

Again, it is important that Steve's language reflects that of position 2, so he would refer to Steve as *"You"* or *"Steve"*.

9. Break state

10. Jenny would guide Steve back to position 1 and ask:

"How's that different now?" or *"How are you feeling now?"*

Jenny would be comparing the mental note she made of Steve's physiology from step 3. Ideally it would be very different and more 'positive'.

11. Jenny may need to guide Steve back to positions 2 and/or 3 if Steve isn't quite where he wants to be in terms of the belief. It may also be useful to introduce a position 4, perhaps that of a person (opponent, team-mate). If so, it is important that Jenny then guides Steve to position 1 and repeats Step 10 – it is important to start and end at position 1.

12. Test the old belief, for example:

"What do you believe now, Steve? How do you feel about that old belief? How do you feel about <playing in the tournament / running against 'so-and-so' in the final>."

Future pace – ask Steve to think about at least three specific situations that previously he was concerned about, and to notice how different it is now. We will cover the visualisation aspects of future pacing in Chapter 10. If appropriate, Jenny would ask Steve what specific tasks he would undertake to embed the new positive belief.

SUMMARY OF THE PROCESS

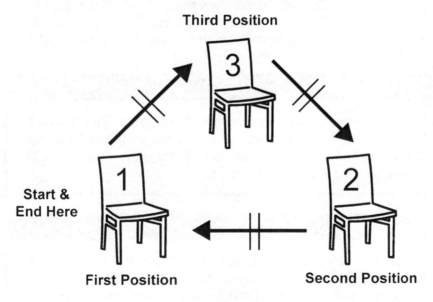

Diagram 9.2

If you intend to use this process, please ensure that you read the previous section at least twice.

Summary Points

Here are some key points to help make the process work every time:

◆ Break state after positions 1, 2 and 3.

◆ Make sure the client's language in each position reflects them actually being in that position.

◆ Coach, stand/sit next to the client. Move with them to each position. Avoid standing or sitting in the spot of position 1, 2 or 3 while the player is at a different position at any time.

◆ Always start and end in position 1 ('at home').

◆ Resist the temptation to suggest or advise or coach. Ask open questions. (The player can't argue with their own advice!)

◆ When back in position 1, draw the client's attention to how things have changed. 'How's that different now?'

◆ If the situation has improved from, say, a '8 out of 10' to a '5 out of 10', and the player would ideally like it to be a '2 out of 10', firstly congratulate the player (and you, secretly!). You could also ask 'how could it get to a 4?' (i.e. reduce incrementally).

Exercise 9.5

Take a relatively minor limiting belief you have. Take yourself through the three perceptual positions, noticing how the impact of the belief has changed by the end of the process when you are back at position 1.

Exercise 9.6

If you are a mental skills coach, take someone else through the perceptual positions process. Ideally get into a practice group of three coaches, and have one observer who can give feedback to the coach. Swap roles so all of you get a turn to be coach. Work with an actual limiting belief.

Tip 9.6

If you are a mental skills coach and intend to work with players' limiting beliefs, I suggest that you either do Exercise 9.6 above or that you do Exercise 12.1 or 12.2 (perceptual positions with some kind of 'conflict' or 'mis-understanding') first so that you become familiar with the process. It then becomes much easier to work with beliefs using this process.

4. Provide the 'Why to' and 'How To'

Robert Dilts, one of the early developers of NLP and who worked closely with John Grinder and Richard Bandler, has written numerous books on the subject of beliefs (see 'Further Reference' section for some suggested titles).

One of Dilts' findings is that often people have limiting beliefs because they lack:

- ◆ the 'why to', in other words the motivation
- ◆ the 'how to', in other words the skills to do a task

'Why to'

Regarding the 'why to', or motivation, remember the examples of the two ladies in Chapter 2 who had the 'why to' to lift up cars. They probably would not have believed they could do it, but because they had the motivation they did it. Sometimes the role of a mental skills coach is to help the athlete be truly motivated. See Chapter 15 for more about motivation.

'How To'

Clearly, the role of a conventional sports coach would be to provide the 'how to', and possibly the 'why to'. From the point of view of a mental skills coach, it may not be in their remit to coach skills, but it absolutely is in their remit to help them identify that there are skills missing and to coach them to find ways to gain those skills.

If you are an athlete using this book for yourself and not coaching others, and have identified a limiting belief, it is worth asking yourself whether your belief relates to lack of motivation in some way (the 'Why To') or a current perceived or actual lack of capability at the moment (the 'How To').

Exercise 9.7

If you are a mental skills coach or player, find opportunities to use an appropriate belief change technique with fellow mental skills coaches and/or players (where appropriate), or by yourself.

Summary

♦ We have covered four ways to change beliefs. There are several other techniques to do this within NLP that are outside the scope of this book because mental skills coaches would need to be trained as NLP Practitioners or Master Practitioners to be able to use these techniques appropriately.

♦ The methods highlighted in this chapter to change beliefs will deal with many of the limiting beliefs that you are likely to face either as an athlete or a mental skills coach.

♦ If you have identified issues which are holding you back, and you are unable to resolve them yourself, then ask a suitably qualified NLP Practitioner, possibly specialising in sports coaching, to assist you.

♦ If you have identified issues which are holding an athlete back, and you are unable to resolve them yourself, or you are concerned that they may be best served by a therapist (see the Introduction to Part III), refer them to someone qualified to help the athlete. This will probably be a qualified NLP Practitioner (for the former) or a qualified counsellor or therapist (for the latter).

Chapter 10
Visualisation
and Mental Rehearsal

An Overview

Visualisation and mental rehearsal are essentially when an athlete sees in their mind's eye (visualisation) a future event or competition, which together with:

- hearing the sounds as they would hear them, both external (for example from the crowd and other competitors) and their own internal dialogue
- feeling the feelings, both emotional and physical/proprioceptive ('proprioception' allows us to be aware of what position our body is in and the movements it is making)
- and possibly even the tastes and smells

make up the mental rehearsal modalities. The term 'visualisation' is often used to mean mental rehearsal, because the visual representational system is the fastest of the representational systems (a picture paints a thousand words), and often an image (be it external or internal) will lead to us hearing, feeling and possibly tasting and smelling things. I've heard athletes say during their visualisation *"it's so close I can almost taste (or smell) it"*. So in effect, mental rehearsal is a more thorough version of visualisation.

This chapter will cover both:

- **why** visualisation and/or mental rehearsal are so important and
- **how** to do it

Unless specifically stated otherwise, the term 'mental rehearsal' will be used to include 'visualisation'.

Why Is Mental Rehearsal So Important?

There are numerous reasons.

1. Champions Do It!

Sally Gunnell rehearsed the 400 meters hurdles race **11-12 times per day for 9 months** before the Barcelona Olympics.[22]

Johnny Wilkinson rehearses his kicks in his mind so frequently that he goes into 'autopilot' when kicking for goal.[23]

Other champions like Roger Black and Steve Backley do it, and former UK National Athletics coach Frank Dick advocates it.[24]

2. Some Research

There was some research done in University of Chicago regarding the impact of mental rehearsal and visualisation on basketball players. The researchers measured the ability of a group of accomplished basketball players to shoot baskets. The researchers split the players into three groups at random and asked them to do the following practice:

◆ group A – practice shooting baskets
◆ group B – do nothing
◆ group C – mentally rehearse shooting baskets **successfully every time.**

The researchers then measured the players' ability to shoot baskets. Group B's performance had, not surprisingly, deteriorated. Group A's performance improved by 24%, and Group C's performance improved by a staggering 23%, even though they hadn't touched a ball since the initial measuring.[25]

---

[22] Jeff Grout & Sarah Perrin, *Mind Games – Inspirational Lessons From The World's Biggest Sports Stars*, Capstone Publishing Ltd, 2004, p.164.

[23] http://news.bbc.co.uk/sport1/hi/rugby_union/get_involved/4204746.stm

[24] Jeff Grout & Sarah Perrin, *Mind Games – Inspirational Lessons From The World's Biggest Sports Stars*, Capstone Publishing Ltd, 2004, pp.153-156

[25] http://www.inq7.net/lif/2003/may/27/lif_22-1.htm

This research showed the importance of mental rehearsal. Just to make it clear, mental rehearsal is not a substitute for appropriate training – these basketball players were already skilled. However, assuming an athlete has done the appropriate physical training, adding appropriate mental rehearsal will almost certainly enhance results.

Mental rehearsal can work in retrospect too, to *'play it better than it was!'* This is covered in Story 10.3.

3. Unconscious Mind Rules, OK!

From an NLP point of view, mental rehearsal trains the unconscious mind to do a particular task or series of tasks effectively. Most physical activities are done unconsciously – do you think about how to walk or drive? In sport, when actually doing the skill or playing in a match, the act of hitting or kicking a ball, or jumping a hurdle, is done UNCONSCIOUSLY. As you will remember from Chapter 2, it is our UNCONSCIOUS mind that runs the body and performs the tasks we do in sport. Obviously the conscious mind will set and targets, think about tactics, and then ideally will leave the rest to the unconscious.

By doing mental rehearsal, you are communicating with the unconscious mind in the way it likes to communicate – in pictures, sounds, feelings, tastes and smells.

And when the physical body AND the conscious mind AND the unconscious mind know what to do and are all aligned to achieve the same thing, it becomes a hugely powerful machine.

Just like the more physical skills, mental rehearsal requires practice! (Remember how often Sally Gunnell practiced).

4. Hurry Up and Improve!

One of the easiest and quickest ways to change someone's approach to sporting situations once the player knows what to do (and assuming he has the requisite ability to do it) is by mental rehearsal.

Story 10.1

I was working with a young professional golfer who had been trying for months to change a habit of letting one bad shot ruin the next five or six holes. He had seen little change. Within one session, he reported that he no longer got angry when he did a bad shot. We will cover how we did this later in this chapter.

Contrast this with a casual, non-professional conversation I had with a coach from a leading professional football club. He referred to one of his leading players who had a particular aspect of his game that the management and coaching staff at the club had spent a long time trying to change. They used video analysis, discussion, practice on the training ground, yet the behaviour was not changing quickly. Whilst I cannot prove it, I am totally confident that if the player mentally rehearsed the new approach to certain situations his results would have improved quickly.

5. Familiarity

By rehearsing mentally, the athlete becomes more comfortable with, and more confident about, the sporting event or competition. Roger Black used to go to the empty stadium before an event and rehearse the event mentally, such that when he walked out in front of a noisy full house a day or two later, he was comfortable – it was like he had been there before.

"I found that if you go into an empty stadium and walk around it, and two days later you're there running, your brain goes, 'Oh yeah, I was here a few days ago', and that's a big help. If you walk into that environment and your brain thinks, 'Oh. I've never been here', you're in trouble."[26]

6. Confidence –
Getting to The Right Place from All The Wrong Places

As well as the feeling of familiarity referred to in the preceding paragraph, numerous athletes and competitors state that a key

---

[26] Jeff Grout & Sarah Perrin, *Mind Games – Inspirational Lessons From The World's Biggest Sports Stars*, Capstone Publishing Ltd, 2004, p.161

aspect of success in sport is being prepared for any eventuality before or during competition. One key way to enhance this preparation is to have rehearsed mentally the different scenarios – again, we will cover some ways to do this later this chapter.

7. Future Pacing

You will remember the sections on:

◆ anchoring (being in THE right state)
◆ submodalities
◆ belief change

where it was important with some of the techniques to 'future pace' the 'change work' so that the athlete would know she was going to do the new behaviour or feel the new way in the future event. With virtually all NLP techniques, having the person visualise and mentally rehearse their own success is a very powerful tool to embed the new behaviour(s).

Keys To Doing Mental Rehearsal

Introduction

Let's move on to how to do mental rehearsal, and some tips to enhance what you do.

Before we begin, it's important to note that there is no definitive way to visualise or rehearse mentally. Everyone is different. If you have found a technique or an approach which gives you the results you want, keep doing it! However, if you have not yet found a way which works for you, or if you want to make what you do even better and are willing to be flexible, then this section may offer you some tips. Remember, if you experiment and it doesn't help the situation, you can always revert to what you were doing!

Also, I sometimes hear people say that they are not very good at visualising anything – the picture they get is not very clear. There are two points I would like to make about that.

Firstly, how clear would you expect the pictures to be? If they were as clear as the ones that you have right now as you are reading the book, how would you tell the difference between what was real and what was imagined!

Secondly, most of us have a preferred representational system (visual, auditory or kinaesthetic), unless we are equally as comfortable using all three. Around 40 percent of people have visual as their preferred representational system. This does not mean that the other 60 percent cannot visualise, it means that they **may** possibly find it more difficult to visualise than to hear sounds or feel feelings. We will touch on and discuss what you can do if you or people you coach find it challenging to visualise.

The rest of this section will cover how to do some of the aspects of mental rehearsal and then will pull it together and explain the processes involved. The first key aspects are association and dissociation.

Association and Dissociation

When we mentally rehearse, we can either be:

- ◆ 'associated' or
- ◆ 'dissociated'

As a reminder, **associated** means that we are living the event as if it were happening, in other words seeing it through our own eyes, and therefore hearing it through our own ears and feeling the feelings.

Dissociated means seeing the situation as if we were watching ourselves in a film. It is more 'detached' and therefore there are less emotions attached. The following exercises demonstrate the impact of association and dissociation.

Exercise 10.1

Choose a mildly unpleasant sporting memory, perhaps one when you did not perform to your best. As you think about that event, notice whether you are looking at it through your own eyes (associated) or seeing yourself in the picture (dissociated). If you are associated, step out of the event so that you are watching it as if you were seeing a film of yourself in the event. Notice the impact it has on how you feel.

If by some chance you feel worse when you dissociate, then re-associate.

Exercise 10.2

Choose a pleasant, successful sporting memory. As you think about that event, notice whether you are associated or dissociated.

If you are associated, notice the impact of dissociating from the event.

If you are dissociated, notice the impact of associating.

Choose to be either associated or dissociated, depending on which is best for you.

I would expect that for almost all readers, dissociating makes the event have less emotional charge, which is probably a useful thing to do when the event is not pleasant and probably not useful when the event is pleasant. Similarly, I would expect that associating gives the event more emotional charge. (This is why I did not ask you to associate into the unpleasant memory in Exercise 10.1.)

So, we can visualise associated or dissociated, or both. I think it is useful to have the athlete do both dissociated and associated rehearsal. There are benefits from doing both. When doing dissociated visualisation, it is an opportunity to learn and notice what that person (i.e. YOU!) are doing well, and what could be improved. You can act as your own coach. By doing associated visualisation, you get to experience the fullness of the event – the what you see, hear, feel, and even taste and smell. It also is a form of training for the body – there have been several experiments done which show that by doing associated visualisation it stimulates the micro-muscles that link to the actual muscles that will be doing the sport.

Tip 10.1

Personally, unless the athlete objects, I would always ask the athlete to do at least one of each – remembering that wisdom comes from multiple perspectives, and there is a lot that the athlete can learn from seeing him/herself doing the particular event (dissociated) from different angles and perspectives.

Also, associated visualisation often adds to the player's motivation because they are experiencing the 'success' or excellent performance.

Exercise 10.3

Think of an imminent unimportant sports event. Mentally rehearse the event as follows:

– see yourself doing it (dissociated), notice how your body is moving and anything else that is relevant to that particular event. Notice that as you see yourself, the person in the picture (i.e. YOU!) is saying things to himself, hearing things (perhaps the crowd or the noise of other competitors) and has some emotions and is aware of how his body feels and is moving.

Repeat the process several times, and look at yourself from different angles – front, behind, both sides, from above. Notice whatever you notice.

– then repeat the process, but this time associated. So see the event itself as if it were happening in real life – see what you see, hear what you hear, feel what you feel (physically and emotionally), notice what you say to yourself.

Repeat the process several times. Notice whatever you notice.

NB.
This is not the full form of mental rehearsal that you will be doing later this chapter – I want you to progress step by step, finding out what works best for you.

From Exercise 10.3, notice which of the two types of mental rehearsal:

+ feels more natural
+ is easier to do
+ gives you more benefit when competing - just because something feels great doesn't mean it's good for you (sorry if I sound like your parent or schoolteacher!)

Exercise 10.4

If you are a mental skills coach, take your athletes through Exercise 10.3. Ask them to tell you which his more easy, comfortable and beneficial.

Other Submodalites

You will remember from the submodalities section that association and dissociation is a submodality. It is useful for athletes to use other submodalities when doing visualisation or mental rehearsal, for example:

+ distance
+ size
+ brightness
+ focus
+ speed of movement
+ location of sound
+ volume
+ direction of sound
+ location of the feeling
+ vibration of the feeling
+ movement of the feeling

Exercise 10.5

When doing the mental rehearsal processes in Exercises 10.3 and 10.4, experiment with changing other submodalities such as those listed immediately above. Notice which ones have the most positive impact on you and your performance, and that of your athletes if you are a mental skills coach.

The purpose is to notice which of the submodalities have the most positive impact and to keep using these when doing mental rehearsal.

For example, if you (or your athletes) find that the results of mental rehearsal are best by making the picture big, bright, clearly focussed and in colour, with volume slightly lower than real life, with a warm anti-clockwise feeling in your stomach, then use these submodalities each time.

Time Distortion

One of the issues regarding mental rehearsal that we need to consider is that of **time.** When rehearsing, do we do it at:

- normal speed?
- slower than normal speed?
- faster than normal speed?

I think this depends on the event itself. Ideally we would do it at normal speed. However, if a marathon runner rehearsed a race 11-12 times per day as Sally Gunnell did, he would have no time for training or sleeping or anything else! Even doing it once per day would be somewhat tedious even for the most committed of athletes. I recommend the use of 'time distortion'. Time distortion is something we all do, especially sportspeople. It is a natural process – Einstein, before the days of 'political correctness', said words to the effect of "a minute spent sitting on a hot stove feels like an hour, and an hour spent talking to a pretty girl seems like a minute".

When referring to specific situations in their sport, many competitors say things like:

- ◆ 'time just slowed down'
- ◆ 'it felt like I had all the time in the world'

Story 10.2

I used to play football in goal semi-professionally, and there were several times when I would make a diving reflex save, and was aware of how time slowed down as I was 'flying' through the air to tip the ball over the bar or round the post.

So we can all do time distortion, both for past events and future events. The next story is particularly illuminating.

Story 10.3 - "Playing it Better Than It Was!"

I worked with an accomplished marathon runner who, as a last resort, used mental rehearsal to compensate for lack of practice, with astounding results. Let's call her Julie.

Julie saw me a few days before a major marathon event, and her outcome/performance goal was to reach the qualifying time to be included with the following year's 'elite' runners. This required her to finish in a time of 3 hours 15 minutes, her personal best being 3 hours 17 minutes.

She expressed some nervousness in the session, due mainly to the fact that she had not been able to complete the 'essential' 20 mile run a few weeks previously. She was concerned about her ability to complete the marathon in the required time because it is common knowledge that runners 'HAVE TO' run the 20 mile race, ideally around three weeks before the Marathon.

I wanted to do some mental rehearsal of the race itself, yet I knew that Julie had some concerns which needed to be addressed.

In the room, we couldn't change the fact that she had not been able to PHYSICALLY complete the 20 mile run, but we could change the MENTAL impact. At the time there were two obvious possible approaches.

1. Some form of belief change regarding the importance of running the 20 mile race.
2. Mentally re-run the 20 mile race.

Given that we did not have much of time left in the session, I asked her to 're-run' the 20 mile race in her mind, associated, but to speed the whole thing up so that it took no more than ten minutes rather than over two hours.

I watched Julie as she did this, eyes-closed and head resting in her hands. I could see from her expressions (reddening face, clenched jaw, involuntary jerking movements) that she was truly doing the race in her mind.

Afterwards, Julie said that she felt as though she had done all she could by way of preparation for the marathon, given that she had not physically run the 20 miles. Julie expressed a calmness about the race, different to how she had been 10 to 15 minutes earlier.

I then asked Julie to do some mental rehearsal of the forth-coming race itself. Before doing it, I asked her what was her target time (3 hours, 14 minutes), and to tell me about the key points of the race. Julie had mentioned previously that there were some key moments in the race. For example, after around 20 miles she would reach the 'wall' and, in her words, *'I'll need to have a word with myself and tell myself to keep going and grit my teeth'*.

I also asked Julie to tell me what was the very last thing that would have to happen for her to know UNDENIABLY that she had achieved her goal. She said it would be running down *The Mall* with less than 100 yards to the finish line and seeing less than '3 hours and 14 minutes' on the clock. I asked her to make sure that when she did the two types of visualisation (associated and dissociated) that she made sure she saw that picture.

I asked her to begin the mental rehearsals and once again, speed up the run, to do the marathon first dissociated and then associated. I asked Julie to accelerate the mental rehearsals, but to slow them down to normal speed for what she had identified as the few key moments of the race.

At the end of the second rehearsal (associated), Julie got quite emotional. She said afterwards that she say the clock showing 3 hours 10 minutes 11 seconds – a very clear image and message from her unconscious mind, and she could hear the crowd and feel the fatigue and elation. I asked her whether she felt it was achievable: *"yes – it will be a stretch but I can do it."*

I asked Julie to rehearse the race mentally every day up until the morning of the race, and to bear in mind one key aspect which we will cover in the next section of this chapter.

TO BE CONTINUED!!

Getting To The Right Place From The Wrong Places

Virtually anyone can mentally rehearse things going perfectly. One of the keys to successful sports performance is being able to deal with challenges and problems that occur before and during performance, some of which may be unforeseen. Being able to handle these events is essential to successful sporting performance, and having rehearsed them physically AND mentally is essential.

Javelin champion Steve Backley believes it is essential to have a solution to deal with any possible situation. *"I make a list of anything that can happen and then over three months come up with answers."*[27]

Story 10.4

Dr Wyatt Woodsmall, a leading NLP Trainer who worked with the US Olympic diving team in the 1980's and 1990s, speaks of how the Chinese Olympic diving team studied Greg Louganis, the US Olympic Gold Medal Winner at the 1984 and 1988 Olympics. Unbeknown to the diving community, the

[27] Jeff Grout & Sarah Perrin, *Mind Games – Inspirational Lessons From The World's Biggest Sports Stars,* Capstone Publishing Ltd, 2004, p.170

Chinese had been studying the way that Louganis dived, and had managed to coach their divers to copy exactly the way Louganis dived.

Dr Woodsmall and his modelling team modelled how Louganis dived. When asked about how he viewed the Chinese challenge, Woodsmall said that the Chinese were able to do dives that LOOKED like Louganis, but they couldn't do one like Louganis, because they hadn't been able to copy his internal mental process (for example, the way he mentally rehearsed, the submodalities of the pictures, sounds and feelings, and his beliefs).

Louganis was quoted as saying:

> *"I'm a real perfectionist. But that is the irony. In order to do it perfectly, I have to let go of perfection a little. For instance, in diving there's a 'sweet spot' on the board, right at the end. I can't always hit it perfectly. Sometimes, I'm a little back from it. Sometimes, I'm a little over. But the judges can't tell that. I have to deal with whatever takeoff I have been given. I can't leave my mind on the board. I have to stay in the present. I have to be relaxed enough to clue into the memory tape of how to do it. That's why I train so hard - not just to do it right, but to do it right from all the wrong places."*[28]

In effect, Louganis is saying that getting to the right place from the right place is (relatively) easy. To be a champion, you have to know how to get to the right place from all the **WRONG** places.

Here are some thoughts on this subject from champions:

◆ Sally Gunnell, as part of her mental rehearsal before the 1992 Olympics, visualised success regardless of what was happening in the 'race'.[29] Moreover, if things were going wrong in the mental rehearsal, she would re-wind the film and replay it, WINNING EVERY TIME.

---

[28] Quote provided by Dr Wyatt Woodsmall.
[29] Jeff Grout & Sarah Perrin, *Mind Games – Inspirational Lessons From The World's Biggest Sports Stars,* Capstone Publishing Ltd, 2004, pp. 164-5

♦ Matthew Pinsent (rowing) says that, "Ordinary athletes train to give themselves a chance of winning. True champions train to eliminate the chances of losing".[30]

♦ Steve Backley (javelin) suggests making a list of everything that could go wrong and then coming up with a solution.[31]

So, in summary, when doing mental rehearsal or visualisation, run all scenarios that could conceivably happen (think laterally!) and then see yourself winning or performing as you want to, no matter what!

By doing this, assuming they have done the physical preparation (also see Story 10.3!), athletes can go into the race feeling fully prepared and confident of their performance.

Story 10.3 Continued

Before Julie left my consulting room, I asked her to consider what could go 'wrong' before and during the race, and to have plans and incorporate those events and plans into her mental rehearsal, so that she was fully prepared for what might happen on the day.

I had a text from Julie on the Sunday afternoon during the break-time from an NLP Practitioner training I was running. She did a time of less than 3 hours and 7 minutes – more than 10 minutes inside her personal best and more than 3 minutes better than her 'dream time'. She was ecstatic at the success and the achievement of being in the 'elite' group of athletes for the following year's Marathon.

Exercise 10.6

Prepare for a sporting event that is important to you. Using what you learned in Exercises 10.3, 10.4 and 10.5, Mentally rehearse the event or competition, remembering to:

---

[30] Jeff Grout & Sarah Perrin, *Mind Games – Inspirational Lessons From The World's Biggest Sports Stars,* Capstone Publishing Ltd, 2004, p. 170
[31] ibid p. 170

- do some dissociated and associated rehearsal

- adjust the submodalities of the associated rehearsal to give you the most positive feeling

- rehearse numerous scenarios, always making sure that you get to where you want to get to ("the right place from all the wrong places")

If you are a mental skills coach, coach your athlete(s) to do the same.

Tip 10.1

If the event you are competing in takes a long time to complete (for example the marathon), identify key stages of the race (for example 'the wall' after 20 miles), or key events that could go wrong (for example, being tripped up or falling over).

Speed up the race, and slow it down to normal speeds for these key stages or events, so that you can mentally rehearse (dissociated and associated) getting to the right place from all the wrong places.

What Happens if Visualisation is Difficult?

Some athletes may not find mental rehearsal easy to do at first. Here are some common problems and tips to help make things easy. These are tips, and of course cannot deal with every single possible difficulty.

i. Difficulty: "I can't visualise."

Suggested Solution: In NLP we have a technique called 'overlapping representational systems'. This is where someone has difficulty in accessing a particular representational system because, perhaps, it is their least preferred representational system. Typically, the mental skills coach would guide the 'client' from their most preferred representational system, through their next most through to their least preferred.

In this situation, let's say that an athlete's most preferred system is kinaesthetic, then auditory, and finally visual. The mental skills coach could say something like:

"feel what it is like to be in the stadium, walking along the track, the feeling of excitement as you take off your track-suit bottoms (the kinaesthetic words and phrases are underlined for your reference, not to be overly stressed when speaking).

And hear the crowd's roar as the announcer announces the athletes' names, the sound of spikes on the track as the other athletes warm up (auditory words and phrases, apart from 'warm up')

And have a look and see the stadium lights and the crowd, and the silver starting blocks etc etc."

Another choice for the coach would be to ask the athlete to describe what he is feeling for a little while, and then what he is hearing and feeling, and then draw his attention to what he is seeing.

ii. Difficulty: *"I can't visualise myself doing it properly because I don't know what it would look like."*

Suggested Solution: Find someone who can do it the way you want to do it, and then 'super-impose' yourself on that picture.

Story 10.5

An athlete client of mine wanted to improve her weight training in order to prepare for the forthcoming race season. During a session we spoke about visualisation.

The following session she reported that she had lifted a 'personal best' during a weight session after our coaching session. She saw a colleague doing a particularly excellent weight lift, and in her mind she super-imposed her own self onto the picture she had of excellence. This led to her own excellent session.

> ## Story 10.6
>
> I had a one-off session with another athlete who wanted to improve a particular aspect of his sprinting technique. I asked him who he knew who could do that particular aspect. The only person he could think of was Carl Lewis (not a bad person to model!). I asked the athlete to see Carl Lewis in his mind and then to super-impose himself onto that mental image.
>
> He was able to do that and reported much improved results at his next sprint training session.

iii. Difficulty: *"I can't make a movie – I only have a still shot (or shots)."*

Suggested Solution: Make a series of still images. Then put them together in a sequence and create a film, even if it is a stuttering film initially. The more the film runs, the smoother it will get as the player gets used to this new type of mental processing.

> ## Story 10.7
>
> The athlete referred to in Story 10.6 was initially barely able to make a still picture when asked to do associated rehearsal. Gradually he was able to make a series of stills, in sequence.
>
> Finally, he was able to put the whole set of stills together into a film as if it were 'real life'.

iv. Difficulty: *"I can't see myself getting to the finish – the film stops."*

Suggested Solution: Initially, check with the athlete that it is absolutely OK with him or her to complete the event (use the ecology questions from the well-formed outcome process referred to in Chapter 4). Also, check that the athlete believes it is possible for him or her to do it. If there are issues around limiting beliefs, secondary gain or ecology issues, these need to be dealt with using techniques covered previously in this book.

Assuming there are none, ask the athlete to make a still image of themselves at the end of the event. Even if it is de-focussed, black & white and dim, make a picture. Gradually ask the athlete to add some colour and/or focus, and possibly some movement or sounds if appropriate.

Ask the athlete what messages or advice that athlete at the 'finishing line' (ie them) is giving to the 'them' doing the race or competition.

As soon as the athlete is giving useful advice, ask if it is OK to begin the film again at or just before the point that it previously stopped, and assuming it is OK, do so.

Story 10.8

I was coaching a cross-channel swimmer for two sessions – let's call her Suzanna. The previous year Suzanna had attempted the swim and had to stop due to adverse weather conditions.

During our second and final session, three days before the swim, I asked her to do the mental rehearsal process, speeded up, firstly as if she were on the accompanying boat watching herself, and then as if she were actually doing it. After a few moments she became a little upset because the movie kept stopping at the point that she had to stop the previous year. The film would not go past that point.

I asked Suzanna to visualise herself actually standing on the beach in France (i.e. dissociated). After a little while she was able to do that. I asked her how that Suzanna on the beach felt, and to be that Suzanna on the beach (i.e associated). Then I asked her what advice she (standing on the beach) wants to give the Suzanna actually swimming. After a few moments Suzanna said 'I'm saying "hurry up Suzanna, it's cold here!"'. I asked Suzanna to let the film continue while she (on the beach) watched Suzanna swim towards her.

Suzanna was able to do that.

Then I asked Suzanna to start the film again, this time associated and really speed it up until she got to the point where the film had stopped, at which point to make it in 'real-time' until she had got over that hurdle and then speed it up to the end.

She was able to do that, and left the session far more confident that she would complete the swim. I asked Suzanna to repeat the visualisation two or three times per day before the day of the swim. I stressed the importance of 'getting to the right place from all the wrong places'.

Suzanna managed to swim the Channel (and become one of only around 250 women to have done so) even though it took almost 20 hours (an amazing feat of endurance!) – the final 400 meters took an hour and a half due to the head wind and adverse currents.

Where and When Should Visualisation Be Done?

I would suggest that the mental rehearsal be done at a time and place when the athlete is alone and able to concentrate, knowing there will be no interruptions.

In terms of how often, there is no hard and fast rule. I would suggest that each athlete finds what works for him or her. As a guideline, I would prepare as far in advance as practical, and do it every day for around 10 to 15 minutes.

Summary

- ◆ Visualisation or mental rehearsal are key skills that will give sportsmen the edge.
- ◆ As with any skill, practice is essential.
- ◆ Make sure that you visualise the event turning out the way you want, regardless of what happens before and during the event. Rehearse mentally how you would handle each of these conceivable instances. It is easy to get to the right places from the right places. Champions know how to get to the **right** place from all the **wrong** places.
- ◆ Knowing that you are prepared to handle anything that comes your way will give you added confidence in your preparation, and will help should any of those events happen.

- Be prepared to speed up events or slow them down if necessary and appropriate.
- Experiment with the kind of visualisation that works for you, especially associated and dissociated.
- Use other submodalities to enhance the mental rehearsal.

Chapter **11**
Dealing with
Setbacks and Difficulties

Introduction

Sport can be regarded as a metaphor for life. Many aspects of life are encompassed in sport, whether you play for fun or for a living, in a sport that is predominantly individual or a team sport. And in life, there will be ups and down, highs and lows.

In sport, the key types of disappointments and the ones that we will deal with in this chapter are as follows:

1. Dealing With Defeat and/or Poor Performances

2. Injury

3. Difficult relationships

Let's take each in turn.

1. Dealing With Defeat and/or Poor Performances

Clearly, losing is part of sport. Some people are better at handling it than others. And playing at our best every time, never making mistakes, is something that is clearly unrealistic. Many sportspeople get upset about mistakes and defeat – whether the upset is some form of anger, or sadness, and possibly leading to some fear of repeating it and/or guilt for letting people down in the future.

So how can we handle this? There are four key ways to do this, and they are not mutually exclusive.

i. 'Acknowledge and learn'
ii. Just 'let it go'
iii. Get back into the same state as when you were playing well
iv. Focus on what you want

It is important to say that if you are already happy with the way you handle defeat and/or poor performances, just keep doing it! If you are not, or if you are a mental skills coach who wants to have more 'tools' in your toolkit, then read on.

i. 'Acknowledge and Learn'

Bearing in mind the NLP presupposition that 'there is no failure, just feedback', if we can consider each 'non-success' as an opportunity to learn, it will help us to feel differently about the situation.

From a basic point of view, 'what you resist persists', so by denying there is a problem or fighting it can just lead to it persisting. It is better to acknowledge if things aren't going the way you would like, for example during a match, and then make any necessary changes to what you are doing.

Taking a somewhat less simple approach, it could be considered that there are four aspects of every 'disappointing' event:

- ◆ the event itself
- ◆ the memory of the event
- ◆ the emotions attached to the event
- ◆ the learnings

We know from the NLP Communication Model that the memory of the event is **never** the event itself, due to the deletions, distortions and generalisations. Often the emotions arising from a disappointment dispel quickly as we 'get over it', and get 'older and wiser' – in other words, we take the learnings from that event and move on.

However, sometimes the emotions are more like **EMOTIONS**, and hence we are not able to take the learnings from the event because we are so upset. (How many tennis racquets have been smashed, or golf clubs tossed away in anger? How many cups of tea have been thrown across football dressing rooms?)

So whether it is a 'bad shot' in tennis or golf, or a defeat in a match, or just a bad performance, by treating it as a learning experience, we can manage our emotions and get over the disappointment much more quickly.

So how can we do this?

One of the most useful techniques I have used with athletes to overcome disappointments is a combination of dissociation and visualisation. This is best explained by way of the following example.

Story 11.1

I was working with a professional golfer who sometimes got extremely angry with himself if he did a bad shot. It often caused him to produce results which did not reflect his true potential.

I explained the concept of 'no failure, just feedback', and that if we treat each 'disappointment' as a learning experience, it becomes an asset to help us improve our game rather than a liability to ruin it.

We agreed that a far more useful strategy for dealing with a bad shot would be for him to be able to dissociate and advise himself of what to do next time, as if he were coaching a stranger or someone he had no emotional attachment to. In order to do this new strategy, I asked him to run it firstly dissociated (yes, run the dissociative strategy dissociated), then associated, then finally dissociated. In more detail, the steps were:

1. Set up a film screen and see himself (i.e. dissociate) having just done a 'bad shot'.
2. See himself in the film mentally step back from the situation i.e. watching himself watching himself (double dissociation).
3. See himself advising himself as if he were talking to (or coaching) someone else who had just done that shot.
4. Give sufficient advice so that the person (i.e. him) would

know what to do next time and that the person (i.e. him) will feel no negative emotions about the shot (see Tips 11.1 and 11.2 below).

5. See himself step back into himself (watch himself re-associate) and take on the 'advice'.

6. Watch himself move forward when there is no emotion on that event, only the learnings for what to do differently next time.

7. Repeat steps 2-6 above several times (10-15) in different scenarios (different courses, tee shots, bunkers, putts etc) so that he felt very comfortable that he knew what to do in those situations.

8. Repeat the process 10-15 times, but this time do it all associated. In other words, actually experiencing himself
    - stepping back in the moment and advising himself, after having done a 'bad' shot, and
    - taking on the advice and
    - feeling no negativity towards himself or the shot and
    - leaving the bad shot behind and moving forward to the next shot in a relaxed state.

9. I asked him then to repeat steps 1-7. This step is optional.

10. Finally, I tested and future paced by asking him now to imagine having done a bad shot, how does he respond? He was able to run the new strategy successfully.

A few weeks later he told me that he had been able to use this new strategy with repeated success, and was consistently scoring below par.

Tip 11.1

Remember, the unconscious mind runs the body, does the golf shot and does not process negatives directly – so say it how you want it to be! For example, when giving advice in the above exercise, saying, "keep your right elbow straight" is a far better way to coach someone than, "don't bend your right elbow".

Tip 11.2

Using the so-called 'feedback sandwich' may be useful here. This is a model for giving someone (including yourself) feedback in a way that empowers rather than dis-empowers. This is covered in Appendix 7.

Exercise 11.1

Think of a behaviour you would like to change. Decide how you would like to behave instead. Check the ecology of this new behaviour.

1. See yourself doing this new behaviour on a film screen in your mind's eye. See yourself in different situations where you will do this new behaviour. Repeat at least five times.
2. As 1 above, but this time do it 'associated' – see it, hear it, feel it.
3. Repeat 1.
4. Test and future pace (the future pace should be easy – in effect you have been doing it in the exercise!).

If you are a mental skills coach, take an athlete through this exercise for a behaviour that he or she would like to change.

ii. Just 'Let It Go'

Another approach is just to 'let go' of a bad shot. Some athletes are just able to do this naturally, others need an approach like that outlined above to assist them. Here are three other approaches to help you to 'let it go'.

It is **essential** with these three approaches to ensure that the athlete takes any appropriate 'learnings' (if any) from the event or situation, such that by taking those learnings the athlete will know what to do and not do next time. By doing so, the event can be a resource rather than a forgotten mistake that is repeated.

Approach 1

The first one uses submodalities. Think of a less than successful sporting event that happened a long time ago and about which you have no emotions and can barely remember. Notice the submodalites of that event – in particular the size, location, distance and focus of the picture, plus any sounds and feelings that are important. Think of a current disappointment, and change the pictures, sounds and feelings into the same submodalities as the old event. Notice the difference.

Exercise 11.2

Think of a current or very recent event that is causing you a problem and for which it would be appropriate for you to treat it as an old event that is long-gone.

Think of an old disappointment that is long-gone and which does not affect you negatively. Notice the submodalities. (If it helps, refresh your memory of submodalities before you notice them by using the submodalities checklist in Appendix 2.)

Bring to mind the current situation, and change the submodalities to be the same as the old situation.

Notice how you feel about it now.

If you are a mental skills coach, take an athlete through this exercise for a behaviour that he or she would like to change.

Approach 2

An alternative to the method above is to take the mental image of that event and just let it disappear into the breeze or the dim distance (or however the athlete wishes to make it disappear). Please make sure that if it is appropriate to take any learnings from that event (i.e. what should be done differently next time) that this is done before letting the mental image disappear.

Exercise 11.3

Think of a very recent event that is causing you a problem and for which it would be appropriate and ecological for you to banish from your mind. If necessary, take the learnings before you do so.

Experiment with ways to 'remove' that memory, for example make it float out into the distance.

Approach 3

Do a context reframe on the event – go forward in time and notice just how unimportant that little mistake was. Or, notice that in the context of your life – perhaps you have children – that it really isn't that important. Clearly, this approach has to be treated with common sense and sparingly. Most sportspeople are motivated and their sport is important. Sometimes there is nothing to do but accept what has happened and move forward.

Tip 11.3

As philosopher Reinhold Niebuhr said: "God grant me the serenity to accept the things I cannot change, the courage to change the things I can and the wisdom to know the difference".

It is useful to bear this in mind.

iii. Get Back Into The Right State

Remember the NLP Communication Model (get into the appropriate physiology – are you walking, breathing and moving like you do when at your best?) and the material you learned in Chapter 7 on 'state management' (anchoring, peripheral vision). You can use these techniques to get back into a 'physiology of excellence'.

iv. Focus on What You Want

Often when we are playing badly, we dwell on it and focus on the mistakes. In addition to the suggestions above, remember that what you focus on increases, so **FOCUS ON WHAT YOU WANT!**

2. Dealing With Injuries

The second area of setbacks and difficulties to look at is injuries. This section is in no way intended to replace medical advice from a qualified medical doctor, specialist or physiotherapist.

One of the challenges that face some athletes is persistent injuries and/or a long-term or serious injury. Apart from receiving appropriate medical treatment, the athlete can assist herself by maintaining a positive mental approach. There are a couple of ways to do this.

Firstly, once again, **FOCUS ON WHAT YOU WANT.** Keep seeing, hearing and feeling what it will be like when you are fit and recovered. Do this visualisation every day.

Norwegian international footballer Ole Gunnar Solskjaer, a centre forward for Manchester United, scored his first senior goal for three years on 23 August 2006 after a succession of injuries over the three-year period. Solskjaer was quoted as saying, "the prospect of doing it was one of the major things that motivated me over the past three years."

Secondly, there is an overwhelming amount of evidence of the 'mind-body link', in other words, what and how we think has an impact on our body. (There are some references in the 'Further Reference' section.) With this in mind, it has been known for athletes and non-athletes to accelerate the body's natural healing process. One approach would be to work with a suitably qualified and experienced hypnotherapist on this. In any event, please make sure that you consult your medical practitioner regarding the suitability of seeking any complementary health treatment.

Another approach would be to visualise the part of the body healing itself. The unconscious mind is responsible for running the body, and has a 'blueprint' of the body in perfect health, in other words it will 'know' what perfect health looks, sounds, feels, tastes and smells like.

3. Difficult Relationships

In Chapter 6, I mentioned two situations where athletes had been 'put-off' by people who weren't opponents. In Story 6.1, a tennis player felt intimidated by her partner in a mixed doubles final. In Story 6.2, a male athlete was distracted by a comment made by a female athlete acquaintance.

In both situations, I asked the athletes to think of the person, and then adjust some of the key aspects of the pictures, sounds and feelings (i.e. the submodalities).

Story 6.1 Continued

With the tennis player, because the tennis coach partnering her was not in any way intending to negatively affect her, I wanted to ensure that she was left with a good mental image of partnering him. I asked her to adjust the picture she had of him by making it a little smaller, lower and further away. She said this helped a little. Normally adjusting just the visual submodalities is sufficient. In this case, it did not seem to be, and so I widened the approach slightly.

I asked what she particularly noticed about the sound, picture and feeling she had when thinking of him, and she said it was his voice.

I elicited some of the key auditory submodalities, and asked her to adjust them individually as covered in Chapter 8, 'Method 2'.

Within two or three minutes she was feeling much more comfortable about playing with him, and, as I later found out, won the match and played really well.

Story 6.2 Continued

With the athlete, because the female athlete was being incon-siderate and unpleasant, and the male athlete had no desire to befriend or mix with her in any way, I was not concerned with leaving him with a 'pleasant' mental image of her.

I asked him to think of her and hear her voice and the sorts of things she had said to him. I then asked him to 'experiment' by:

- imagining her saying those words but in the same voice as characters like Donald Duck or Mickey Mouse, or in a very slow groaning drawl
- and to hear the voice but with circus music in the back ground
- or someone blowing raspberries

and to notice which one(s) worked best for him. And as he was hearing these 'different' voices, to notice what happened if he made the picture he had of her become flat rather than 3-D (which tends to 'de-personalise' the person being thought about), and (one by one) make the picture smaller, lower down and further away.

He was left with an image of a tiny little clown-like figure with a squeaky voice saying rude things, and he burst out laughing when I tested. I asked him to future pace this new response by seeing himself (i.e. dissociated) meeting her in the future and her making the type of comments she would make just before he raced. Again, he was fine and was laughing and had a broad grin.

As far as I am aware she did not bother him again.

Summary

- ◆ Remember, every seemingly negative event is a learning opportunity, even if it doesn't feel like it at the time! 'It's not what happens to us that counts, it's how we deal with it', in other words we cannot always control how competitions and matches will go, but we can control our response to it.

◆ Take those learnings, use them, and let the event itself go.

◆ Focus on what you want and what that will bring for you when faced with challenges and set-backs.

Chapter 12
Gaining Other Perspectives

This chapter covers one of the most valuable aspects of the 'How To' of NLP coaching in a sports context – that of gaining other perspectives on a situation. We will touch on the perceptual positions technique we covered in Chapter 9 (Belief Change). There is a detailed example in Appendix 13.

It is so useful because, as you will remember from earlier chapters, 'wisdom comes from multiple perspectives'. Many times people have 'challenges' which can be overcome by using this simple yet powerful approach. I have used perceptual positions (either in its pure form or a variation of it) with just about every single client I have ever worked with, and my students have all found it an extremely useful technique.

This chapter covers the following:

- The perceptual positions technique, both its pure form and some variations
- Examples of when you can use it, either with yourself or with others, for specific situations
- How to use a variant of it to improve your performance and that of others

The Perceptual Positions Technique

Why Use it?

The perceptual positions technique can be used in the following types of situations:

♦ where you (or someone else) wants to gain insight into another person's (or team's) point of view.

♦ to resolve or prevent conflict or misunderstandings.

♦ to improve your ability to get the most from other people.

♦ to negotiate more effectively.

♦ to improve our ability to coach others to deal with situations similar to those above.

What Is The Perceptual Position Technique?

As you will remember from Chapter 9, there are three main perceptual positions:

♦ **Position 1** is 'us', looking at a situation from our own point of view, feeling what we feel and speaking our thoughts.

♦ **Position 2** is the other person(s). In this position, we literally look at the situation from the perspective of the other person(s) involved, feel how they feel and speak as if we were them.

♦ **Position 3** is the neutral, impartial, objective observer, noticing what 'those people' in positions 1 and 2 haven't noticed because they are too involved in the situation.

Particularly where there is some inter-personal 'conflict', one of the key reasons why there is a conflict is because both people are stuck in their own mindset, i.e. stuck in position 1. There is a kind of 'inter-locking of ideas' and thinking between the two people (some people call it a 'system' from the concept of 'systems thinking'). By one person changing their mindset towards the other person, the 'system' will change. If one person stops being 'locked' in his or her thinking, it is almost inevitable that the other person will change.

You will probably have experienced situations, in sports or in life generally, where you have had a particular opinion of someone and noticed all the 'evidence' that supported your opinion; then, some time later, something happens and you change your opinion about that person and gather new evidence to support that new belief (the NLP Communication Model explains this).

Or, you will have a negative opinion about someone's character and yet someone else has a completely different opinion about that same person. This person who you both have differing opinions about is not truly the way you perceive him to be, nor truly the way the other person perceives him to be.

The perceptual positions technique helps us to see that person from a different perspective, and where there is some 'impasse' or 'locking of ideas' the technique helps us to find new ways to approach the situation or 'unlock' our thinking.

It will probably require us to make some changes in our behaviour or approach, which is a good thing because, from the concept of 'cause and effect', it absolutely puts us 'at cause' in changing situations. Most people when stuck in a 'conflict' or 'misunderstanding' will blame the other person. Rarely are they willing to change their own approach.

How Do We Use The Technique?

The approach is similar to that used in the belief change exercise in Chapter 9, and is detailed in Appendix 13. Please read Appendix 13 in conjunction with Exercises 12.1 and 12.2.

Exercise 12.1

Find a challenge you have regarding someone else, or a situation where you would like to have greater insight. Do the perceptual positions exercise.

If you cannot think of one, think about playing a match against your next opponents – put yourself in their shoes and notice how they are thinking and feeling about the prospect of playing you, and what their tactics may be. Please resist the temptation to over-analyse and get concerned about what opponents may be thinking – however it is a useful exercise to give more insight.

If this is not appropriate, pick a context outside of sport, for example friends, partners, family, work colleagues.

Exercise 12.2

If you are a mental skills coach, where appropriate take someone else through the perceptual positions exercise for an issue they have or a situation they would like greater insight into.

Examples of When You Can Use Perceptual Positions

Earlier in this chapter in the section headed *'Why Use It?'* there were some examples of the types of issues that you could use the perceptual positions technique. As a generalisation, the perceptual positions technique involves being able to put yourself in someone else's shoes and also resolving conflicts between you and others. Apart from using it formally as shown in Appendix 13, it can be used 'conversationally', for example asking questions like:

◆ "if you were in their shoes, what would you think?" (i.e. putting them into position 2)

◆ "if you were advising someone else in a similar situation to you, what would you say to them?" (i.e. putting them into position 3)

Story 12.1

I was working with a very successful tri-athlete (let's call him Jeff) whose pulse rate just before the start of swimming event (the first event) was around 140. This is far too high, and caused Jeff to feel overly anxious before the race and caused him to feel physically tired earlier in the race than necessary. He said that a pulse of around 80-90 per minute would have been more appropriate.

I asked Jeff what concerned him so much at the start of the race that his pulse would be so much higher than appropriate. He said his friends always made journeys to see him compete and he didn't want to let them down. This is a statement from 'position 1'.

I asked him to consider the situation from his friends' point of view (i.e. position 2). I suggested that Jeff consider for a moment what his friends were thinking about him before, during and after the race. I could tell he was considering something he had never considered before – his face went blank and there was a marked change in his facial colour.

Jeff said that he realised that his friends simply loved him, regardless of whether he won or lost, and just wanted to be there for him (like all good friends do). I asked him what his friends would say if they thought Jeff was nervous on their account. Jeff said that his friends would just laugh and tell him not to worry about them.

I asked Jeff to imagine what would be happening as he lined up for future events. He said that he would only be focussing on getting to grips with the race, not on what his friends would be saying or thinking.

Subsequently, Jeff reported significantly lower pulse rates before events.

Another way that the principles of perceptual positions can be used is to put yourself into position 3 and consider the following two key questions:

◆ 'what are the attributes of a champion in your particular field?' List around ten. For example, if you are a tennis player, you would probably list the main shots, plus other attributes like playing big points well and winning when not necessarily playing well.

◆ 'If 10 out of 10 is the ideal score, where are you on each of those attributes?' (be impartial – step to position 3 for this one!).

Exercise 12.3

In your sport, pick someone who you would like to model or emulate. Make a list of around ten traits or attributes they have, both from the technical/sport point of view and from a character point of view.

Rate your score on a scale of zero to ten for those attributes and traits (from the point of view of a neutral observer with no axe to grind).

Based on this, decide what you specifically need to do to improve your performance. Make a plan.

If possible and appropriate, ask someone who knows your performance (for example your sports coach) to look through the list of attributes, and possibly add one or two. Also ask this person to score you against those traits and attributes.

Discuss this with your sports coach, and make a plan or take action accordingly.

One final point is that you can improve your own performance by visualising your performance from different perspectives, for example:

- ◆ your team mates
- ◆ competitors
- ◆ seeing yourself from numerous angles for technical improvements

Story 12.2

I had the privilege of listening to a talk given by a world champion martial artist. He mentioned that during his training his coach would often 'freeze' situations when he was sparring, and ask him to notice how this looked from other angles, so that he could be aware of when there were gaps in his defences.

Being able to compare your actual performance with the aspects of your performance when you are at your best enables you to provide guidance to yourself at times when you are not performing at your best, and then to take appropriate action. This is particularly useful when doing sports where there is limited or restricted input from your coach during competition.

Exercise 12.4

Think of a time or series of times when you performed at your best. Take a 'personal inventory' of what was happening, including:

- relevant aspects of your physiology, both before and during competition, for example, the way you stand, your breathing, movement and gestures. (Remember the coaching that Tony Robbins gave Andre Agassi regarding the way he walked onto court.)
- your self-talk, including the words and tonality of those words
- your beliefs
- the mental images you have

Ensure that you know these aspects of peak performance so that if you are not 'on form' you can do a comparison of 'you' at peak performance and 'you' in the moment, and make necessary changes.

Summary

- ◆ Remember, there is always another way of looking at a situation. Or as people often say, there are three sides to the argument – yours, mine and the 'truth'!
- ◆ Having more insight into situations is normally better than not having enough.
- ◆ Develop the acuity to know when you are not at your best and what you need to do to get back on track.

Chapter 13
Preparation
and Other Topics

In this chapter we will touch on some ideas regarding preparation and some other sundry thoughts that supplement what you have learned in the other chapters. Some of the points made in this chapter are repeated from previous chapters to re-enforce the new points made in this chapter. Please remember as you read this chapter that this book will be read by amateur as well as professional athletes, and so some of the ideas may be 'obvious' to professional sportspeople. Please also remember that *'knowing what to do'* and *'doing what you know'* are two different concepts – I can think of at least one situation that received a fair amount of publicity where an experienced international sportsman admitted that the reason for his poor performance in the international match was lack of preparation.

If what you are doing works well for you, keep doing it!

Why Is Preparation So Important?

Remember, I did say earlier in the book that there would be some 'obvious' issues touched on and 'obvious' points made!

From the point of view of a successful non-professional athlete, who will probably be working and have to squeeze practice and competition into their spare time, being properly prepared for competition **and** training is an essential component of getting the most from yourself within your sport. This includes all forms of preparation, such as:

- having the right equipment for training
- having the right equipment for matches and competition
- knowing the directions to the venue
- being mentally prepared for training
- being mentally prepared for matches and competition
- having the right nourishment during the week and available for the competition

I remember being told the '6 Ps' many years ago by a former professional American Football coach. I quote:

*"**P**roper*
***P**rior*
***P**lanning*
***P**revents*
***P**iss-poor*
***P**erformance"*

Some Thoughts On How To Prepare

1. Get Organised!

Let's start with equipment. Depending on your sport and the level at which you choose to play, there could be a minimal level of equipment and clothing required at one end of the spectrum or it could be relatively complicated to prepare.

The simple answer is to plan and if appropriate make a checklist. The plan could be anything from keeping all your essential kit in your kit bag, to something more elaborate. If your system works for you, remember to stick to it!

Story 13.1

This simple approach helped take some the anxieties away from one of my tri-athlete clients. She would sometimes not train as effectively as she would like because she did not have the appropriate training equipment with her when she went to the gym straight after work. This impacted on her confidence levels before and during competition (for example, "have I done enough training?", "I wish I could have run more last week – silly me for not having the right shoes!").

Also, she would get anxious before events, sometimes rushing around before she left home to get the right equipment, food and directions, wondering during the journey whether she had forgotten something.

Also, she would sometimes not eat properly before competition because she did not have the right food in the house.

By:

- making checklists
- keeping them in her kitbag
- getting all her equipment ready the night before competition (using the checklist!)
- making a shopping list for food and drink
- having and using a checklist for training equipment

she was able to be far more relaxed and perform even better.

Story 13.2

You will remember from Story 10.3 the marathon runner called Julie, who was unable to complete the 20 mile run a few weeks before the Marathon. The reason she was unable to complete it was because she did not have the right food and nutrition before the event. She was relying on someone else to provide it, and it did not happen.

This could easily have ruined her results – fortunately we did the work explained in Story 10.3 to help her overcome it.

She was adamant that she would take full responsibility for her own preparation in future!

In terms of physical preparation, ensure that you have the appropriate amount of sleep and nutrition (sorry to sound like your parents again!), and of course, the appropriate amount and type of training.

Moving on to mental preparation - by now you will have realised the importance of mental rehearsal and preparation. Create time to do this - it will not happen by chance. If necessary, book a slot in your diary for this!

2. Training

Clearly, the appropriate amount and type of physical training is essential to be able to perform at your best and to improve. As we covered in Tip 2.1, conventional wisdom is that *'Practice makes Perfect!'* This is NOT true. The truth is:

Practice makes PERMANENT!

Perfect Practice makes *Perfect*

So please ensure that when training, you practice the techniques correctly.

Also, please take practice seriously. What happens during matches is a direct reflection of what happens in training. Less than excellent practice will lead to less than excellent performance in competition. Make practice as true a reflection of what will happen in competitive situations as possible – make it realistic. For example, if you are a golfer playing 'stroke-play' competition (in other words, where the golfer with the fewest shots wins), ensure your practice rounds are stroke play, not 'match-play' (where the person who wins most holes in the match).

3. Focusing

Especially when training for a big event, remember to FOCUS ON WHAT YOU WANT. Will the party with friends, or that half-bottle of wine, get you to where you want to be? If it will, then fine. Generally, it is better to keep distractions to a minimum, although remembering the 'Inverted U' curve (Performance and Arousal – Diagram 7.1), it will be important for the athlete to manage their arousal level. For some people, it may be productive to spend time before a competition doing activities which take your mind off of the competition and which do not impair your performance. Ultimately, each to their own – it is up to us all as individuals to find out what works best for us.

Some Other Thoughts

1. Learning

There is always more to learn! Ask experts, read relevant books and publications, observe experts. Be hungry for knowledge.

Tip 13.1

Find someone who does a particular aspect of your sport well, and ask him/her how they do that. Sometimes the sportsperson will not want to give away their 'secrets' – in which case you have lost nothing by asking. Often people are willing to talk about what they love and do well.

It may be useful to use your scores from Exercise 12.3 (where you gave yourself marks out of ten for the key attributes of your sport) for this exercise.

2. Improving

There are always things we can do to improve. Remember the champion marksman in Story 3.3 who worked on the weakest element of his performance until it became the strongest, and then repeated the exercise so that he was constantly ratcheting up his performance.

3. Staying Present

There is always a temptation when playing sport to be thinking about what you have done and/or will do. Clearly, this is an important thing to do so that we can learn and plan for success. However, during the actual event, we need to stay present, in other words be in the moment.

If we have made a mistake during a manoeuvre (for example the take-off for an ice-skating jump or the feet position for a backhand in tennis), by dwelling on it we cannot correct it. This is because we will be thinking about the past (even if it is a few split seconds ago). We can only correct it in the moment by making adjustments based on where we are RIGHT NOW. Remember Greg Louganis' thoughts (Story 10.4) – champions can get to the right places from the wrong places, in other words they make adjustments in the here and now.

4. Evaluating Performance

Some people evaluate the quality of their performance based on the quality of the result. Whilst sport, especially professional sport, is very results driven, it is important that we evaluate what works and what could be done even better. Frank Dick, former UK National Athletics Coach, held the view that if you don't know why you won or did well, then it was just an accident![32]

In sport, there is an element of luck in the short term or in a particular match, for example injuries, referee's decisions and unexpected illness can greatly influence the result. In the long term it is probably better to do the right things and make decisions which give you the best chance of winning, rather than having the attitude of 'we won so everything is OK' or 'we lost so it's all terrible'.

Summary

+ Remember the 6 P's about preparation.
+ Practice makes **Permanent**, so take practice seriously.
+ Use checklists and plan ahead.
+ Get to know yourself and what works for you in terms of the level and types of distractions that are acceptable before events.
+ If you take your sport seriously, find ways to keep learning and improving.
+ Stay 'present' to help you get to the right places.
+ Avoid confusing the quality of a decision or performance with the quality of the result or outcome.

---

[32] Jeff Grout & Sarah Perrin, *Mind Games – Inspirational Lessons From The World's Biggest Sports Stars,* Capstone Publishing Ltd, 2004, p. 214

Chapter 14
Finding a
Mental Skills Coach

I declare a vested interest here – of course I believe it is useful for all sports people to have a mental skills coach, and essential for all prospective or actual professionals to have one. And I believe it is useful for all coaches and essential for all professional coaches to be trained in many of the techniques I have outlined so far and will outline in Part IV.

Why do I say this? Simply because the NLP and related techniques have been proven time and again to work, provided that the mental skills coach is skilled and that the athlete wants to improve. Often, we can help ourselves, and other times it is useful to have the perspective of an impartial professional, someone who has a vested interest in us performing at our best without having the pressure that many team managers or traditional sports coaches have.

This chapter deals with what to look for in a mental skills coach, so that you can ask the right questions to be able to hook up with someone who will be an ally in your search to improve results. If finding a mental skills coach is not on your agenda, move to the next chapter.

Characteristics of a Mental Skills Coach

Firstly, I would like to say that there is no 'correct' or 'absolute' criteria when selecting a mental skills coach. To a large extent it is subjective. The following are some guidelines.

You would probably want the mental skills coach to:

◆ be qualified in NLP (probably at least an NLP Practitioner or an NLP Sports Diploma) or a similar field such as applied sports psychology.

◆ have some awareness of sport, so that he or she has some understanding of what happens during a sporting competition. The mental skills coach would not necessarily need to have much knowledge of your particular sport, nor to have played to any particular level. They are not advising you the way a traditional sports coach does.

◆ have experience of working with athletes and sportspeople.

◆ be a good listener to find out what YOU want and what stops YOU from achieving the results YOU want, rather than telling you what he thinks you should be doing. Clearly, when doing the NLP 'processes', the mental skills coach will need to be 'in charge', but it should ideally be that they are doing processes *with* you, rather than *to* you.

◆ be completely trustworthy, and keep whatever is said between you and him/her, unless you give him/her written permission to repeat what has been said during the session. Please note that where the mental skills coach is being employed by a team, it is important that the team manager knows that confidentiality will be maintained. Really effective work can normally only be done when there is a foundation of trust and confidentiality.

In addition, you would want to feel that you can get on with him or her and there is a natural rapport between the both of you.

Exercise 14.1

List the benefits to you of having a mental skills coach.

Exercise 14.2

List the attributes you would look for in a mental skills coach.

CONCLUDING COMMENTS

We have now completed the three main sections of this book. The remaining part is primarily for sports coaches or mental skills coaches, although it will be useful for athletes and players to read it if you are looking to improve your communication skills, particularly sections 1 and 2 in Chapter 16 and section 9 of Chapter 17.

If you choose not to read Part IV, I suggest that you skip it and move straight on to Chapter 18.

Part IV

What They Probably Don't Teach You at Coaching School

This final part of the book is written primarily for sports coaches and mental skills coaches, although athletes and sportspeople will almost certainly find it useful. As you will no doubt have realised by now, many of the ideas, concepts and techniques mentioned in this book are relevant not just to sport, but also to other aspects of life such as work, families and all relationships.

The purpose of this final part is both to cover some essential aspects of working with people that are not normally taught unless you attend specialised NLP and related courses, and to recap on the essential points we have covered that relate specifically to coaching others.

Many of the topics covered in Part IV are worthy of books in their own right – indeed many books have been written about the individual topics. In keeping with the intention of this book, I will give you the essential aspects – further references are provided in a separate section at the end of this book.

Part IV is split into three chapters. The first covers 'meta programs', which I refer to as 'fundamental filters', and other aspects of motivation. The second covers language tips (I promise it will not be like English classes at school!). The third covers the following topics:

- Logical Levels – one of the keys to being focused
- Metaphors – the use of stories and analogies that influence people
- Walking your talk
- The Wheel Of Life
- Some tips on one-to-one coaching where the sportsmen is a 'client'
- Feedback

- ◆ Emotions
- ◆ Stages of Group and team development
- ◆ Personal Transitions

Remember too that unlike traditional sports coaching, where the coach is the expert in the sport, mental skills coaching is not about knowing the answers. Mental skills coaching is more about being able to help the player find his or her own resources and answers to truly empower them. As you will see later in this part, it is often more important to know the right **question** than the **answer.**

Chapter 15
Fundamental
Filters and Motivation

We will cover the following topics in this chapter:

◆ Meta programs – key personality traits and filters we all have, how to identify and use them, and how they relate to motivation. We will refer to meta programs as 'fundamental filters'.

◆ Other aspects of motivation.

1. Fundamental Filters and Motivation

Have you ever said something innocently or innocuously to an athlete which led to a response that seemed very out of proportion to your comment or question? Have you ever said the same thing or used the same approach with two sportsmen and had completely different results or responses from them? If so, the chances are that you have unwittingly mismatched their 'fundamental filters'.

As you will remember from Chapter 1 and the Communication Model, fundamental filters (meta programs) are one of the filters that determine what and how information is filtered. They can be thought of as 'preferences' for dealing with and presenting information. The fundamental filters describe the range of responses along a spectrum, as will become apparent shortly.

A working knowledge of fundamental filters is an extremely important tool when dealing with people; if you 'match' someone's fundamental filters (preferences) you will have much more chance of influencing them the way you intend than if you 'mismatch' them.

Also, many disagreements arise when people have one or more fundamental filters that are at the opposite end of the spectrum to someone else's.

I have heard it said that there are up to 65 fundamental filters, although it is generally accepted within NLP that there are around 15 to 20 fundamental filters that are useful. In this chapter we will be covering in some detail five of the fundamental filters that relate primarily to motivation, which, together with the information you have from Chapter 5, will provide you with extremely useful information regarding motivating and communicating with individuals and teams. For each of these fundamental filters, I will describe and explain:

◆ what it is

◆ how to 'elicit' or recognise where someone is on the spectrum of each of the fundamental filters (preference)

◆ how to use it

I will also briefly summarise some other fundamental filters so that you can be aware of them and seek more information if that would be useful to you as a coach.

One of the benefits of utilising fundamental filters to understand someone is that you can do so conversationally without any need to do a 'personality profile' or any questionnaire, which can be time consuming, costly and which a player or athlete can manipulate.

There are five key points to make before you learn more about these fundamental filters.

i. For each fundamental filter there is a question to elicit someone's preference. The question has been carefully selected to give the most useful, accurate and user friendly information. I strongly urge you to use the question and resist any temptation to make up your own.

ii. The first fundamental filter we will discuss will be in some detail to give you enough information to grasp the concept and feel confident about using fundamental filters. The remaining fundamental filters will be covered in less detail.

iii. There is no right or wrong, nor good or bad place to be on any fundamental filter spectrum. Whatever someone's fundamental filters are, they are useful in some contexts and not so useful in other contexts. Good communicators (and of course good mental skills coaches and sports coaches) will be flexible enough to utilise players' natural personality preferences to get the best from the player.

iv. It is important to be aware of your own fundamental filters so that you know how you operate and can build more flexibility if you desire. We often deal with and treat others the way we would like to be dealt with ourselves. As you know, everyone is different and responds better to some approaches than others.

v. Being at one end of the spectrum for some of the fundamental filters below may seem to you irrelevant for your particular sport. Please remember that this book is written for sports coaches and mental skills coaches for all different sports, and that just because it seems irrelevant to you does not mean that there are no players or athletes with that particular filter preference!

Let's take each fundamental filter in turn. I will then discuss how to pull this together to be able to easily use this information.

1. Towards or Away From?

We have already touched on this in Chapter 5. To remind you, we all have values, which are key to our motivation. For each of these values, we are motivated either to move 'towards' having it or 'away from' not having it, or some combination of the two. We will go into the necessary detail for you to be able to understand and use this fundamental filter effectively.

As with all of the fundamental filters we will cover, this is a spectrum, with 'towards' at one end and 'away from' at the other. Given that this is an art and not a science, we will not endeavour to get too specific – we will simply say that there are the following other categories:

♦ Mainly towards

- ◆ Equally towards and away from
- ◆ Mainly away from

and these will exhibit a combination of the characteristics referred to below.

As a mental skills coach, given that you want a player to feel motivated, knowing where they are on the spectrum will give you a big advantage.

Spotting 'Towards' and 'Away From'

The characteristics of 'towards' and 'away from' are shown in the following table:

Towards	Away From
◆ Stays focussed on their goal. Hence, tends to be good at managing priorities.	◆ May have trouble focussing on goals and prioritising, because whatever is wrong will attract their attention.
◆ Thinks in terms of what they can achieve – they want to win because they want to win!	◆ Aware of what should be avoided or got rid of.
◆ Often has difficulty in recognising problems to be avoided.	◆ Motivated by problems to solve or avoid – they want to win because they don't want to lose!
◆ Energised/motivated by their goals.	◆ Motivated by threats.
◆ The absence of goals to move towards may leave them de-motivated.	◆ Good at trouble-shooting and spotting possible problems in the planning stages.

The best way to elicit this fundamental filter is to ask someone what is important to them in the context of their sport (i.e. elicit some of the 'values') and then ask them the following questions:

"Why is <value> important to you?" "And why is *that* important to you?" "And why is THAT important to you?"

'Towards' and 'away from' motivation is indicated by words and phrases such as those shown in the following table:

Towards	Away From
mentions what they would ♦ gain, ♦ achieve, ♦ win, ♦ get, ♦ have.	mentions what situations they would ♦ avoid, ♦ get rid of, ♦ not have, ♦ undesired situations, ♦ problems, ♦ negations, ♦ words indicating necessity such as 'have to', 'must', 'should', 'ought to', and possibly comparisons such as 'more', 'less', 'better' (than what?).

In the example below, I will highlight where the athlete mentions a likely 'towards' statement (T) or an 'away from' statement (A).

Coach: "What is important to you in the context of sport (or running, tennis, hockey etc)?"

Athlete: "Winning trophies, having fun, improving all the time."

Coach: "What is the order of importance? (The reader will recognise this as an extract from Exercise 5.2 – Values Elicitation.)

Athlete: "'Improving all the time' is first, then 'winning trophies', then 'fun' third."

Coach: "Why is 'improving all the time' important to you?"

Athlete: "Because it makes me feel good (T) and stops me from feeling I'm stagnating (A)."

Coach: "And why is that important to you?"

Athlete: "Because it gives me energy (T) and makes me happy (T)."

Coach: "And why is that important to you?"

Athlete: "Because I feel good (T) and it stops me from getting bored (A)."

From the above, we can guess that the athlete is 'mainly towards' (four T's and two A's). We would ideally repeat the exercise with one of the other values ('winning trophies').

How to Influence Using This Filter

So with this athlete, we would use mainly 'towards' language, with some 'away from', to motivate them. For example, a coach could say something like: *"here is what we want to achieve – breaking the club record (T), and doing a personal best (T), whilst making sure that you don't ruin your chances for next week (A)"*, or *"here are our goals and objectives (T) and what we want to achieve (T) from this tournament, and we have to make sure that we avoid peaking too soon (A)"*.

By using appropriate influencing language, you will have the best chance of motivating the athlete, and minimise the chances of switching him or her off. (In case you didn't notice, there was a 'towards' and an 'away from' statement in that last sentence!)

Tip 15.1

Where you are speaking to a group or someone you don't know, use language from both ends of the 'towards' and 'away from' spectrum.

The remaining fundamental filters that we will cover are even easier to grasp than 'towards' and 'away from'.

2. Internally or Externally Referenced?

Some people are motivated from external sources, and others are motivated by internal standards and beliefs.

Spotting 'Internal' or 'External'

The key characteristics of each end of the spectrum are as follows:

Internal	External
◆ Provides their own motivation.	◆ Needs other people's opinions and direction.
◆ Decides on the quality of their work.	◆ If they don't get opinions, they may not know how they're doing.
◆ May have difficulty accepting other people's assessment, feedback and input.	◆ Takes information as instructions.
◆ They will decide for themselves who they take notice of – others need to demonstrate credibility.	◆ Motivated when someone else decides.
◆ Gathers information externally, but decides themselves about it.	◆ Have trouble starting or continuing a task without some feedback.
◆ Takes instruction as information, hence may be difficult to supervise.	

Again, the other categories within the spectrum are:

◆   Mainly internal

- ◆ Equally internal and external
- ◆ Mainly external

The question to elicit this fundamental filter is:

"How do you know you have done a good job?"

People who are internally referenced will say something like, "I just know". People who are externally referenced will reply indicating that there are external factors, such as results or other people's feedback.

How to Influence Using This Filter

In terms of how to use this information, here are some tips:

- ◆ Give lots of feedback to players who are externally referenced to a significant extent.
- ◆ Where applicable and appropriate, involve people who are internally referenced in setting standards and deciding on tactics, to get their 'buy-in'.
- ◆ Make sure you demonstrate credibility when meeting internally referenced people (otherwise, they will be asking themselves 'why should I listen to this person?').
- ◆ When meeting players or athletes for the first time, or when meeting a group of them, assume that they are internally referenced and explain your credentials. Externally referenced people will listen to you anyway!

In addition, there is the following 'influencing language' that can be used:

Internal	External
◆ only you can decide,	◆ others will say...
◆ you know it's your choice,	◆ the feedback will be...
◆ what do you think?	◆ the recognition you'll get,
◆ you may want to consider...	◆ others will notice,

- a suggestion for you to think about,

- I have an opinion that may be different from yours. Would you be interested?"

- I can't convince you of anything. Only you will know for sure.

- the (XYZ newspaper or magazine) reported that...

- consider what others involved will think.

As with all fundamental filters, you can use an appropriate combination to suit players' individual preferences.

Only you can know whether fundamental filters will be useful for you when coaching. On the other hand, if you want to know what some other experts have written, please see the 'Further Reference' section. (You probably spotted the phrase for internally referenced people and the subsequent one for externally referenced people.)

3. Options or Procedures?

Some people are motivated by the chance to do things in new or different ways ('options'), others prefer to follow established procedures ('procedures').

Spotting 'Options' or 'Procedures'

The key characteristics of each end of the spectrum are as follows:

Options	Procedures
- Motivated by opportunities and possibilities to do something in a different way. - There's always a better way to do something.	- Likes to follow set procedures. - Believes there's a 'right' way to do something. - May feel lost without a procedure to follow.

◆ May be able to create procedures, but will have difficulty following them. ◆ If you offer them a guaranteed formula for success, they'll probably try to improve it! ◆ Breaking the rules is almost irresistible for extreme options people!	◆ 'I've started so I'll finish.'

Again, the other categories within the spectrum are:

- ◆ Mainly options
- ◆ Equally options and procedures
- ◆ Mainly procedures

The question to elicit this fundamental filter is:

"Why did you choose your current work (or sporting pursuit, or <name of discipline>)?"

For those of you who are at the 'options' end of the scale, bearing in mind that you like breaking the rules, you will probably want to make up your own questions for each of the fundamental filters. My simple advice is **resist the temptation!** By following this procedure, you will have **far** more options regarding the use of these fundamental filters with your athletes because you will have useful information.

Players who are at the 'options' end of the spectrum will answer by giving you criteria or values (for example "more interesting", "challenging") or they will refer to options, choices and opportunities. People who are at the 'procedures' end of the spectrum will answer the 'why' question as if it were a 'how' question, in other words they will give you the story (or procedure) of how they came to do this type of sport, or they will indicate that it wasn't really their choice, it was more of a necessity or they just fell into it.

How to Influence Using This Filter

In terms of how to use this information, here are some tips:

- ◆ Allow (and even encourage) 'options' players alternative ways to do something (such as some training practice) as long as it gives you and/or the team the same results and benefit.
- ◆ Provide sufficient repetition for 'procedures' athletes – they believe there is a 'right way' to do things.

In addition, there is the following 'influencing language' that can be used for players at either end of the spectrum – please mix according to where players are in the spectrum:

Options	Procedures
◆ break the rules just for you,	◆ speak in procedures – first, second, then, …last,
◆ opportunity,	◆ the right way,
◆ choice,	◆ tried and trusted,
◆ expanding,	◆ obligations,
◆ options,	◆ *"Consider the obligations we have... We really must do this."*
◆ the sky's the limit,	
◆ alternatives,	
◆ possibilities.	
◆ *"Consider the possibilities in this event... we really can do this."*	

So the opportunities and options to use these fundamental filters are endless – I'm sure you can think of alternatives yourself. And in order to have the best chance of using fundamental filters in the right way, the way that has been tried and tested, just follow the procedures for eliciting and using these filters. (Did you spot the 'options' and 'procedures' sentences?)

4. Proactive or Reactive?

Some people are motivated to take immediate action ('proactive'), whilst others prefer to wait, analyse and consider ('reactive').

Spotting 'Proactive' or 'Reactive

The key characteristics of each end of the spectrum are as follows:

Proactive	Reactive
◆ Tends to act with little or no consideration, to jump into situations without analysing.	◆ Prefers to wait for others to initiate, or until the right situation before acting.
◆ May upset people because they can bulldoze ahead with what they want.	◆ Wants to fully understand/ assess before acting, and may spend a lot of time waiting.
◆ Good at getting the job done.	◆ At the extreme, suffers from analysis/paralysis.
◆ Does not wait for others to initiate.	◆ Believes in fate/destiny – some things are just the way they are.
◆ Believes you make your own luck.	

Again, the other categories within the spectrum are:

◆ Mainly proactive
◆ Equally proactive and reactive
◆ Mainly reactive

The question to elicit this fundamental filter is:

"When you come to a situation, do you usually act quickly after sizing it up, or do you make a complete study of all the consequences and then act?" (Often, it is not necessary to ask the question – just listening to the responses to other questions will give you the information.)

Players and athletes who are mainly 'proactive' will respond with 'act quickly'. They will also:

◆ speak in short sentences
◆ speak as if they are in control of their world
◆ use a crisp, clear sentence structure
◆ be direct
◆ at the extreme, they 'bulldoze'
◆ have body language which shows signs of impatience or inability to sit still for long periods

Players and athletes who are mainly 'reactive' will respond with 'do a study first'. Also they may speak with:

◆ passive verbs or verbs transformed into nouns
◆ lots of infinitives
◆ language that suggests that the world controls them
◆ long and convoluted sentences
◆ conditionals – could, would, might
◆ also, they are usually able to keep still for long periods

How to Influence Using This Filter

In terms of how to use this information, here are some tips:

◆ allow 'reactive' players time to think about what they are doing (within the context of the sport, of course!)
◆ resist the temptation to over-analyse when speaking with 'proactive' players'

In addition, there is the following 'influencing language' that can be used for athletes at either end of the spectrum – please mix according to where athletes are in the spectrum:

Proactive	Reactive
◆ do it,	◆ understand,
◆ jump in,	◆ assess,
◆ now,	◆ consider,
◆ get it done,	◆ wait,
◆ don't wait,	◆ could,
◆ go for it,	◆ might,
◆ *"Let's go and do this. There's no need to wait."*	◆ *"If you think about it and you've analysed it, then you'll be ready to make up your mind now".*

So, let's move straight on to the next section now, unless you'd like to pause and consider what we've done thus far!

5. Big Picture or Detail?

Some athletes, players and coaches like and prefer a summary and get annoyed with too much detail ('big picture'). Others like and respond best to details ('detail').

Spotting 'Big Picture' or 'Detail'

The key characteristics of each end of the spectrum are as follows:

Big Picture	Detail
◆ Prefer to work on an overview, conceptual or big picture level.	◆ Prefer to handle small pieces of information.
◆ May present ideas in random order.	◆ May have difficulty in seeing the big picture.

◆ Dealing with details for a long time irritates them.	◆ May have difficulty prioritising because they see so much detail. ◆ Excellent in situations where attention to detail is crucial.

The other categories within the spectrum are:

- ◆ Mainly big picture
- ◆ Equally big picture and detail
- ◆ Mainly detail

The question to elicit this fundamental filter is:

"If we were going to do a project together, would you want to know the big picture or the details first? Would you really need to know the (other)?" (Often, it is not necessary to ask the question – just listen to responses to other questions.)

For example, if they answer 'big picture' to the first question and 'yes' to the second question (i.e. 'would you really need to know the details?'), then that suggests mainly 'big picture'. If they answer 'no' to the second question, that suggests 'big picture'.

You can generally tell where someone is on this spectrum by the amount of detail they give you when answering this or other questions, and remember, everything is relative.

Story 15.1

I did a business–related project in 2001 which involved interviewing and eliciting fundamental filters of a group of people. One particular man answered this question with 'big picture', but he took twice as long as anyone else to be interviewed because he gave and was interested in so much detail! If he was interested in the 'big picture' of a project, goodness knows what his idea of 'detail' is!

People who are 'big picture':

- ◆ may present things in a random order
- ◆ will present summaries/overview
- ◆ will talk about concepts and in the abstract
- ◆ often have simple sentences with few details

People who are 'detail':

- ◆ talk in or about sequences
- ◆ give step by step answers
- ◆ use lots of adverbs/adjectives
- ◆ if they lose the sequence, will probably start the sentence over again

How to Influence Using This Filter

You can use this information as follows:

- ◆ for 'big picture' people, start with an overview, tell them the purpose, give them an outline of how the 'situation' (training session, tactical talk etc) will go.
- ◆ For 'detail' people, provide enough detail, take them through step by step what they will do or what needs to happen.
- ◆ Remember that too much detail will annoy a 'big picture', as will not enough detail for a 'detail' person.

You can also use the following types of language:

Big Picture	Detail
◆ the big picture,	◆ exactly,
◆ essentially,	◆ precisely,
◆ the key aspects,	◆ specifically (give lots of detail in sequence),
◆ in general,	◆ plan,
◆ conceptually,	◆ schedule,

◆ idea,	◆ define,
◆ concept,	◆ structure,
◆ typically,	◆ *"Here are the details."* (Be specific. Don't use abstractions.)
◆ overall,	
◆ overview,	
◆ *"Here's the big picture..."* (Don't give too many details, stay abstract.)	

(Here it comes!) You may wish to make your own summary of this section. The rest of the fundamental filters will be shown in brief below. To obtain even more information about how to use this material, or to learn more detail about the fundamental filters referred to below, refer to the 'Further Reference' section.

6. Summary of Other Key Fundamental Filters

The purpose of this section is to make you aware of some of the traits that people have, so that you can at least recognise them, both in others and yourself. Remember, for each filter below we only cover the extremes – there are normally combinations or points on the spectrum.

Name of Filter	Summary of Traits
Sameness or Difference	Some people like change to be slow and gradual. They notice how things are similar to what they know. Others like change to be frequent and/or radical. They notice how things are different to what they know or expect.
Stress Response ('Choice', 'Associated', 'Dissociated')	Some people are extremely vulnerable to normal levels of stress in their work or competition. ('associated')

Name of Filter	Summary of Traits
	Other people do not feel much stress – they are almost dissociated from it. ('dissociated') Most people feel it but can 'overcome' or 'deal' with it. ('choice')
Affiliation ('Independent', 'Team', 'Management')	Some people like working alone. ('independent') Others like being part of a team, sharing responsibility ('team') Others like working with others around them, yet either being in charge or having their own specific area(s) of responsibility ('management').
Work Preference ('Person' or 'Task')	Some people focus on people's thoughts and feelings. At the extreme, keeping people happy becomes the task in itself. ('person') Other people focus on the task at hand, or are more interested in systems, tools, objectives and facts, believing that people's feelings are not important. ('task')
Convincer 1 (See, hear, do, read)	We all have ways that we are convinced about someone's competence. We initially gather information about something or someone either by: ◆ seeing or ◆ hearing or ◆ doing with/experiencing or ◆ reading about Normally there is one preferred way to gather information.

Name of Filter	Summary of Traits
Convincer 2 (Automatic, never, number of times, period of time)	Then, to be convinced, we have to gather that information either: ◆ a number of times (three is a common number) or ◆ over a period of time or ◆ some people are automatically convinced ◆ some people are never truly convinced (you are only as good as your next performance!)
Speaking Style and Listening Style (Literal/Direct or Inferential/Hinting)	Some people when they speak are very direct. Others prefer to drop hints. Similarly when listening, other listen literally, others infer. So if a 'literal speaker' says "I'm thirsty", they may be surprised when an 'inferential listener' brings them a drink. When an 'inferential speaker' says "I'm thirsty" and a 'literal listener' doesn't do anything (because the 'literal listener' will take it literally as information and not as a request) the 'inferential speaker' may get upset. ***Tip for Coaches:*** **Be aware of your own speaking and listening style, and that of others. A 'literal listener' may not realise that an 'inferential speaker' has paid them a compliment, or actually wants them to do a specific aspect of the sport (for example, tactics). An 'inferential listener' may read meaning into comments, or may misinterpret even a 'literal speaker' (let alone an 'inferential speaker' – you know what I mean, don't you?!!!)**

Name of Filter	Summary of Traits
Introverts and Extroverts	Some people recharge the batteries by being with others ('extroverts') and often think out loud to clarify their ideas, whereas other people prefer time alone or quiet time to recharge their batteries and think things through alone to clarify their ideas ('introverts'). ***Tip for Coaches:*** **Allow for athletes' differing needs regarding 'recharge' time. An 'introvert' may not be being a 'party pooper' – they may just get 'pooped' by the party as being with people too much tires them out! An 'extrovert' will need to spend time with other people to recharge.**
Planned or Open-ended	Some people like to plan and be organised, have things completed and finalised. Others like to 'go with the flow', appear disorganised and prefer to avoid 'closure' in case a better option comes along.

The 'Further Reference' section will provide information on how to find out more about these fundamental filters.

2. How to Use Fundamental Filters in Practice.

Knowing all this information above is **interesting**. To be able to use it is extremely **useful**, which is of more benefit to us.

In order to be able to feel comfortable identifying or eliciting and using these fundamental filters, here are some suggestions and alternatives. If you prefer a set way of doing this (procedures), there are exercises shortly!

1. Treat any attempt to identify someone's fundamental filters as a 'guess and test' exercise. This takes the pressure off you. Even now I occasionally guess incorrectly, and I treat it as a learning experience.

2. Notice where you are on the spectrum of the five fundamental filters detailed above. Where you are at one end of a spectrum (as opposed to being in the middle), take special note.

3. Take one or two fundamental filters at a time and listen to a conversation, a chat show or interview, listening for clues as to which end of the spectrum the speakers are at.

4. Build up to listen out for all five fundamental filters.

5. Use the fundamental filters worksheet in Appendix 8 as a guide. Feel free to copy it or create your own. In steps 3 and 4 above, every time you hear an indication of one of the ends of the spectrum, make a mark next to the relevant line on the worksheet. For example, if the chat-show guest said, "I just knew what to do," make a line (like a number '1') next to 'internal'.

Exercise 15.1

Find two willing people (perhaps other mental skills coaches) and elicit each other's fundamental filters. Have one person as coach (A), one as 'athlete' (B) and the other as observer (C).

1. Pick one context of life, for example 'work', and 'A' asks 'B' the question to elicit the fundamental filter. 'A' and 'C' make notes as suggested in point 5 above.

   Normally, you only need to spend 20-30 seconds per question – once 'B' has given you the answer, just move on.

2. When 'A' has finished, 'A' and 'C' compare notes and their 'guesses' about where 'B' is on the spectrum for these five fundamental filters.

   As 'A' is the Coach, he/she has 'the final say' regarding the next step.

3. 'A' spends a few moments preparing to offer 'B' two choices in the context used (in this case, two different pieces or types of work). The first offer will be based on the OPPOSITE end of the spectrum for each fundamental filter, the second will match 'A's guess of the fundamental filters.

Appendix 8 gives a worked example and guideline script.

Clearly, in 'real life' you would not deliberately 'mismatch' someone's fundamental filters. The purpose of this is both to give 'A' the practice of using language at both ends of the spectrum and also to make all three of you aware of the impact of mismatching someone's fundamental filters. In 'real life', you would make your guesses and use language accordingly. If you noticed that the guess 'missed the mark' slightly, you could refine your guess.

4. Discuss with 'B' the impact of 'mismatching' fundamental filters compared to 'matching' them.

5. Swap roles, so that you each take the roles of 'A', 'B' and 'C'. Ideally, repeat the exercise three times in different contexts to increase the level of practice.

Tip 15.1

As the coach in the above exercise, also notice how it feels using statements that are in line with your own fundamental filters compared to using statements which are at the other end of the spectrum.

It probably feels unnatural to do the latter at the moment, yet with practice you will develop your flexibility to communicate in a way which appeals to and motivates your athletes.

Exercise 15.2

Identify the fundamental filters of your athletes, either formally (per Exercise 15.1 above) or by listening out for the language and/or noticing behaviours which indicate where they are on the spectrum of the five main fundamental filters.

It is also useful to be aware of some of the other fundamental filters mentioned above.

3. Some Other Thoughts on Motivation

1. Achievement, Affiliation and Power Motivation

There are numerous studies and theories about motivation. One which is particularly useful in a sporting context was developed by American psychologist David McClelland, a former Harvard University lecturer.

Essentially, he states that there are three types of motivating forces which drive people. They are the need for:

◆ Achievement
◆ Power
◆ Affiliation

'Achievement' relates to attainment of realistic but challenging goals, and advancement in the job. There is a strong need for feedback as to achievement and progress, and a need for a sense of accomplishment. In a sporting context, 'achievement' motivated people will always be looking to improve on what they have done, for example improve their technique or track times or score.

'Power' relates to the extent to which someone is 'authority motivated'. This driver produces a need to be influential, effective and to make an impact. There is a strong need to lead and for their ideas to prevail. There is also motivation and need towards increasing personal status and prestige. In a sporting context, 'power' motivated people will want to win and beat opponents.

'Affiliation' relates to the extent that someone has a need for friendly relationships and is motivated towards interaction with other people. The affiliation driver produces motivation and the need to be liked and held in popular regard. These people are team players, and value the personal interaction within sports.

McClelland said that most people possess and exhibit a combination of these characteristics. Some people exhibit a strong bias to a particular motivational need, and this motivational or needs 'mix' consequently affects their behaviour and working/managing style.[33]

---

[33] http://www.businessballs.com/davidmcclelland.htm

The way that McClelland assesses an individual's motivation is by giving him or her a picture and asking him or her to write about it. People's preferences will show in the way they interpret the pictures. For example, someone who is 'power' motivated will refer to aspects of control and directing. Someone who is 'affiliation' motivated will mention feelings and relationships between the people in the picture, and someone who is 'achievement' motivated will refer to accomplishing and improving.

So, from the point of view of mental skills coaches or sports coaches, being aware of a player's motivational type can be useful in choosing how to motivate him/her and how to treat or not treat someone. As a stretch, you could also map 'towards' and 'away from' onto McClelland's three types to give six types of motivation. For example, knowing that someone is 'achievement' motivated is useful. Knowing that they are 'towards' and 'achievement' would give you even more ideas of how to have them improve and achieve their goals, whereas if they were 'away from' and 'achievement' you would want to help them make sure they did not miss out on ways to improve.

2. Changing Values

Values change naturally as we mature. Are the things which are important to you now the same as were important to you when you were 18? Some will be, yet other values will have changed.

In Chapter 5 we touched on whether 'away from' values can be changed by mental skills coaches. They can, usually with extremely beneficial results (see Story 5.1), although this is best done by someone highly trained in NLP. Changing 'away from' values will often change the relative importance of values in any given context of a player's life. There are also other advanced NLP techniques to change values.

The purpose of writing this is to let you as a sports coach or mental skills coach know that 'yo-yo' results (see Diagram 5.2) and other seemingly difficult challenges with players can be addressed, relatively quickly, so that you can refer players for some deeper 'change work' if it is necessary.

3. Values – Deeper Levels of Understanding and Motivation

In Exercise 5.2, the 'values' of a player were elicited. This gives you as the coach excellent information about how to motivate him or her. Yet there are deeper aspects to this.

Knowing that for example 'recognition' is important to a player is useful information. However, do you know what the player means by 'recognition', and what you (as the mental skills coach or sports coach) need to do in order to fulfil the value of 'recognition'? The answer is "no". You know what YOU mean by 'recognition', but you do not know what anyone else means by it nor how anyone else would like to be treated in order that their value of 'recognition' is fulfilled and hence that the player is motivated.

In NLP, we call the meaning or 'equivalent' of these values or criteria 'criteria equivalents'. The best way to find out someone's 'criteria equivalents' is simply to ask the player the following types of questions:

a) "What has to happen for you to know that you are/have a _____?"
b) "How do you know when you're _____?"
c) "What does _____ mean to you?"
d) "How do you know when someone _____ you?"
e) "What is your evidence procedure for _____?"
f) "What causes you to feel _____?"
g) "What would have to happen for you to feel not _____?"

The answer to these questions lets you, the coach, know what to do and not do in order to keep the player motivated.

Exercise 15.3

Refer back to Exercise 5.2. Take the top three or four values that you elicited and ask some of the questions in a) to g) above to elicit the criteria equivalents.

For your athletes, make sure you know exactly what to do to motivate them, and what not to do so that you do not de-motivate them.

4. Using Submodalities to Motivate

In Chapter 8 we discussed how to use submodalities to change our mindset, and in Chapter 10 we touched on how to use them to enhance mental rehearsal.

In a similar way, submodalities can also be used to enhance motivation. By thinking of a goal you want to achieve and adjusting the submodalities of it (for example, making the picture bigger, brighter and with a crowd cheering loudly) the goal can become even more motivating.

Exercise 15.3

Think of something that motivates you. Adjust the submodalities until you feel really fired up!

Do the same with your athletes.

Summary

- There are several fundamental filters which impact on our results and behaviours.

- An understanding of the existence of different approaches, and a recognition that none of these are inherently bad or wrong, form a key aspect of a coach's ability to get the best out of people.

- Becoming more fluent in recognising and utilising these fundamental filters in coaching, and by knowing and recognising your own, will improve your performance and that of your athletes. This links back to some of the NLP 'presuppositions' in Chapter 3, for example being flexible in your behaviour and communications.

- Being aware of whether an athlete is motivated by affiliation, achievement or power will give you additional insights into how to motivate.

- Using criteria equivalents can help you as the mental skills coach or sports coach to gain even greater insight into how to motivate your players.

Chapter **16**

Language Tips for Coaches

A few years ago I thought I knew quite a lot about language – I speak French extremely well, and passable German and smatterings of Spanish, plus having spent four years at a leading management consultancy firm in London I thought I had honed my English skills.

But then I started learning NLP, and realised just how much I didn't know and how much fun it was to learn new linguistic skills. As you can probably guess from the name 'Neuro Linguistic Programming', the words we use are extremely important when influencing ourselves and others. You remember from the Communication Model in Chapter 1 that language is a key filter.

With every client I have ever coached, the language they have used has given me invaluable tips about how to structure my approach to them. This, plus the NLP tools, helped me know the language to use and avoid using with them.

Now in case you are thinking "Oh no, I hate grammar, I'll skip this chapter", just STOP……., and think again now, and remember my promise at the very start of this book to give you the important points with minimal theory. Hang on in there!

This chapter is divided into four sections

1. **Small words with big meanings**
2. **Speaking the athlete's language**
3. **How to use the language of time**
4. **Power questioning**

As with other parts of this book, some of what you will read may seem basic, yet I have heard numerous intelligent and experienced fitness professionals, coaches and trainers misuse the English language in a way that limits their players, athletes and clients.

1. Small Words With Big Meanings

Here are several small words which, as you will discover, have disproportionately big meanings.

i. Try

'Try' is one of my favourite words to avoid using. What does the word 'try' imply? Well, it implies two things. Firstly, that what you will 'try' to do will be difficult, and secondly that you may well not succeed. Compare the following two sentences:

Statement A:
"I will try to improve my bunker shots."

Statement B:
"I will improve my bunker shots."

Which of the two sentences is more convincing? Probably statement B – there is a statement of intent to improve, whereas in statement A there is a statement of intent to 'try'.

Let me put this another way. Most of the readers either are or will be parents. As parents, are you going to *try* to ensure your child or children have enough food to eat, or are you going to ensure they have enough food to eat?

The only time I use the word 'try' is when I want someone not to succeed at something! For example if I have done some 'change work' with a player, and have tested to make sure they have made the change in their mind, as a final convincer to me and them I may say something like *"try really hard to get anxious* (for example) *about playing in the final"*. They usually say *"I can't get anxious"*, at which point we have pretty much completed the work.

Tip 16.1

Banish the word 'try' from your vocabulary unless you actually want someone not to succeed.

Do the same with your players and athletes, pointing out to them the impact of the word 'try'.

As Yoda said, "Do. Or do not. There is no try."

ii. But, However, Although, And

The effect of the words 'but', 'however' and to some extend 'although' is to negate or minimise what has been said. The effect of 'and' is to agree with or add to what has been said.

Compare these two pairs of sentences:

Statement A:
*"You played well today, **but** (or **'however'** or **'although'**) you faded a little near the end."*

Statement B:
*"You played well today, **and** you faded a little near the end."*

Statement A:
*"You're a very effective coach, **but** your use of language could be improved."*

Statement B:
*"You're a very effective coach, **and** your use of language could be improved."*

Which statements make you feel better as a listener? Probably statement B, because the 'positive comments' in statement A are followed by a 'but' or 'however' or 'although', which negates what has been said, whereas the 'and' adds to it.

So, use words like 'but' if you want to negate or minimise what has been said, for example:

"Yes, that's true, we did not play well, but given the young side we had there were some very encouraging signs."

Tip 16.2

Use words like 'but', 'however' and 'although' only when you want to negate or minimise what has been said. Use 'and' when you want to add to or agree with what has been said.

    iii. Don't.....

As you will remember from Part I, the unconscious mind, which is the aspect of our mind that accesses the skills we use during sport, cannot directly process a negative (don't think about your best friend now!).

So when working with athletes, avoid telling them what you don't want, tell them what you **do** want. If for some reason it is important to make them aware of what you don't want them to do, follow it up immediately with what you do want them to do, and **emphasise it** by voice tonality or by repeating what you want them to do, or both.

Compare these two pairs of sentences:

> **Statement A:**
> *"Don't take your eyes off the ball."*
>
> **Statement B:**
> *"Keep your eyes on the ball."*

Statement A:
"Don't listen to what your critics are saying."

Statement B:
"Ignore your critics. Remember how well you played last week and know that you can repeat that."

Both statements A leave you thinking about what you don't want to do or think about. Statements B leave you knowing what to do.

Tip 16.3

There are many ways not to do a skill well. There are very few (if only one) ways to do it properly.

Say it how you want it to be!

The only exception to the above is when I want someone to do what I'm asking them not to do.

Story 16.1

I was working with a sportswoman who used to get anxious in certain situations. We did some 'change work', and instead of feeling anxious when she thought of those situations she started laughing. In the context of what we were doing this was a good thing.

After she had laughed a couple of times when thinking about the event, I said, *"Don't laugh, this was a serious issue for you,"* with a slight smirk and a playful tone of voice. Of course, she laughed even more!

After doing this two or three more times, she changed her mindset and associated laughter with the event she used to be anxious about.

iv. STOP!

The word 'STOP' actually stops the train of thought someone is having. As a mental skills coach or sports coach, you can use it to ask someone to stop what they are doing and do something else instead. For example, if someone is talking about how things are not working for them, you could say something like:

"Now I want you to STOP……….. and tell me what you would like instead."

v. Or

Often when people use the word 'or', they imply that there is one choice or another, but not both and not anything else. In other words, it limits their thinking and possibly the thinking of those involved in the conversation.

As a sports coach and/or mental skills coach and/or athlete (and/or any other capacity in life), it is really useful to be able to think 'outside the box'. So notice to what extent words such as 'or' limits your thinking. Notice also to what extent it limits your players or team-mates and 'challenge it' appropriately.

For example, if the options presented are 'X or Y', here is a list of what could actually be done:

- ◆ X only
- ◆ Y only
- ◆ X and Y only
- ◆ X and Y and other options
- ◆ X and other options
- ◆ Y and other options.
- ◆ Other options (but not X or Y)
- ◆ Nothing at all.

There are numerous choices within the 'other options' bracket. Yet often people limit their thinking and that of others by this little word 'or'.

vi. If, When

'If' implies that something is conditional or in doubt. 'When' implies that something with happen, it is merely a question of time.

Compare the following statements:

Statement A:
"If you run the 100 metres in less than 10.2 seconds today, you will be set up nicely for the next race."

Statement B:
"When you have run the 100 metres in less than 10.2 seconds today, you will be set up nicely for the next race."

Which is more certain? Statement B. Clearly we need to apply common sense when using these words – for example there may be situations where it is more appropriate to use 'if' when talking about future good performance, possibly to avoid putting undue pressure on an athlete.

Tip 16.4

Use 'if' when you want to imply doubt, and use 'when' when you want to imply certainty.

vii. Yet

'Yet' is such a useful word if someone has a perceived block, especially if the tone of voice, or inference suggests that they believe they not only cannot do it now but will not be able to do so in the future. For example, a budding pole-vaulter might say "I can't land the pole with as much precision as I'd like". You as the sports coach or mental skills coach could simply reply "Yet", which takes the athlete beyond the present to a time when they could or will be able to do it.

The following story illustrates some of the points covered so far in this chapter.

Story 16.2

I was in a gym around the time that I was planning this book. I walked past a class where a fitness class was taking place.

I heard the instructor say the following comments:
(My comments to you (some are 'tongue in cheek') are in brackets):

"Don't think about how tired you are." (I wasn't but now you mention it... 'Keep going, think of how great you'll feel when you've finished' would be better.)

"Don't bend your knees when you do that." (So what do I do instead?)

"When your knees start aching, just have a five minute break." (My knees don't normally ache, perhaps they will today – oh dear. NB. If it is important to make this point from a safety or health angle, then 'if' would be better than 'when'.)

"You're doing well, but there is much more to do." (I think I'll give up now! Am I really doing well? 'You're doing well, keep going' would be better.)

"Try to get your knees higher." (I am trying, I'm not sure if I'll be able to, and it will be so hard to do it! And anyway, how high? 'Lift your knees another three inches so they are level with your sternum' is clearer.)

---

2. Speaking The Athlete's Language

You will remember from earlier in the book that there are five representational systems plus auditory digital, our 'self-talk'. Generally, people have a preferred representational system, or will favour one any given moment to process information.

People trained in NLP know that we all use words and phrases which indicate which representational system we are using at any given moment, and there is much evidence that we are more likely to build rapport with and influence people if we use words and phrases which match the representational system they are using, and or present information using methods aligned with that representational system.

Athletes who process primarily visually will prefer to be *shown* what to do, and will prefer to hear words and phrases linked to visual concepts such as *see, look, show, clear, viewpoint,* and *mental image*. For example, when explaining a poor performance, they may say something like, *"I just couldn't see how I could win today. My mind went fuzzy".*

Athletes who process primarily auditorily will prefer to *listen* to what to do, and will prefer to hear words and phrases linked to auditory concepts such as *hear, listen, rings a bell, tune in,* and *manner of speaking*. For example, when explaining a poor performance, they may say something like, *"I just can't explain it. I wasn't on the same wavelength as the others".*

Athletes who process primarily kinaesthetically will prefer to *experience* or *walk through* what to do, and will prefer to hear words and phrases linked to kinaesthetic concepts such as *feel, touch, solid, concrete idea, get a handle on* and *firm foundations*. For example, when explaining a poor performance, they may say something like, *"I felt all washed up today. I couldn't get to grips with the conditions".*

Athletes who prefer the auditory digital system will prefer to understand what to do (it is important that things 'make sense' or are logical to these athletes), and will prefer to hear words and phrases that are non-specific to any particular representational system, such as *consider, think, perceive, decide,* and *process*. For example, when explaining a poor performance, they may say something like, *"It's just not rational. I don't understand what happened".*

Thus, by becoming well-versed in the different 'languages', mental skills coaches and sports coaches are more likely to:

◆ See eye to eye, have the same viewpoint and be able to paint a clear picture with athletes.

◆ Speak the same language, be on the same wavelength and sing from the same hymn-sheet as our players.

◆ Feel comfortable, kick some ideas around and get to grips with sportspeople.

◆ Understand the ideas and be more aware of what athletes think.

Appendix 9 gives more examples of such words and phrases.

As a generalisation of the population overall, 35 to 40 percent of people prefer to use the visual system, 20 to 25 percent prefer to use either auditory or auditory digital, and 35 to 40 percent prefer to use the kinaesthetic system. Given that sport is inherently a kinaesthetic activity, the percentages may be slightly weighted towards kinaesthetic for sportspeople. (Please note that athletes will use all of their representational systems, but will tend to have one which they prefer using.)

So, for example, a mental skills coach who tends not to use visual-type words or who does not *show* (i.e. does not use the visual representational system) athletes what to do, may risk not seeing eye to eye with up to 40 percent of athletes.

Exercise 16.1

Review the words and phrases in Appendix 9. Choose one representational system per day, and notice when people use words which represent that system during the day.

Repeat the exercise the next three days for the other systems.

As you become more adept at hearing the relevant words and phrases, pick two, three or four systems each day until you can easily notice which representational system an athlete is using.

> ### Exercise 16.2
>
> This is similar to Exercise 16.1, except that instead of listening out for each representational system, make a conscious effort to use a different one each day, so that you become equally comfortable and 'fluent' in each.

Tip 16.5

As a mental skills coach, present information in a way that your athletes prefer to receive it. When in doubt, or when speaking to a group or team, use a combination of all four.

3. How To Use The Language of Time

As we discussed in the 'context reframe' section of Chapter 9, one way to change the meaning of an event is to change the time frame. We can extend this when dealing with 'issues' that athletes and players have. Broadly, by using words that directly or indirectly imply a change in time frame, we can change players' thinking about issues.

We need to cover a little theory (only a little!). Let's consider the three main tenses in any language – past, present and future. For each, there is a form of the tense which implies that a situation is 'static', and another which implies that the situation is ongoing. Here are some examples to illustrate this with the verb 'to play'.

Static or Ongoing	Past	Present	Future
Static	I played I have played I did play	I play I do play	I will play
Ongoing	I was playing I have been playing	I am playing	I will be playing

Generally, we want to put any 'problems' into the static past, so that it appears to be completed, and make any resources or advantages into the ongoing present and future (ongoing or static, depending on the circumstances). As with all coaching and especially NLP coaching approaches, it is important that there is rapport and that the coach uses 'common sense'.

Let's take some examples of conversations between a player (P) and a coach (C):

Putting Problems into the Completed Past

P: "My javelin throwing is really bad."

C: "OK, so your javelin throwing has not worked as you'd like recently."

Here, the coach acknowledges the player's concern, and puts the problem into the completed past ("has not worked"). For good measure, the coach reframes 'really bad' into 'not worked as you'd like'.

P: "I can't seem to get the hang of doing a drop shot."

C: "OK, so up to now you haven't been able to get the hang of drop shots."

Again, the coach puts the problem into the completed past ('up to now, you haven't...')

Taking Resources into the Present or Future

P1: "I've been getting anxious about the hockey final."

C1: "Have you been anxious in the past about something that actually went well for you?"

P2: *Pause* "Yes – a few occasions actually."

C2: "How did it feel afterwards?"

P3: "Great."

C3: "Imagine some time in the future looking back at this. Could this be just another one of those situations when you thought you were anxious but actually the event turned out really well and you felt great about it?"

P4: "Yes it could."

C4: "How does that feel?"

P5: "Good – I feel more confident now."

C5: "Imagine how well you will be playing in that final now that you are feeling more confident."

The comment at C1 'paces' the player and his 'problem', putting it into the past, and together with C2 identifies some resources from the past. At C3, the coach does a temporal shift, asking the player whether this current anxiety could be just another example of when things have turned out well. At C5, the coach takes those resources and puts them into the future using the ongoing resource ('will be feeling', 'will be playing').

Exercise 16.3

Find one or two fellow coaches to work with on this. Assign coach A to be 'client', coach B to be 'coach' and coach C to be observer.

'A' states a relatively minor problem or limitation he/she has.

'B' reflects back the problem/limitation such that it's in the past.

'C' observes, and possibly adds on of his/her own suggestions.

'A' and 'C' give feedback on the effectiveness of the intervention.

For Example:

A: "One of my players is causing me a real problem at the moment and I don't know how to deal with it."

B: "One of your players has been (or 'was') getting on your nerves and up to now you haven't found a way to deal with it."

Exercise 16.4

'A' states a relatively minor problem or limitation he/she has.

'B' reflects back the problem/limitation such that it's in the past and asks for a desired outcome.

'A' responds.

'B' places the outcome/resources into the future.

'A' gives feedback. 'C' observes and gives feedback. 'C' only helps 'B' as a last resort!

For Example:

A: "I don't feel confident with floor exercises."

B: "So, you have not felt confident with floor exercises. What would you like instead?"

A: "I'd like to feel empowered and light."

B: "So, once you've put your (temporary) lack of confidence behind you, you will be feeling empowered and light."

Permanence, Factual, Temporary, Automatic

You will have realised that there are times when it is useful to be able to suggest that something is:

◆ **Permanent,** for example to highlight positive changes that the player has made, skills, confidence and generally good traits. Words and phrases such as 'lasting', 'continuous', 'ongoing', 'always', 'never-ending' and 'secure' are examples.

◆ **Factual,** for example to highlight the benefits of mind coaching and the techniques included in this book. Words and phrases such as 'genuine', 'undeniable', 'obvious(ly)', 'absolute(ly)' and 'definite' are examples.

◆ **Temporary,** for example to minimise loss of form, setbacks and problems. ('Temporary lack of confidence' was used in Exercise 16.4.) Words and phrases such as 'fleeting', 'for a little while', 'short term' and 'like a shot' are examples.

◆ **Automatic,** for example to re-enforce the ease with which players can use new skills and feel confident in certain situations. Words and phrases such as 'automatically', 'constant' and 'second nature' are examples.

You will **no doubt** have realised that any **fleeting** concerns you may have had about the long-term benefits of these **proven** NLP techniques will give way to **lasting** confidence in their usefulness. Soon, if not already, using the **tried and tested** techniques in this book will become **second nature.** (The highlighted words are for your purpose as the reader. When speaking, it is preferable to speak in your normal tone of voice as opposed to emphasising these words.)

Exercise 16.5

List as many words and phrases as you can for each of the four categories covered in this segment (permanence, factual, temporary, automatic).

Think of the kinds of statements denoting problems that you hear from players.

Create responses based on incorporating the words and phrases from the first part of this exercise. If appropriate, incorporate the language skills from Exercises 16.1 and 16.2.

Do this exercise either alone or in small groups.

Practice using the new responses.

4. Power Questions

Sometimes clients and sportspeople ask me if I have the answers. My reply is that as a mental skills coach, I don't necessarily have the answers (although I may do), but I do have the questions to allow the clients or athlete to find their own answers. Remembering the points made in the Introduction to this book and in the Introduction to Part IV, knowing the right question is every bit as important as knowing the answer, because knowing the answer is often your answer or someone else's, not that of the player in front of you.

Based on the Communication Model discussed in Chapter 1, we all delete, distort and generalise information that comes to us. These three internal processes are reflected in our thinking and language. Given that people make many deletions, distortions and generalisations (DDGs) in order to ascribe meaning to the events happening in their life, we could waste a lot of time asking questions that don't provide information of any real use. If we could ask questions which uncover the most relevant information, we'd be able to 'cut to the chase' and get to the key, relevant points, and uncover other people's DDGs that could provide an opening or other useful information to accelerate progress and results.

NB. Please remember to use common sense. The questions are to be used for a purpose, not just to score points or appear 'clever'.

Below are examples of DDGs and how to deal with them.

i. 'Mind Reads'

Claiming to know what someone is thinking, for example *'I know you're wondering', 'I know she thinks I'm lazy'.*

Suggestion: Question how someone 'knows' what someone else is thinking.

Example: '(I know) he doesn't like me.'

Response: 'How (specifically) do you know he doesn't like you?'

ii. *'Causation & Equivalences'*

Words and phrases such as: *causes, because, makes, if..then, means, is/are.*

Suggestion: Question the linkage, or find counter-examples.

Example: 'My coach shouting at me makes me feel stupid.'

Response: 'How (specifically) does your coach shouting at you make you feel stupid?'

'Have you ever shouted at someone who you thought was intelligent/clever/not stupid?'

Example: 'My running badly today means I won't run well next week.'

Response: 'How (specifically) does running badly today mean that you won't run well/will run badly next week?' 'Have you (or someone else) ever run badly one week and turned it round the next?'

iii. *'Anonymous Judgements and Rules'*

Phrases where there is no mention of the person doing the judging, such as *'it's bad to...'*, *'it's good to....'*.

Suggestion: Question the source of the judgement - Example (a).

Phrases where there are words like *must, have to, got to, should, ought to, can, can't.*

Suggestion: Question the consequence of not following the rule or counter-examples (b), or the validity of the rule (c), or what prevents us (d).

Example (a): 'It's essential to run a 20 mile race before a marathon.'

Response: 'According to who?' 'Who says it's essential?' 'How (specifically) do you know it's essential?'

Example (b): 'We have to get anxious to perform well.'

Response: 'What would happen if we didn't get anxious?' 'Have we ever played well and not been anxious?'

Example (c): 'We've got to do this.'

Response: 'According to who?' 'What would happen if we didn't?'

Example (d): 'I can't improve my backhand.'

Response: 'What stops you?' 'How do you know?'

iv. Generalisations

Words and phrases which imply groups or several times or never, such as *never, no one, nobody, everybody, always, all, every.*

Suggestion: Question the 'generalisation', or find a counter-example.

Example: 'My coach never praises me.'

Response: 'Never?''

Example: 'None of my team-mates seem to concern themselves about me.'

Response: 'None of them? Not one single person?'

Example: 'Players always struggle when they go up a standard.'

Response: 'Can you think of a player who hasn't struggled, or has adapted well?' 'What about <name> - she adapted well.'

v. Hidden Comparisons

Words and phrases such as *more, better, less, faster, stronger.*

Suggestion: Question against who, what or when the comparison is being made.

Example: 'He's much better.'

Response: 'Better than who/what/when?'

Example: 'Let's run faster.'

Response: 'Faster than who/what/when?'

vi. Abstract Nouns

Words such as *communication, relationship, decision.*

Suggestion: Turn the noun back into a process or a verb and then ask an appropriate question.

Example: 'There's no communication around here.'

Response: 'Who is not communicating (verb) what to whom?' 'What would you like to be communicated (verb)?' 'How would you like to communicate (verb) instead?'

Example: 'There are a lot of decisions to make.'

Response: 'What (specifically) needs to be decided (verb)?'

vii. Other Nouns

Suggestion: For general nouns, gain specificity.

Example: 'I like Nike.'

Response: 'What specifically do you like about Nike?' (is it the brand or the company itself?) 'Which particular product(s) do you like?'

viii. Verbs

Where verbs are used which have a powerful meaning in the context of the situation yet are unspecified, such as *rejected, challenged, disagreed.*

Suggestion: Get specific!

Example: 'They rejected me.'

Response: 'How specifically did they reject you?' 'What did they do or not do specifically to reject you?'

Example: 'She challenged my authority.'

Response: 'How specifically did she challenge your authority?'

ix. This, That, It, They, We, You etc

These pronouns can cause confusion. For example, who exactly is included in 'we', or 'you', or 'they'? Numerous times I have heard people say phrases like 'I want you to do it' when they have been talking about several points and it is not clear exactly what this 'it' is.

Suggestion: The solution is simple – ask or clarify your understanding. It might be useful to include the word 'specifically'.

x. Other Power questions

There have been several examples of other very useful questions throughout this book. For example, the 'ecology' questions are extremely powerful when setting goals, as are many of the other well-formed outcome questions.

When seeking to find the positive intention of a behaviour, asking 'for what purpose?' or 'what will that do/get for you?' will usually provide extremely useful information.

Exercise 16.6

'Challenge' the following statements (please resist looking at the answers in Appendix 10 until you have done the exercise – and where there is more than one aspect that you could 'challenge', choose the one (or occasionally two) which is likely to be most useful:

I know you think he's a good player.
I know you came here for a purpose.
I can see you believe this.
I know you're not concerned about this.

I'm looking for a new track-suit.
I saw the report in the newspaper.
The relationship has broken down.
I don't have enough knowledge.

They rejected us.
They were toying with us.
It's creating havoc.
They challenged me.

It's good to play it hard.
We have to make a decision today.
We can't ask them for more.
You should really go to that training session.

Everyone does it that way.
We always take our time when making decisions.
We've tried everything to make this happen.
I can't trust anyone with this.

We do more.
That's expensive!
We're faster.
We try harder.

They make me feel so annoyed.
Her being late means she doesn't care about the team.
If they don't do the paperwork today, then they're not serious about the contract.
You're disagreeing, so you can't be interested in doing this.

Summary

- Remember the small words with big meaning.
- Putting 'problems' into the past (preferably the completed past) by using verb tenses and putting resources into the present and/or future is an excellent and neat way to coach without appearing to do much.
- Remember to use 'power questions' appropriately – using them too often or inappropriately, or trying to be 'clever' will probably break rapport and could intensely annoy players.
- Becoming even more fluent at language will pay huge dividends, I promise!

Chapter 17
Other Advanced Coaching Tools and Tips

In this chapter we will cover the following topics:

1. 'Logical Levels' – one of the keys to being focused
2. Metaphors – the use of stories and analogies that influence people
3. Walking your talk
4. The 'Wheel Of Life'
5. Some tips on one-to-one coaching where the sportsmen is a 'client'
6. Feedback
7. Emotions
8. Stages of group and team development
9. Personal transitions

1. 'Logical Levels'

In Chapter 5 (see Diagram 5.1) we touched on an extremely useful model for coaches. In NLP it is called 'logical levels'.[34]

Essentially, the 'logical levels' model is a very useful way for us to structure our thinking, and can be applied to many situations, particularly when doing some kind of one-to-one coaching work and where any kind of individual or organisational change is required.

The model has six 'levels':

---

[34] Developed by Robert Dilts based on work done by Gregory Bateson, an anthropologist

1. Mission or Purpose
2. Identity
3. Beliefs and Values
4. Capabilities
5. Behaviours
6. Environment

The principles of the model are as follows:

- A perceived problem, challenge or limitation at any particular level can only be dealt with by addressing it at a higher level, or possibly the same level, but never lower.

- Where all levels are in 'alignment', there will be a powerful energy generated. Where there is lack of alignment, it is likely that there will be a lack of congruence and focus.

- Changing higher levels will impact on levels lower down.

- Each level has a key question implicit for that level. These questions will be shown in the example below.

1. **MISSION / PURPOSE** - refers to the larger system of which you are part. Successful organisations pay attention to the bigger system. The key question for this level is 'Who else?'

2. **IDENTITY** - how you think of yourself as a person or how an organisation, team or club defines its identity or its unique value. The key question for this level is 'Who?'

3. **BELIEFS** - emotionally held views. Beliefs in an organisation, team or club are viable only if supported by the behaviour of its entire members (players, employees etc).

    VALUES - criteria or qualities held to be important and are used as a basis for daily action. Organisation, team or club values are only valid if covert and overt values are the same. Agreed values can be a code of practice if they are genuinely shared. The key question for this level is 'Why?'

4. **CAPABILITIES** - becoming increasingly known as competencies, these are the skills, qualities and strategies, which we use in our life and in our sport. The key question for this level is 'How?'

5. **BEHAVIOUR** - what you do and say, the external expression of the self. Behaviour is not identity; an individual is not their behaviour (as you will remember from then NLP presuppositions in Chapter 3). This is a useful distinction to make. The key question for this level is 'What?'

6. **ENVIRONMENT** - refers to what is outside yourself such as the place where you train and play, the people around you. We often react to our environment. The key questions for this level are 'Where?' and 'When?'

To illustrate these points and how the model works, let's use the following example.

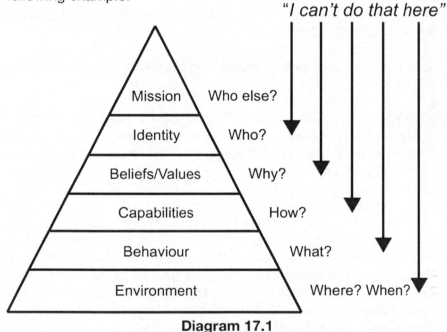

Diagram 17.1

So if someone were to say "I can't do that here', the meaning of this sentence would depend on where the emphasis is.

- ◆ If the emphasis is on the word **'here'**, that implies it is something about the environment, i.e. *'Where'* or possibly *'When'*.

- ◆ If the emphasis is on the word **'that'**, that implies the person does not know what behaviours to do, i.e. does not know *'What'*.

◆ If the emphasis is on the word **'do'**, that implies the person does not have the capabilities, i.e. does not know *'How'*.

◆ If the emphasis is on the word **'can't'**, that implies the person either does not believe they can do it, or it is against their values, i.e. there is no reason (or not enough reasons) *'Why'*.

◆ If the emphasis is on the word **'I'**, that implies it is something about the person's sense of identity, i.e. *'Who'* they are.

Please note that sometimes *behaviours* and *capabilities* are lumped together and known as *skills* and *abilities.*

The concept of 'mission' or 'purpose' implies that there is a reason beyond themselves. You often hear professional players talk about pushing themselves 'for the fans', in other words it is about other people, not them – they have a 'mission'.

There are three **key points** about 'logical levels' from a coaching perspective.

1. To effect a change (which is fundamentally what coaching and especially mental skills coaching is about) you have to operate from at least the 'logical level' that the problem is on, and probably at a higher level.

   For example, if a golfer says in practice, "I can't putt here", and the explicit or implicit emphasis is on *'here'*, you might ask, "where/when can you putt?" and move to a different location or practice at another time. If the same golfer says, "I can't putt here" and the explicit or implicit emphasis is on *'can't'*, then practicing at another time or location will not solve anything. You would need to deal with this at the 'beliefs and values' level, and possibly even at 'identity' or 'beyond identity'.

   If we consider the two ladies referred to in Chapter 2 who lifted cars to help save someone, what enabled them to do it from a 'logical levels' standpoint was that it was about someone else (son or friend). Even though they did not think they had the 'capabilities' or 'behaviours' to lift the car, because it was so important to them and there was a 'purpose' (beyond themselves) in doing it, they were able to lift the cars.

Some sample questions for doing coaching at each of the levels are shown after Tip 17.1.

2. Having an alignment of the 'logical levels' provides a powerful force to achieve goals, whether for individuals or teams. In other words if goals or targets are supported by an appropriate sense of 'identity', which in turn is supported and aligned with the appropriate 'beliefs and values', and there are the appropriate 'capabilities' to do the necessary 'behaviours' and the training is done in the right 'environment' (time and place), then there is far more chance of success than if there is a lack of alignment.

    Another way of thinking of this it to imagine the 'logical levels' of an individual or a team being like 100 watts of energy. When this energy is dispersed like a light bulb, you get a particular result. Yet when this energy is truly focused, aligned and pointing in the same direction, rather like a laser beam of 100 watts, it has immense power to break down barriers and cut through obstacles. We will refer to this a little later in this chapter.

    We often hear of people who 'walk their talk' – from a 'logical levels' perspective this means that their 'behaviours' tie in with their stated 'beliefs and values'.

    Frank Dick, the former UK National Athletics coach, says, *"The real achievers, the champions, the gold medallists, the record breakers will be nothing short of 100% who they are"*.[35] In other words, their sense of 'identity', a major aspect of the 'logical levels', is aligned with their success. They are being totally true to themselves.

3. Please be aware of when someone (including you!) is operating at a level which is inappropriate. For example, if an athlete were to say 'If I don't win, I am a failure', this implies that they are in some way linking the result to them at an **identity** level. It would be more useful to keep this at a **behaviour** and **capability** level, by re-framing it to, for example, 'if I don't perform as I expect to, I will need to change some aspects of my performance/training'.

---

[35] Jeff Grout & Sarah Perrin, *Mind Games – Inspirational Lessons From The World's Biggest Sports Stars*, Capstone Publishing Ltd, 2004, p.94

Story 17.1

During one of the coaching sessions with the swimmer referred to in Story 10.8, she said 'if I don't do it, I am a failure', and was quite upset. She was linking the behaviours and capabilities of swimming the Channel to her as an individual (identity level).

I explained the 'logical levels' model to her, asking her at what level were the statements 'if I don't do it (i.e. swim the Channel)' and 'I am a failure'. She realised the first was 'capability' level and the second was 'identity' level. It took little prompting from me for her to realise that she had mixed up the levels, mistakenly taking a 'capability' to mean an 'identity'.

She was then able to separate the two notions, and realise that whatever the outcome, as a person she is courageous, committed and determined. This helped significantly reduce the pressure she had put on herself – perceived negatives and threats at an 'identity' level often have a negative effect on people.

Tip 17.1

When giving feedback that could be taken negatively, make it about *behaviour,* not the individual *(identity)*. For example, it is better to say, 'when you do X, I feel Y', or even, 'when you do stupid things like X, I feel Y', (both statements are at *behaviour* level, albeit one more judgementally expressed) than to say, 'You are stupid for doing X'.

Avoid making negative 'identity' statements such as 'You are stupid / useless etc'.

Some Useful Coaching Questions for Different Levels

In the table below are some sample questions if it is necessary or useful to coach at a specific level. Please note that these are suggestions – you would have to use your common sense to judge the correct approach or appropriate question to ask.

Level	Sample Questions
Mission/Purpose	◆ Who else would benefit from you changing? ◆ Who else is (or would be) affected by your actions? ◆ What impact would this have on your family?
Identity	◆ Who (what type of person) would you need to be to win/achieve this? ◆ How can you find it in yourself to overcome this challenge? ◆ What are the personal attributes of a champion? Where and how have you demonstrated that you have these attributes? ◆ What do you believe about yourself?
Beliefs & Values	◆ What is important to you about doing X or being X? ◆ What do you believe about this situation? ◆ Can you change the situation? ◆ For what purpose are you doing this – what will it get for you? And what will that do for you/get for you? ◆ What stops you?

Level	Sample Questions
Capabilities	◆ What are your main skills in this area? ◆ What parts of your game do you need to work on? ◆ If you developed XYZ skill, what impact would it have on your performance?
Behaviour	◆ What do you need to do differently next time? ◆ Do you know what to do? ◆ What changes do you need to make to your stance / take off / swing / technique?
Environment	◆ Where would you like to practice to give you the best chance of winning/ success? ◆ When would you like to practice to give you the best chance of winning/ success?

Exercise 17.1

When listening to your athletes or players, start noticing which 'logical level' they are coming from at different times, both when they discuss 'successes' and 'non-successes'.

Make a mental note and, if and when appropriate, coach them at a 'logical level' which is above where their 'issue' or 'challenge' is.

2. Metaphors and Analogies

Metaphors are telling stories ('telling' is both an adjective and verb here!). Analogies are where we draw parallels between two situations. The purposes of using metaphors and analogies when coaching are:

i.   to assist us in explaining concepts and ideas

ii. to help players remember what we have told them

iii. to help overcome players' resistance to our ideas

Taking the first point, if someone tries to explain to you a concept that you may not currently fully understand by using technical language or other concepts that you don't understand, that will probably confuse you even more! However, if that person uses analogies that you can understand to explain what you don't yet understand, that makes it far easier for you to grasp. My guess is that your understanding of the potential benefits of having 'logical levels' aligned was enhanced by the analogy of 100 watt light-bulb compared to the 100 watt laser beam.

Regarding the second point, as children, we all loved stories, and even as adults many of us can remember the 'fairy stories' we were told as children. One of the ways that the unconscious mind works is by making links and connections between aspects of a story and the individual's present situation in life. So by telling a story about how someone else (sportsman or otherwise) overcame or dealt with a particular challenge, the athlete you are coaching will be more likely to remember it than if you just tell him or her how to do it, and they will also be able to (unconsciously) apply it to their own situation.

Regarding the third point, overcoming resistance, sometimes when coaching athletes they may resist (for whatever reason) suggestions you have made. One way to bypass this resistance is to tell a story about how someone else overcame a block or dealt with a situation that is similar to the one your athlete is facing. This 'other person' could be an athlete you know – remember not to mention names unless you have their permission or it is information in the public domain.

I have used metaphors and analogies at some point during the coaching with virtually every single client I have worked with. Also, notice how you responded as you read the stories in this book – were they useful in explaining the points being made? I use metaphors and stories also during my training courses, and delegates seem to value them as a learning aid.

Story 17.2

Paul, a hurdler, initially was reluctant to do any form of visualisation. I explained how other three clients had used visualisation successfully to enhance their performance (Paul had a 'three times' convincer fundamental filter - see Chapter 15).

This overcame the resistance he had. In addition, because I gave sufficient information during the metaphor about HOW the clients did the visualisation, he was able to do it successfully himself.

Tip 17.2

Listen to other people when they explain something. Do they use metaphors and analogies? Use theirs if and when appropriate, and develop your own.

Exercise 17.2

When explaining concepts to athletes, practice using metaphors and analogies. Over the next month, use at least five metaphors and analogies, preferably in your coaching.

If you feel you need to practice in a 'safe' environment, do so with friends and family (I assume that is safer than at work!), or any other situations you feel is appropriate.

3. Walking Your Talk

Didn't you just hate being told as a kid or an adolescent, "don't do as I do, do as I say!" It's a little hypocritical, to say the least. Your players and athletes will pick up from you any 'incongruencies' you have, even if you think you hide them well. In Appendix 1 on 'rapport', I explain that the vast majority of communication is 'non-verbal' and from body language and voice tonality.

By not walking your talk, players may think, 'well, why should I?' or 'you can talk', or words to that effect, even if they don't express it. Given that many athletes will be teenagers or in the twenties, this type of attitude may not be surprising.

By walking your talk, you send a message to athletes and players that what you are asking them to do and the way you are asking them to behave and think is something you are prepared to do.

The difference that walking your talk makes to players may be relatively small and subtle, and in most sports there is very little to choose between the top teams or players, so every little helps!

The main areas for you as a mental skills coach or sports coach to walk your talk are covered in Part I, particularly:

◆ The Mindset for Success (particularly the NLP presuppositions)
◆ being 'at cause' - if **you** make excuses, your players will
◆ taking responsibility for yourself and your results

Exercise 17.3

If you looked at someone who was in a similar situation to yourself and behaved the way you do, what advice would you give him to make what he does even better, particularly with respect to walking his talk?

Take your own medicine!

In addition, given that you are asking players and athletes to look at themselves and have some mental skills coaching, I would strongly urge you to find yourself a mental skills coach for the following reasons:

- ◆ To fully appreciate what it is like for your players to receive mind coaching. This knowledge will certainly make you an even better coach.

- ◆ To be able to take advantage of all the benefits of coaching. Managers and coaches often experience the kinds of issues that players are facing. Being able to deal with them makes it significantly easier for your players to do so.

- ◆ Also, it is useful to have a neutral, independent person committed to your success for you to bounce ideas off and to help you think 'out of the box'.

- ◆ Sometimes it is useful just to 'offload'. As with the business world, sometimes the more senior the person is, the more difficult it is to find a neutral person with whom the manager can discuss issues and challenges he or she is facing. If you are carrying minimal, if any, unresolved or unaddressed 'work' problems, your athletes are more likely to do the same.

- ◆ To keep you on track. Often, senior people in any organisation (including coaches and managers of sports teams) have such a position of power that people around them are too scared to challenge their thinking for fear of losing their jobs. Yet senior people are fallible too, and one of the roles of a good mental skills coach will be to challenge the thinking of coaches and managers.

As a final point in this segment, it is absolutely essential that you believe your players and athletes will achieve the goals they set. David Hemery says in his book, 'One of the greatest gifts a coach can give is a sense of belief in the performer'.[36] Experienced mental skills coaches and therapists have known for a long time that clients have an uncanny knack of being able to read what you are thinking, so if you don't believe in your athlete either change your beliefs or resign as their coach, especially if there is a professional relationship between you.

---

[36] David Hemery, Sporting Excellence - What Makes a Champion? CollinsWillow, 1991. p.66.

4. The Wheel Of Life

If a sportsperson is not performing to their potential on a frequent or prolonged basis, and there is no obvious reason for this, the chances are that he or she will have some issues in other areas of their life. In general coaching, there is a concept called 'The Wheel of Life'. Essentially, this is a diagrammatic way of representing the areas of someone's life and the level of satisfaction that person has in each of those areas.

The Wheel of Life

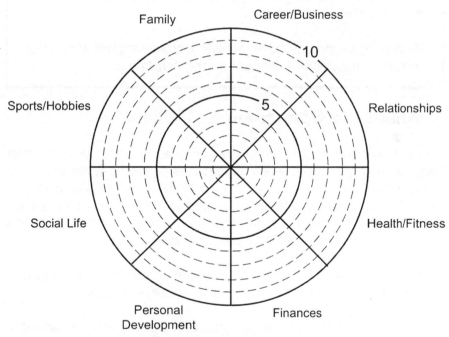

Diagram 17.2

As you can see from Diagram 17.2, imagine that someone's life is split into between six and nine segments (here we have taken eight) representing the key areas of life. These areas may change from person to person, but the principle is the same.

By asking the player to rank each segment on a scale of zero to ten, where ten is massively satisfied with that area of your life and zero is 'the pits', you as the mental skills coach can get a sense of how the player's life is going and whether there could be some factors outside sport that are interfering with performance. Even by just being aware of these other areas, were a player to be under-performing you could ask how aspects in the rest of his or her life are, specifically asking about family, friends, relationships, money etc. Please make sure that it is appropriate to have this type of conversation with the player beforehand.

Exercise 17.4

Do your own 'wheel of life'. What do you need to change to improve each segment, particularly the ones with scores below six or seven?

Where appropriate, have similar conversations with your athletes, especially if they are underperforming.

---

5. Where The Sportsman Is A 'Client'

If you work with sportspeople as clients, in other words either they come to you for a series of sessions or they pay for your time in discrete blocks (normally an hour or two), as opposed to you being their regular sports coach/manager who does some mental skills coaching, here are some thoughts about how to set up the relationship so that it has the best chance of success.

i.   On the first point of contact, interview them to make sure that they are ready to make changes to improve results.

     Also, make sure that you feel you can work with them, and that they can work with you. A client/coach relationship requires mutual trust and respect for it to work effectively.

     Where professional players are 'sent' to you, they may be reluctant to deal with a 'mental skills coach'. You may need to spend some time up front to find out what motivates them and for them to feel that they can trust you.

Tip 17.3

As one of my mentors taught me, the secret to being a successful coach is to choose your client wisely. It is better to be discerning and refer a potential client to someone else than to take on a client who you regret working with, especially when you had a gut feel at the start that it was not appropriate for you to work together.

Work with clients who are motivated to succeed and want to work with you. This makes it easy for you to coach the client to get the results that the client wants.

ii. Set up the coaching agreement at the start, including the 'rules', payment terms, penalties for cancellation, approach to doing tasks that you set, and that everything is confidential. Ask the client to sign a written agreement. The intention is not to create a legal contract, more to be a statement of how you will work together. It should also make reference to the fact the client is fit and healthy both physically and psychologically to undergo coaching. Appendix 11 provides a sample agreement purely as a guideline for you.

Make sure you stick to the agreement and that the client does too, particularly at the start of the relationship. If you let them off the hook, you could be setting up a situation where they don't stick to the agreement and lose some of the benefits of coaching. It is essential that you enforce your boundaries. If you allow clients to get away with lying to you or not keeping their word, they will probably do it with others and themselves, for example not doing all the physical and mental training they say they will do.

iii. Before the first session, ask them to do some pre-work. I normally ask them to answer four questions:

a) What do you want to achieve?
b) How will you know when you have achieved it?
c) What will achieving it do for you?
d) What stops you from achieving it?

This gets them to start to really think about what they want, and to have a goal beyond the goal (remember, a key reason for non-achievement is the lack of a goal beyond the goal). It also gives you an idea of what has stopped them so far, and the types of coaching approaches and techniques you may need to use.

Finally, you can get a good idea of the level of motivation a client has by the quality of their answers and the effort (or lack of it) they have put in.

Exercise 17.5

Answer the following four questions:

1. What do you want to achieve?
2. How will you know when you have achieved it?
3. What will achieving it do for you?
4. What stops you from achieving it?

Assuming you use the services of a mental skills coach, these questions will be useful as a starting point.

---

iv. At the start of the first session, take them through some of the key NLP presuppositions, and also the principles of 'cause and effect' and 'responsibility for results' (i.e. THEY, not you, are responsible for achieving the results) that we covered in Part I. Make sure they understand the concept of being 'at cause' and that you will be pointing out when they make excuses (they probably won't realise when they are doing it!).

Tip 17.4

Tell them you are totally on their side, and that it doesn't mean that you will always be 'nice' to them. You may need to be extremely challenging and ask them questions they may not want to answer. Check that this is OK with them.

If and when the time comes for you to ask them such a question, and were they to get upset, you can remind them that they agreed to this and that you are being totally on their side by asking that question.

Exercise 17.6

Review Chapter 3. Explain the following concepts to someone who will give you useful feedback:

- 'Cause and Effect'
- 'Results and Reasons'
- Each of the NLP presuppositions covered in this book

Practice until you can comfortably explain them to clients/ athletes/players.

v.   Begin the mental skills coaching by reviewing the answer to the four questions mentioned in paragraph iii) above. Ensure that the goal(s) is 'well-formed' (it probably won't be, so you may need to do a little work there). Also, it may be useful to ask which of the blocks to success represent the biggest issue(s) for the client, and then deal with those first. Sometimes you may find, especially as you get more experienced, that it is obvious to you which is the key block which, when progress is made with that, other issues will become less pressing.

It may be appropriate to design small wins first, i.e. initially pick an issue which his relatively small and which will be relatively simple and quick to make progress with, so that the athlete gains confidence in the coaching process and you as a coach. Then you can move on to bigger issues.

What Happens if the Client Breaks their Agreement?

Breaking agreements includes not turning up, not giving you enough notice of postponement and not doing the tasks they agree to do. I would take the following approach:

♦   Ask them if they realised they had made an agreement. There could have been a genuine misunderstanding.

♦   Assuming they say 'Yes', ask them if they realised they broke their agreement. Again, there could have been a genuine misunderstanding.

- ◆ If they either didn't realise they had made an agreement, or that they had broken it, then you may need to spell it out to them and satisfy yourself that they know they have made an agreement for the next time.

- ◆ If they did realise they broke their agreement, then I would adopt the 'three strikes and you're out' policy, in other words resign them as a client if they do it three times. As another former mentor advises:

  - the first time it happens, it's a mistake, it can happen to anyone
  - the second time it happens, shame on them
  - the third time it happens, shame on you!

Clearly, one has to use common sense. If there are, for example, genuine medical emergencies, the above will not apply. As I mentioned earlier, if you let clients off the hook too easily, they will lose the benefits of coaching. To succeed in sport, discipline is required. They are coming to you because they are not getting the results they want in their sport. For them to continue doing things their way will almost certainly not work!

6. Feedback

Please review Appendix 7 on how to give feedback. It is an essential skill in developing athletes and clients.

7. Emotions

Sport is an emotional business. Often, people invest their heart and soul into achieving a sporting goal, whether it is to win the British Open or to reduce their handicap to 12. Sometimes they will experience strong emotions, and express them in ways ranging from sobbing to smashing their putter. As a mental skills coach, it is essential that you are able to deal with players expressing their emotions.

Obviously you are the one who knows the situation with your particular athlete. Here are some tips that I have found useful:

i.   Accept that someone getting upset is natural and will pass. Allow them to express the emotions. (Clearly, it must be done in a way that is not dangerous or harmful to themselves or others.)

ii.   Gently explore the reasons for their upset. Remember, mental skills coaching may be therapeutic, but it is not therapy. If it is outside the 'contract' you have with the athlete or beyond the scope of your experience or competence, explore with the athlete whether it is appropriate for them to see someone more qualified in dealing with their emotions, and if so, how to find an appropriate person.

Tip 17.5

Find a handful of counsellors and therapists and NLP Practitioners/ Master Practitioners to whom you could refer clients and athletes in the unlikely event that you need to do so.

8. Stages of Group and Team Development

As mental skills coaches and sports coaches, there may be times when you are involved in groups and teams. There is an excellent and widely referred to model of group dynamics which was developed by Dr Bruce Tuckman in 1965. It is known as Tuckman's 'Forming Storming Norming Performing team-development model'.[37] (The following is taken from the source indicated in the footnote). Whilst some of the following may not be applicable in a sporting context, it is worth sports coaches and managers being aware of the stages below.

As the name implies, there are four key stages to this model.

1. forming
2. storming
3. norming
4. performing

---

[37] http://en.wikipedia.org/wiki/Forming-storming-norming-performing

Tuckman later added a fifth phase, *adjourning*, that involves completing the task and breaking up the team. Others call it the phase for *mourning*. We will consider only the four stages listed above.

Stage 1 - Forming

In the first phase, the 'forming' of the team takes place. The team meets and learns about the opportunity, challenges, agrees on goals and begins to tackle the tasks. Team members tend to behave quite independently. They may be motivated but are usually relatively uninformed of the issues and objectives of the team. Team members are usually on their best behaviour but very focused on self. Mature team members begin to model appropriate behaviour even at this early phase. Sharing the knowledge of the concept of "Teams - Forming, Storming, Norming, Performing" is extremely helpful to the team.

Supervisors of the team during this phase tend to need to be directive.

Stage 2 - Storming

Every group will then enter the 'storming' stage in which different ideas compete for consideration. The team addresses issues such as what problems they are really supposed to solve, how they will function independently and together and what leadership model they will accept. Team members open out to each other and confront each other's ideas and perspectives.

In some cases 'storming' can be resolved quickly. In others, the team never leaves this stage. The maturity of some team members usually determines whether the team will ever move out of this stage. Immature team members will begin 'acting out' to demonstrate how much they know and convince others that their ideas are correct. Some team members will focus on minutiae to evade real issues.

The 'storming' stage is necessary to the growth of the team. It can be contentious, unpleasant and even painful to members of the team who are averse to conflict. Tolerance of each team member and their differences needs to be emphasised. Without tolerance and patience the team will fail. This phase can become destructive to the team and will lower motivation if allowed to get out of control.

Supervisors of the team during this phase may be more accessible but tend to still need to be directive in their guidance of decision-making and professional behaviour.

Stage 3 - Norming

At some point, the team may enter the 'norming' stage. Team members adjust their behaviour to each other as they develop work habits that make teamwork seem more natural and fluid. Team members often work through this stage by agreeing on rules, values, professional behaviour, shared methods, working tools and even taboos. During this phase, team members begin to trust each other. Motivation increases as the team gets more acquainted with the project.

Teams in this phase may lose their creativity if the 'norming' behaviours become too strong and begin to stifle healthy dissent and the team begins to exhibit 'groupthink'.

Supervisors of the team during this phase tend to be participative more than in the earlier stages. The team members can be expected to take more responsibility for making decisions and for their professional behaviour.

Stage 4 - Performing

Some teams will reach the 'performing' stage. These high-performing teams are able to function as a unit as they find ways to get the job done smoothly and effectively without inappropriate conflict or the need for external supervision. Team members have become interdependent. By this time they are motivated and knowledgeable. The team members are now competent, autonomous and able to handle the decision-making process without supervision. Dissent is expected and allowed as long as it is channelled through means acceptable to the team.

Supervisors of the team during this phase are almost always participative. The team will make most of the necessary decisions.

Even the most high-performing teams will revert to earlier stages in certain circumstances. Many long-standing teams will go through these cycles many times as they react to changing circumstances. For example, a change in leadership may cause the team to revert to 'storming' as the new people challenge the existing norms and dynamics of the team.

9. Personal 'Transitions'

Throughout an athlete's career there will be various changes in their situation and status. Being able to facilitate the athlete's transitions is an extremely useful skill for a coach to have. Using an example of a professional player or athlete, here are some of the stages that he or she could go through:

- being signed as a junior by a professional club for the first time
- being picked for a junior representative team (for example, county or country) for the first time
- signing a professional contract having been an amateur
- moving from being a full-time employee/part-time player to being a full-time player
- breaking into the first team having been in the reserves or youth team
- being left out of the team for a prolonged period having been an established first choice
- being picked to play for one's country having been 'just' a club or county player
- being transferred to a significantly bigger or smaller club
- winning one's first major tournament, medal or trophy, becoming a 'favourite' to win future tournaments rather than an 'outsider' (in betting parlance)
- playing in a different country
- being seen as an experienced player and a role model for youngsters, rather than a younger or regular member of the team
- approaching the end of one's career
- finishing one's career

Some players and athletes will be able to take all of this in their stride. Others may find some transitions extremely difficult to make. For example, in most sports there have been many youngsters who showed immense promise but failed to develop or maintain their progress. Some successful sportspeople manage to find successful second careers once their playing days are over, whereas others go on a downward spiral.

There are two aspects covered in this book that could be particularly useful to all coaches (not to mention the athletes themselves) to help them manage this transition. These are 'logical levels', covered at the start of this chapter, and 'perceptual positions', covered in Chapter 12/Appendix 13.

i. Logical Levels

Stephen Gilligan, an extremely well respected NLP trainer, refers to many of the important events in our life as 'identity events'. For example, for many people becoming a parent is an 'identity event', in other words who they perceive themselves to be has changed in some significant way *('I am a father/mother/parent')*.

In a sporting context, becoming an 'international', winning a major tournament, trophy or medal, ending one's career are examples of events that are potentially identity events. Statements or thoughts such as *'I am an Olympic champion', 'I am an established International',* and *'I am a professional athlete'* (with the emphasis on 'I') are all 'identity' statements using the 'logical levels' model. In other words the athlete's sense of 'identity' is strongly tied to the statement.

When someone holds a concept at 'identity' level, as opposed to at 'capability' or 'behaviour' level, there is the potential for upset if and when the situation changes. ('Capability' or 'behaviour' level statements would be, for example, *'my current profession is a golfer', 'I play rugby for a living', 'I have won some trophies'.*)

By being aware of this, mental skills coaches and sports coaches can explore with the players what the change or transition or new status means to them as a person. Ideally, this is best done in advance of the transition, or as soon as is practical afterwards. Where it appears that the player could respond negatively to a transition, the mental skills coach and/or sports coach can at least begin to point the player in the right direction, for example:

- ◆ raising the player's awareness of the impact on them of the transition
- ◆ discussing possible implications and ways forward
- ◆ involving other specialist professionals who are experienced in dealing with players in similar situations

The above does not represent an exhaustive list.

ii. Perceptual Positions

Mental skills coaches and sports coaches could also use the concept of perceptual positions. Position 1 could represent where they are now, position 2 could represent where they would like to be in five or ten years time, and position 3 could be an observer noticing how the player could make the transition from position 1 to position 2.

Another perceptual positions exercise could be done using the player's family (partner and/or children) in position 2, helping the player to gain insight into what his family could be thinking.

Summary

- ◆ Practice listening for which 'logical level' a player is at. Remember that a problem needs to be solved at least at the level where the 'problem' is held, normally at a higher level.
- ◆ Remember, we all love stories – they are a powerful way to get a message across. Practice using metaphors and analogies.
- ◆ Walk your talk as a coach. The more congruent and aligned you are within yourself, the more likely the players and athletes will be so. The opposite applies.
- ◆ If someone is persistently under-performing, there could be issues in other areas of the 'Wheel of Life'.
- ◆ Select your 'clients' wisely. Set yourself up for success by having firm agreements and sticking to them.

Chapter 18
Final Comments

Firstly, thank you for getting to this stage of the book. It is somewhat different to many others on the subject of successful sport, in that there are exercises for you to do to embed the knowledge and learnings.

Whether you are a:

◆ recreational competitor
◆ seasoned professional
◆ somewhere in between
◆ a coach or mental skills coach

I sincerely hope that you have benefited from the knowledge within this book and exercises contained within it.

I know from my own personal journey in arriving at a point where I have the knowledge and experience to be able to write this book, there is always more to learn. I continue to learn from my clients and students, as well as from formal learning such as reading and attending courses myself.

I sincerely hope that you use this material to enhance your own learning, re-visiting the material as and when necessary, and practicing what you have learned.

As you have probably realised, one of my passions is helping other people to perform better and to help others to do the same. I would be honoured if you would share your success stories and learning experiences with me – my website address is *www.thelazarus.com*, and personal contact details will be shown there. By doing so, I will be able to pass this knowledge to others, in order to continue to 'raise the bar' of mental skills coaching and its application by athletes, just as athletes courageously seek to raise their own physical performance levels.

Thank you.

Appendices

Appendix 1
Building Rapport

Introduction

Rapport is a term used in NLP to describe a feeling of mutual trust and respect between two or more people, such that the people involved will be willing to co-operate with each other.

Why Is Rapport So Important?

Many of us are able to unknowingly build rapport with friends and partners. Being able to build and maintain rapport is essential to any good sporting relationship. Rapport is not the same as agreeing with someone. In fact, it is completely appropriate and possible to maintain rapport even when disagreeing. By doing so, it maintains the mutual trust even if there is disagreement. Also, sometimes as a sports coach and a mental skills coach we need to challenge our players and clients. By having this underlying trust and rapport, they will be far more likely to go that extra mile and accept our challenging requests, demands and questions than if there is a lack of rapport.

The founders of NLP noticed that hypnotherapists were able to quickly build so much rapport with clients that the clients would relatively easily go into a trance having only recently met the hypnotherapist. How did the hypnotherapist create that level of rapport?

The rest of this appendix deals with how to build and maintain rapport.

Some Background Information

There are two key principles of building rapport. The first is that people tend to like people who are like them. Secondly, the majority of communication is non-verbal. There have been studies which show that:

- ◆   55 percent of communication is based on body language
- ◆   38 percent is based on voice tonality
- ◆   only 7 percent is based on the words we say

This means that up to 93 percent of communication is non-verbal and out of our conscious awareness. Whether these figures are 'correct' is not the issue. We have all experienced a gesture or look (body language) from parents, teachers and partners which means everything is fine, and another which means we are in trouble! Or they say our name (just one word) in a certain tone, and we know everything is OK, and in another tone and we know we better hide!

Equally, we have all been in situations where someone says something and we just have a 'gut feeling' they are not being totally honest. If the words say one thing and the voice and/or body language say something different, we will believe the non-verbal signals.

How Can We Build and Maintain Rapport?

So, the question is, "how can we use non-verbal communication to demonstrate that we are like someone and hence build rapport?"

The answer is by 'matching' aspects of their body language and/or voice tonality. For example, if someone had their hand on their hip, you would be 'matching' their posture if you had your hand on your hip.

What aspects of body language and voice tonality can we match? There are several aspects, and we will cover some of the more obvious and easy to use. If you are interested in finding out more, please see the section on 'Further Reference Material' at the end of this book.

Please note when reading the following that matching is best done subtly and out of the other person's conscious awareness.

i. Body Language

We can match the following:

- ◆ **gestures,** such as nodding, arm or hand movements
- ◆ **posture,** such as leg crossing, arms folded, leaning forward or back or to one side

It is OK to match certain aspects of someone's **posture** when they are talking – remember, please do it subtly. However, please only match someone's **gestures** when it is **YOUR** turn to talk! Matching someone's arm-waving while **they** are talking will really annoy them and break rapport!

ii. Voice Tonality

We can match the following:

- ◆ Speed of speech – fast or slow
- ◆ Volume of speech – loud or soft
- ◆ Pitch – high or low in the normal range for men and women. So for example, if a woman is speaking to a man who has a relatively low pitch voice, she could adjust her voice pitch so that it is in the relatively low-pitch range for female voices.

Pacing and Leading

In NLP, we call matching someone's body language or voice tonality for a period of time 'pacing'. This period of time can range from a few seconds to several minutes, possibly even longer depending on circumstances. One very useful way for us to know whether we have built rapport is to slowly/gently/subtly change aspects of our body language and or voice tonality and notice whether the other person follows. This is called 'leading'. If the person you are communicating with follows your lead unconsciously you probably have a good level of rapport. If the person does not follow your lead go back to matching again, observing more attentively (pacing) before leading again.

Tips:

Here are some tips about rapport:

◆ Pick one or two aspects to match. Attempting to match everything will probably overwhelm you, and even if you do it, the other person will probably spot it.

◆ Be subtle. If someone crosses their arms, don't cross your arms immediately. Wait a few moments.

◆ A little goes a long way. You don't have to completely match the full extent of someone's gestures, posture or voice tonality. For example, if someone makes big circular hand movements with both hands when they speak, when it's your turn to speak you can use smaller circular hand movements with one or both hands.

◆ If things are going well and you both feel comfortable, assume that you are in rapport. If you don't feel comfortable, the chances are that the other person doesn't, and hence you may need to use some of the above to build rapport.

◆ Be patient. 'Pace' the other person by, for example, speaking at their pace or volume, and then when you feel in rapport adjust the pace to one that is more comfortable. If the person follows, that is an excellent indicator that you are in rapport. In NLP, the rule of thumb is 'PACE, PACE, PACE' then 'LEAD'

◆ As an exercise, observe friends and partners in conversation in restaurants, cafes or bars. Notice how they automatically seem to match each other. Friends will reach for a glass of wine at similar times or lean forwards or back at the same time. This is the equivalent of the above point – when you are in rapport with someone, you can 'lead' them, and they can 'lead' you.

◆ Even when disagreeing with someone, or delivering a difficult message (for example giving some feedback on poor performance), if it is appropriate to stay in rapport (which it probably will be), stay in rapport! Even though the message may be unpleasant for the other person to receive, there will be an underlying sense of trust if you stay in rapport.

◆ If someone is angry and you do not want it to flare up, match their energy levels (for example loud voice, fast speech) with 'non-confrontational' language.

◆ Use your common sense!

Appendix 2

List of Submodalities

Here is a list of submodalites. This is not an exhaustive list, although these are the main submodalites that will be useful for you. Occasionally athletes may get very specific about certain of the submodalities, for example the size of the picture of a person they feel comfortable with may be a 2 feet square picture, whereas for a person they feel uncomfortable with it may be 3 feet square.

Visual

- Black & White or Colour
- Near or Far
- Bright or Dim
- Location in the person's visual field e.g. top right, bottom left
- Size of Picture (big, small, medium)
- Associated (looking through your own eyes) or Dissociated (seeing yourself in the picture)
- Focused or Defocused
- Is the Focus changing or steady
- Framed or Panoramic
- Moving or Still
- If Moving - Fast/Normal/Slow
- Amount of Contrast
- 3D or Flat
- Angle Viewed From e.g. straight ahead, looking down, looking up

Auditory

- Location e.g. left ear, right ear, behind you
- Direction e.g. moving towards you, moving in circles
- Internal or External
- Volume, i.e. Loud, medium, soft
- Speed, i.e. Fast or medium or slow
- Pitch - High or low
- Timbre i.e. clear or raspy
- Pauses or Continuous
- Any Rhythm?
- Duration – how long does the sound last?
- Any Uniqueness of Sound

Kinaesthetic

- Location – where is the feeling?
- Size of feeling – big, medium, small
- Shape
- What Colour (some people report that feelings have a colour, even though 'Colour' could be deemed a visual, not kinesthetic, submodality).
- Intensity of feeling e.g. very intense, not intense
- Steadiness of intensity
- Still/Moving
- If Moving, what Speed i.e. Fast, medium, slow
- If Moving, which direction e.g. clockwise
- Duration e.g short or long
- Humidity i.e. dry or wet
- Any Vibration?
- Temperature i.e. Hot, warm or cold
- Any Pressure? If so, is it high or low?
- Texture e.g. rough or smooth
- Weight i.e. Heavy or Light
- Is the feeling Internal or External?

Appendix 3

Elicitation of Submodalities

Steps:

1. Have a copy of the submodality checklist to hand (See Appendix 2).

2. Identify the situation to be addressed, and how the player would like to feel instead. It's helpful to put numbers on these, so for example the player may feel 8 out of 10 on the 'anxiety scale', and would like to feel 3 out of 10. Doing this helps the player have a goal to aim at, and lets you both know when they are there.

3. Check that it is OK for the player to feel the desired way. Make sure there are no negative consequences of making the change. For example, check that the player would not be overly–minimising a situation which does need some attention, or that she would not lose the 'edge'.

4. Ask the player to think of the situation and ask, "when you think of <that situation>, do you have a picture?"

5. Once they say 'Yes', elicit the visual submodalities. Phrase the questions openly, without favouring one option or another, for example

   ◆ "is it bright or dim?" is preferable to "is it bright?"
   ◆ "where is it located in your visual field – top left, bottom right, where is it located?" is preferable to "is it in then top of your field of vision?"

   As you elicit, make a shorthand notation on the checklist, e.g. 'B' for 'big'. You'll need to elicit the submodalities quickly, for reasons that will become apparent shortly.

6. When you have finished eliciting the visual submodalities, elicit the auditory submodalities – ask, "and when you think of this situation and have that picture, are there any sounds?" If there are, repeat step 5 for the auditory submodalities. If there are none, move on to step 7.

7. Elicit the kinaesthetic submodalities as you did at steps 5 and 6.

Here are some tips to make the elicitation go smoothly.

- Elicit as opposed to install! For example ask, 'is it near or far?' in a neutral voice, with no emphasis on either the 'near' or 'far'. Avoid giving just one option such as 'is it near?' Also, ask, 'When you think of (say) chocolate, *do you have a picture?*' as opposed to '*make a picture*'. You want to find out how they actually represent (say) chocolate internally.

- Elicit the submodalities quickly. Because the unconscious mind processes quickly, it is important that you elicit quickly to get a true reflection of the submodalities. Go as fast as you can, and then some. As a guide, the elicitation of the visual, auditory and kinaesthetic submodalities should take less than five minutes. The elicitation of the visual submodalities should take less than one minute.

- Sit at an angle of roughly 90 to 120 degrees to the athlete. Make sure you can see them, and avoid sitting opposite them – allow them to visualise without you being in their face!

- Familiarise yourself with the submodalities checklist, and avoid having your head buried in the paper, so that you can make sure that you can have your attention on the athlete. Look up at him/her so that they feel you are 'with them'. It will help maintain rapport.

- If by some chance the player cannot get a picture of the 'situation', start with a different representational system, probably their most preferred (for example kinaesthetic), and elicit the kinaesthetic submodalities, then move on to (say) auditory and then to visual.

Appendix 4

Submodalities
'Mapping Across'

'Mapping Across' is when we elicit two sets of submodalities, one for the 'problem' situation and the other for the 'desired' situation, and then ask the player to change the submodalities of the 'problem' situation to be the same as those of the 'desired' situation. Bearing in mind that submodalities give meaning to our experiences, by changing the submodalities to those of the desired situation, the player will now relate to the situation in the desired way.

It is essential to pick an appropriate desired situation. Here are some guidelines by way of examples:

◆ if a fitness trainer's client has a strong liking for a food (say chocolate) and wishes they only liked it a little or even not at all, then find a food that they holds the same level of appeal as they wished chocolate would hold. So if they like chocolate 9 out of 10, and wish they liked it only 1 out of 10, find a food they like only 1 out of 10. Remember, the two sets of experiences must be of the same logical type – food and food, drink and drink, people and people. Ideally, the food would be as similar as possible to chocolate. So 'Marmite' would be better than red peppers, but if red peppers are the only food that the person likes 1 out of 10, then use red peppers.

◆ If a badminton player is apprehensive about partnering an excellent player, ask the player how they would like to feel instead (let's say 'comfortable and excited') and ask then to think of a good or excellent player who they feel comfortable and excited about playing with.

I will assume that the reader will be guiding someone else through the process, although as previously mentioned it is possible to do this process on yourself. Let's take chocolate and Marmite for the fitness trainer's client as an example. The submodalities table later in this appendix highlights this.

Steps:

1. Check that it is totally OK with the client to make the changes, and that it is ecological. Explain the process briefly, including that you will be going quickly as this is the best way to make the process work.

2. Elicit the submodalities of chocolate as discussed in Appendix 3. (Column 1 in the table later in this appendix). *"When you think of chocolate, do you have a picture?"* Notice their face and general physiology.

3. Once you have elicited the submodalities of chocolate, it is important that the client goes into a neutral state before they consider the next picture of Marmite. To help the client to get into a neutral state, ask the client an unrelated question about, say, holidays or films or their last cup of coffee. Then, elicit the submodalities of Marmite as discussed in Appendix 3 (Column 2 in the table). *"When you think of Marmite, do you have a picture?"* Notice their facial expressions and general physiology.

4. Take a few moments yourself to compare the two sets of submodalities and mark the differences in Column 3. (In NLP this is called 'contrastive analysis'.)

    Using the example shown in the following table, the picture of chocolate is in black & white and near, and the picture of Marmite is also black & white but is far. Hence there is an asterisk in the same row as 'near/far' in column 3. The same principle applies to all the submodalities.

5. Ask the client to bring back the picture of chocolate. Direct the client to change the submodalities of chocolate to be the same as that of Marmite. Do it one by one, and ask the client to let you know when they have made each change by, say, nodding. Explain that you will be going quickly as this is the best way to make the process work. Using the example below say something like "as you think of chocolate, make the picture far away (pause

slightly until they nod), make it dim, (pause slightly until they nod), move it to the left side middle height (pause slightly until they nod)", etc.

You will probably find that a point will come during the process when the client will show the same physiology as they did when thinking of Marmite (secretly congratulate yourself at this point!). This is because there are normally one or two key submodalities (called 'drivers') which when they change all they other submodalities change. Let's assume in this example that 'location' is a 'driver' (as it often is). You would continue with the process, probably saying something like, "Make sure the picture is medium size, make sure the focus is steady, make sure the picture is panoramic", continuing quickly with the other submodalities.

6. Test by asking what the person thinks of chocolate. Not only should they say that they don't want it, they should show similar physiology and voice tonality as they did for Marmite. If you have any chocolate available, offer it to the client and notice their reaction. Test thoroughly, and ask for the 0-10 score for chocolate.

7. Future pace by asking them to consider a situation in the future where in the past they would have eaten or wanted chocolate. How do they respond now? Do this at least three times for situations in the short, medium and longer term. Continue until you and the client are convinced they don't like chocolate!

SUBMODALITIES EXAMPLE

	Chocolate	Marmite	
Visual	**1**	**2**	**3**
Black & White or Colour	B	B	
Near or Far	N	F	*
Bright or Dim	B	D	*
Location	Front - upper	Left side - mid	*
Picture Size-big/med/small	B	M	*
Associated / Dissociated	A	A	
Focused or Defocused	F	F	
Focus (changing/steady)	C	S	*
Framed or Panoramic	F	P	*
Movie or Still	M	M	
Movie-Fast/Normal/Slow	N	N	
Amount of Contrast	Lots	A little	*
3D or Flat	3D	3D	
Angle Viewed From	Straight on	Straight on	
# of Pictures (Shift?)	1	1	
Auditory			
Location	Left side	Right side	*
Direction	Towards ear	Circular	*
Internal or External	E	E	
Loud or Soft	L	S	*
Fast or Slow	F	F	
Pitch (high/low)	H	H	
Timbre – clear/raspy	C	R	*
Pauses	No	N	
Cadence/Rhythm	No	N	
Duration	Long time	Long time	
Uniqueness of Sound	No	N	
Kinesthetic			
Location	Chest	Throat	*
Size	B	B	
Shape	Round	Square	*
Colour	Blue	Green	*
Intensity (high/low)	H	H	
Steady	Yes	No	*
Still/Moving	S	M	*
Fast/Slow	-	F	*
Duration (short/long)	S	S	
Humidity (dry/wet)	D	D	
Vibration	Yes	Y	
Hot/cold	H	Warm	*
Pressure? (high/low)	Y – High	N	*
Texture (rough/smooth)	R	R	
Heavy/Light	H	H	
Internal/External	I	I	

Are there any sounds that are important?

Are there any feelings that are important?

Appendix 5

Examples of Limiting Beliefs

This is a list of possible limiting beliefs, not an exhaustive list.

Examples of Unrealistic Beliefs

◆ We must be thoroughly competent and achieve important goals in sport if we are to consider ourselves worthwhile.

◆ Our unhappiness is externally caused and we have little ability to control our emotions.

◆ We should not have problems. If we do then it is a sign of incompetence, weakness or lack of ability.

◆ We must depend on others and rely on someone stronger than us.

◆ It is always easier to avoid rather than face certain difficult situations in life.

◆ Disagreement and conflict are a disaster, and must be avoided at all costs.

◆ We are the way we are and perform the way we do because of our past experiences, and we cannot change.

◆ Crises are invariably destructive and no good can come out of them.

◆ People are basically bad and out to get me.

◆ There is something wrong with money. People who have it are greedy.

◆ I have the truth and no one else has.

◆ My group has the truth and no other group has.

Examples of Unrealistic Beliefs about Self

To be acceptable:

◆ I must be liked by everyone – people should love me.

- I must not show my fearful/angry/sad feelings.
- I must do everything perfectly, and never make mistakes.
- I must make a good impression on others.
- I must win the race/game/competition at all costs.
- I should do what I am told.
- I must not think bad thoughts.
- I should say what other people want to hear.
- I must put up a good front.
- I must keep up with my colleagues, neighbours and friends.
- I will grow frailer, sicker and lose my powers as I grow old.
- I am not creative.
- I have no imagination.

Appendix 6

Collapsing Anchors

'Collapsing anchors' is a technique which gives people new choices of behaviour rather than feeling negative about a particular situation.

With 'resource anchors' as explained in Chapter 7, the player anchored him- or herself. With textbook 'collapse anchors', the mental skills coach applies the anchors, normally kinaesthetically by touching the player's knuckles. It is important that the mental skills coach feels comfortable that he or she can detect when the player is in the state (see *'How Do We Do Anchoring?'* in Chapter 7) and therefore knows when to apply and release the anchors. For that reason, it may be beneficial to practice with other mental skills coaches before working with players. If the mental skills coach is on doubt, there are other ways to do the 'collapse anchors' technique mentioned in Chapter 7.

If ever the mental skills coach needs to touch a player, it is essential to explain why and to ask permission.

There are 10 Steps:

1. Get into rapport, explain the process and what the player can expect, and seek agreement to proceed.

2. Decide on which negative state is to be collapsed, and on which positive states or resources are needed. Check that the player does not have any existing anchors on his/her knuckles.

3. Anchor the positive states several times i.e. set a 'resource anchor' (see Chapter 7) on one knuckle. (Remember, get into the specific positive state you're eliciting.) Make sure that the person is in a fully associated, intense, congruent state. You as the mental skills coach will need to apply the 'anchor' as you

see the player go into the state, and release it as you see him or her come out of state.

4. Break state and test to make sure the anchor is strong.

5. Anchor the negative state, only once, on an adjacent knuckle.

6. Break state and test to make sure the anchor works.

7. Fire both anchors (i.e. touch both knuckles) at the same time. You will probably see signs of both states and after a few seconds the player will show signs of that the 'integration' is complete – there will be little facial movement, and if there is it will be of the resourceful state.

8. Release the negative anchor.

9. Hold the positive anchor for 5 seconds and then release.

10. Test & future pace.

Test by asking the player how he or she feels about the situations which were causing a problem previously. Where possible, ask about specific situations that the player mentioned to you.

Future Pace by asking the player to consider a situation in the future which, if it had happened in the past, the player would have behaved or felt negatively, and for the player to notice how they respond. Repeat this for at least three future events stretching out several months or even years into the future, until you and the player are convinced that the old 'problem' is gone and that they have new, appropriate choices of behaviour in these circumstances.

Appendix 7

Giving Feedback

The so-called 'feedback sandwich' is a model for giving someone (including yourself) feedback in a way that empowers rather than dis-empowers. When the competition has gone well, feedback is easy to give and receive. However, when results or the performance are disappointing, feedback is harder to give and receive.

Here is a model for giving feedback:

Step 1 – say what worked or what went well.
Step 2 – give two or three things that the player should do to make it **even better** next time.
Step 3 - give an overall positive comment.

By giving some positive comments at the start (step 1), it makes the athlete (and particularly the athlete's unconscious mind, which after all runs the body) willing to listen.

Then, when they are listening, you can let them know what to do to make it even better (step 2), which implies it is already good! If the performance is poor, here are four tips to deliver useful feedback.

◆ Make sure that the player is in a state of mind to take on board the feedback. There are some schools of thought which suggest that feedback is best given within five minutes of the event or as soon as possible, so that the event is fresh in the player's mind. This is probably ideal where the feedback can be given and received without emotion. Where the coach and/or player are likely to be upset or have some negative emotions, it is probably better to wait until feelings have calmed down so that the match or event can be considered rationally.

- Remember to give feedback at the **behavioural** or **capability** level (see 'logical levels' in Chapter 17) rather than at **identity** level. It is better to say, 'I want you to take into account the state of the match when deciding to go all out attack rather than do it at random' than to say, 'you're an idiot!' The first lets the player have some idea about what to do next time and makes it non-personal. The latter is just a personal insult.

- Give no more than three areas of improvement at a time. More than that risks the player 'tuning out'. If there are numerous areas for improvement, pick a couple that would make the biggest difference.

- If you have any doubt about whether the player has taken your feedback on board, ask him to tell you what he will do differently next time.

By finishing on a positive note in step 3, it leaves the player with some degree of positivity and more likely to be motivated to improve.

I am aware that the above could be seen as avoiding giving harsh feedback to players. Sometimes giving harsh feedback is necessary and useful, for example if players do not give maximum effort, or if they do not adhere to the agreed system of play or tactics. However, openly criticising, say, a rugby player for dropping a ball, or a footballer for misplacing a pass is pointless. It may give the team's coach or manager a temporary feeling of satisfaction about having vented frustration, but does it help make the player less likely to make an accidental mistake next time? Probably not. On the contrary, it could make him more nervous and likely to do it next time.

If someone is good enough for the team, pick them and encourage them. If they are not, don't pick them! Openly criticising for making mistakes rarely makes someone less likely to do it next time.

Appendix 8 - Fundamental Filters Profile Worksheet and Example

Questions	Category	Patterns - Indicators
When you come to a situation, do you usually act quickly after sizing it up, or do you make a complete study of all the consequences and then act?" Or – just listen to responses to other questions.	**Action** ‗‗‗‗‗ ‗‗‗‗‗	**Proactive** - action, do it, short, crisp sentences **Reactive** - try, think about it, could, wait
What do you want in your (work?)	**Values/Criteria**	
Why is that (criteria/value) important to you? Ask up to 3 times?	**Direction** ‗‗‗‗‗ ‗‗‗‗‗	**Toward** - Attain, get, achieve, target **Away From** - Avoid, not have, notice problems
Why did you choose your (current work)?	**Reason** ‗‗‗‗‗ ‗‗‗‗‗	**Options** - criteria, choice, possibilities, **Procedures** - story, how, necessity, didn't choose
How do you know you've done a good job?	**Frame of Ref** ‗‗‗‗‗ ‗‗‗‗‗	**Internal** - knows within self **External** - told by others, results, facts & figures
"If we were going to do a project together, would you want to know the big picture or the details first? Would you really need to know the (other)?" Or – just listen to responses to other questions.	**Big Picture/Detail** ‗‗‗‗‗ ‗‗‗‗‗	**Global** - overview, random order, big picture **Specific** - details, sequences, precise, exact
"How do you know that someone else (a colleague) is good at what they do?" "How often do you need to see/ hear/ read/ do that to be convinced they're good?"	**Convincer** ‗‗‗‗‗ ‗‗‗‗‗	**See** **No. of Examples** - give number **Hear** **Automatic** - benefit of doubt **Do** **Consistent** - never, every time **Read** **Period of time** - give time period

Example

Assume you guess that 'John' has the following 'fundamental filter' profile in the context of his work:

- Equal 'towards' and 'away from'
- 'Procedures'
- 'Internal'
- 'Mainly Pro-active'
- 'Big picture'

John has also told you that working with great people, fun and challenge are important to him.

Therefore, the first test as a 'mismatch' would be:

- Either 'towards' or 'away from' (either, because our guess is that he is in the middle)
- 'Options'
- 'External'
- 'Reactive'
- 'Detail'

So you could say something like: "John, let me offer you two pieces of work. With the first piece of work:

- it would be important to consider what to do, evaluating and analysing for quite some time before taking any action (REACTIVE)
- there would be very little chance for challenge or fun, and the people will be 'so-so' (Mismatching his VALUES)
- the job would consist almost entirely of problem solving and fire-fighting, avoiding difficulties (AWAY FROM)
- and there would be lots of scope to devise alternative ways to do things, and there would be opportunities to choose how you did things, and you would be encouraged to bend the rules (OPTIONS)
- although you'd need to ask for feedback and approval,

you won't have any idea of the standards that are required, or whether you're doing a good job unless others tell you (EXTERNAL)

- ◆ and there will be lots of details and 'nitty-gritty' to deal with, sometimes you won't even be able to see the wood from the trees (DETAIL)

Do you want the work, John?"

By this time it will be hard for you to keep a straight face!

"So John, with the second piece of work:

- ◆ you'll be expected to just do it, to get stuck in without having too much time for analysis, although there will be some times when a little consideration before action is required (MAINLY PROACTIVE)
- ◆ there will be challenges and you'll be working with some great people who'll make it fun (VALUES)
- ◆ you'll have some clear targets and goals, and deadlines to meet, although in order to achieve it you'll need to solve various problems and be aware of some potential pitfalls (EQUAL TOWARDS AND AWAY FROM)
- ◆ you'll be able to do all this by following the laid down procedures, which has been proven to be the best way to get the job done (PROCEDURES)
- ◆ and you'll be able to set your own standards and know for yourself whether you've been doing well or not. Occasionally you'll check in with others to let you know that you're on track (MAINLY INTERNAL)
- ◆ it will be important to have an overview of what's happening – you won't need to get involved with details (BIG PICTURE)

Which career do you prefer, John?"

Normally you would expect him to say the second one. I'd then ask whether there was anything about the first one which appealed to him, or anything about the second one which didn't appeal, in order to refine my initial guesses if necessary.

As you get more practice, you'll be able to be more fluent in eliciting the fundamental filters and doing the testing.

Of course, in situations where you don't have the willing co-operation of a client and hence where you won't be able to overtly test, you'll have to trust your guesses.

Appendix 9

Representational System Words and Phrases

Here are some words and phrases which indicate which representational system (visual, auditory, kinaesthetic and auditory digital) a sportsperson may be using at any given time. It is not an exhaustive list.

V	A	K	Ad
see	hear	feel	sense
look	listen	touch	experience
view	sound(s)	grasp	understand
appear	make music	get hold of	think
show	harmonise	slip through	learn
dawn	tune in/out	catch on	process
reveal	be all ears	tap into	decide
envision	rings a bell	make contact	motivate
illuminate	silence	throw out	consider
imagine	be heard	turn around	change
clear	resonate	hard	perceive
foggy	deaf	unfeeling	insensitive
focused	melodious	concrete	distinct
hazy	dissonance	scrape	conceive
crystal	question	get a handle	know
picture	unhearing	solid	describe
flash	attune	impression	question
fade	quiet	sensation	perceive
dim view	call on	get to grips with	
in light of	manner of speaking	hang in there	
mental image	unheard of	get in touch with	
mental picture	tuned in	hold it!	
mind's eye	tuned out	hold on!	
naked eye	to tell the truth	lay cards on table	
paint a picture		smooth operator	
short sighted		pain-in the neck	
tunnel vision			
an eyeful			

Appendix 10
Answers to Exercise 16.6

Here are some suggested answers to the statements made in Exercise 16.6. Remember, these questions are to be used when appropriate, not just for the sake of it.

Mind Reads:

I know you think he's a good player.
"How (specifically) do you know I think he's a good player?"

I know you came here for a purpose.
"How (specifically) do you know I came here for a purpose?"

I can see you believe this.
"How (specifically) can you see I believe this?"

I know you're not concerned about this.
"How (specifically) do you know I'm not concerned about this?"

Nouns and Abstract Nouns:

I'm looking for a new track-suit.
"What sort of track-suit are you looking for?"

I saw the report in the newspaper.
"Which report, (specifically)?"
"Which newspaper specifically?"

The relationship has broken down.
"In what way (specifically) are we/they not relating?" (turn the noun 'relationship' into a verb 'to relate')

I don't have enough knowledge.
"What (exactly) don't you know enough about?" (Turn the noun 'knowledge' into a verb 'to know').

Unspecified Verbs:

They rejected us.
"How did they reject you?"
"What (specifically) did they do or not do to reject you?"

They were toying with us.
"How exactly were they toying with us?"
"What were they doing that makes you think they were toying with us?"

It's creating havoc.
"How is it creating havoc?"
"What (specifically) is creating havoc?"

They challenged me.
"How did they challenge you?"
"What are they doing (specifically) to challenge you?"

Anonymous Judgements and Rules:

It's good to play it hard.
"Who says it's good?" "According to who?"

We have to make a decision today.
"What would happen if we don't?"
"Or?"
Depending on the answer, it may be appropriate to challenge the abstract noun 'decision' by asking, *"what do we have to decide?"*

We can't ask them for more.
"What would happen if we did?"
"What stops/prevents us?"

You should really go to that training session.
"What would happen if I didn't go?"

Generalisations:

Everyone does it that way.
"Everyone? Are there no exceptions?"

"What about Fred and Sylvia – they do it differently and get great results."

We always take our time when making decisions.
"Always? Have you ever not taken your time/made a quick decision?"

We've tried everything to make this happen.
"Everything? Name twenty things!"
"Everything? What about XYZ?"

I can't trust anyone with this.
"Surely there is someone who you can trust."
You could possibly challenge the 'can't' by *"what would happen if you did trust someone"* or *"What prevents you?"*

Hidden Comparisons:

We do more.
"More than whom?"
"More than what?"
"More than when?"

That's expensive!
"Compared to what/who/when?"

We're faster.
"Compared to who/what/when?"

We try harder.
"Harder than who/what/when?"

Causation & Equivalences:

They make me feel so annoyed.
"How (specifically/exactly) do they make you feel so annoyed?"
"How does their doing X make you feel so annoyed?"

Her being late means she doesn't care about the team.
"How does her being late mean she doesn't care?"
"Have you ever cared about something or someone and yet been late?"

If they don't do the paperwork today, then they're not serious about the contract.
"How does their not doing the paperwork today mean they're not serious?"
"What happens if they courier it over first thing tomorrow?"

You're disagreeing, so you can't be interested in doing this.
"How (specifically) does my disagreeing mean I'm not interested?"
"Have you ever been really interested about something and wanted to get it right in the long-term, even if it meant a temporary disagreement?"

Appendix 11

Sample Coaching Agreement

The following is a sample coaching agreement. It is not intended to be legally binding, just a document which sets out the roles of both parties. Clearly, it is intended as a guide only. Please feel free to amend this in any way that suits you and your clients.

COACHING AGREEMENT

This agreement is between :

_____ The Client

_____ The Coach

I, The Client, fully understand that:

- The results of the coaching sessions are dependent upon me following the instructions that my Coach gives me during any coaching process aimed at removing any obstacles to my success. The responsibility for making the process work is solely mine, since no one else can do it for me.
- I understand that my Coach is a Practitioner of NLP/ experienced mental skills coach. I agree to allow him to guide me through any processes relevant to me achieving the goals I have set.
- The results of the coaching sessions are dependent upon me completing whatever homework and tasks my Coach gives me.
- The results of the coaching sessions are dependent on me focusing on what I want rather than what I don't want.

- I understand that my Coach is not a mind reader and cannot assist me in resolving issues/blocks to success that I do not share with him, nor achieving goals I do not express to him.
- Coaching in no way replaces a diagnosis or advice from a medical doctor or psychiatrist.
- I acknowledge that I know of no reason, medical, psychological or otherwise, why I should not undertake coaching. I agree that I will inform the Coach if this changes during the coaching relationship.
- I will give my Coach at least 72 hours' notice of cancellation, otherwise I will pay for the session cancelled. I understand that the Coach will give me a free session if he does not give me 72 hours' notice of cancellation. (Genuine medical emergencies excepted for either party)

On this basis I agree to commit to working with my Coach for approximately 1-2 hours per month at an hourly rate of £XXX plus VAT to achieve my outcomes. Payment will be one session in advance. The main outcomes are as follows:

Client's signature: _____ Date: _____

Coach's signature: _____ Date: _____

Appendix 12

Guideline Script for The Peripheral Vision Exercise

Here is a **guideline** to doing the 'peripheral vision' process. Clearly, you as the mental skills coach may wish to modify this slightly to suit your own style.

JL (1): *"You mentioned that you often get anxious during golf tournaments, particularly on the final few holes when you're close to winning, and that you'd like to be able to control your emotions. I'd like to take you through a process which is simple to learn and to do, and which you can use on the golf course whenever you feel a little anxious. It should take us around ten minutes to do. Is that OK with you?"*

Golfer: *"Will it hurt? Just kidding! Yes, let's do it."*

JL (2): *"OK. Let's stand over here."* JL leads the golfer to a point roughly in the middle of the room, perhaps slightly to the back of the room. JL will have noticed that there is some spot on the wall that the player can focus on, or he will fix to the facing wall a piece of paper with a black dot around two inches in diameter, roughly seven feet high.

JL stands next to golfer and observes the golfer during the exercise. *"I'd like you to look at that spot on the wall."*

Pause for around ten seconds - *"and as you keep your eyes on that spot, notice that you can be aware/see either side of that spot. So even though you're looking at that spot, you allow your awareness to expand so that you can see the whole of the front wall, both of the corners of the front wall. Nod or let me know when you can do this. Relax the muscles around your jaw – perhaps open your mouth slightly and let the lower jaw relax."*

Golfer: "Yeah." (or nods)

JL (3):   JL observes the golfer and looks for signs of relaxation such as slower breathing.

"Good. And as you do keep your eyes on that spot, and your jaw relaxed, notice that your awareness spreads along both of the side walls at the same time, so that you're aware of the front wall and both of the side (adjacent) walls. Allow your awareness to spread so that you're aware of everything either side of you, 180 degrees.

So even though you're looking at that spot on the wall, you're aware of everything in front and to the side of you, and maybe you can even allow your awareness to spread a full 360 degrees, so that you're aware of what's behind you too.

You're certainly aware of my hand gently moving in your peripheral vision." (JL gently moves his hand so that the golfer could only see it out of his extreme peripheral vision). *"Are you aware of my hand gently moving?"*

Golfer: *"Yes."*

JL (4):   *"Good. Do you notice just how relaxed you feel?"*

Golfer: *"Yes."*

JL (5):   *"Good. In this state, you're completely relaxed. Just keep like this for a few moments."* JL pauses for a minute or so to ensure the client is really relaxed and holds on to this state.

JL (6):   *"Now I want you to consider the situations where up to now you* have been *getting anxious* **(USE THE PAST TENSE!)***."* JL pauses while the client considers the golfing situations while in 'peripheral vision'. *"Tell me how you're feeling now."*

Golfer: *"Relaxed. It's OK – I can just get on with my game, choose the right shot and execute it well. I'm calm about it, not stressed."*

JL (7): *"Good. Now think of some other scenarios that previously might have made you feel anxious in some way. How do you feel now?"*

Golfer: *"Fine. No problem."*

JL (8): *"Great. Let's walk round the room* **(optional)** *while you tell me how it was for you doing this, and then I'll repeat the exercise. After that, I'd like you to do it by yourself enough times so that you can reproduce it when you need to – I won't be next to you on the fairway! By the time you've done it two or three times in this room, you'll be able to get into the state almost instantaneously.*

Just so that you know, once you're in peripheral vision and relaxed in this room you can lower your eyes as you would normally do when playing. During a match, any time you were to feel anxious, for example before a shot, you would do the process you've done in this room – it will only take a moment, and then you would be ready to start your shot."

Tip App 12

When in doubt, do less initially and build up, rather than doing too much and risk confusing the athlete. So for example, just do the process up to and including JL (5), ask the golfer about his experience and then repeat, adding in steps 6, 7 and 8.

Appendix 13

The Perceptual
Positions Technique

The technique works as follows. We will assume that you are a mental skills coach, fitness instructor or team manager coaching a client or player through a 'mis-understanding' with someone else. (Please remember that you can do the 'perceptual positions' technique with yourself if you are stuck or want to gain some more insights into someone else's thinking.) Let's assume that your player is called John, and the person with whom he has a conflict is called Alan.

Summary Steps:

1. Make sure you are in 'rapport', check ecology, explain the technique
2. Find out present and desired situations, and willingness to change
3. Mark out the three positions
4. Position 1 – 'what are you thinking and feeling, John?'
5. 'Break state'
6. Position 2 – 'what are you thinking and feeling, Alan?'
7. 'Break state'
8. Position 3 – 'what do you notice that they haven't noticed yet? What could they (especially John) do differently?'
9. Position 1 – 'How is that different now?' Recycle if necessary - always end in position 1
10. Test and future pace, and if appropriate gain a commitment from John for specific actions by specific dates

Here are the steps in more detail:

1. Identify the challenging situation that John has. Make sure you are in rapport, and have checked that it is ecological for you to work with John so that he can gain new insights into this challenge. Explain the process in overview. Check also there is no 'secondary gain' (benefits of keeping the situation as it currently is).

2. Get the 'scores on the doors', i.e. marks out of ten for how big the problem is, marks out of ten for where John would realistically like it to be, and how he would know he were there. Also, get the score (out of ten or 100) for how much John wants to move from the current score to the new desired score. NB. If John is anything less than ten out of ten or 100 percent willing for the situation to change, check for secondary gain (question 9 in the 'Keys To An Achievable Outcome' in Chapter 4) and ask him what would be the purpose of not moving from an unpleasant situation, even if it meant him changing his approach.

Tip App 13.1

If John is not 100 percent willing for the situation to change (and by implication willing to change his own approach), then you may need to 'reframe', for example, ask him how his life or sporting career will be in, say, five years' time, if things stay as they are compared to if John makes the necessary changes.

Also, it may be necessary to 'reframe' (i.e. turn a negative into a positive) the concept of 'changing'. Some people, (especially testosterone-filled young men!) feel that is in some way a sign of 'weakness' to change one's approach. Consider drawing the player's attention to how much courage or maturity (or whatever is appropriate for the situation you as the mental skills coach are in) it takes to change your approach to a situation if it will ultimately benefit you.

3. Mark out three positions, possibly with three chairs as shown in Diagram App 13.

Third Position

First Position   **Second Position**

Diagram App 13

4. Take John to position 1, and ask him, "As you look at Alan over there (gesturing to position 2), what are you thinking and what are you feeling?" Stand next to John. Notice his voice tonality and his physiology (posture, breathing). Keep him there for no more than one minute – one of the reasons he has this problem is because he is stuck in position 1 and cannot see other points of view, so there is no merit in asking him to stay there any longer than a minute!

5. Ask him to move from position 1, and do a 'break state'. A 'break state' is where the mental skills coach does or says something which leads the 'client' or 'player' changing his state of mind – clearly for John to see another perspective he would need to be out of the state of mind that he was in when he was in position 1. The 'coach' has 'carte blanche' when doing the break state. I often ask about the player's last or next holiday, or their favourite film, and engage them long enough so that they are clearly out of the mindset and state they were in at position 1. Typically, this lasts around 15 to 30 seconds.

6. Before taking John to position 2, where he 'becomes' Alan, check with John that it is acceptable to do that (see point 6

of the Tip at the end of this appendix for what to do if it is not acceptable). Refer to John as Alan, asking him to stand or sit as he (Alan) normally would. Ask 'Alan', "when you look at John over there (gesturing to position 1), what are you thinking and feeling?"

Listen and possibly make a few notes. (Make sure that there is the appropriate language, i.e. when Alan says "you", he means 'John', and when he says "I" or "me" he means 'Alan'.) Keep asking, "what else (are you thinking and feeling)?" Normally, there will be some interesting 'insights' as you hear 'Alan' say things that suggest that there is another side to the story. Keep going until there are no more useful comments coming from 'Alan'.

7. Break state (see step 5 above).

8. Ask John to go to position 3, where John is a neutral observer from a distance, a wise sage, with a bird's eye view of the situation. Sometimes it is useful for you and John to stand on a chair to gain this overview (make sure it is safe to do so and that the player is comfortable doing so!). Ask the neutral observer questions like:

   ◆ "from this detached position, what do you notice about the situation of those two people John and Alan over there (or down there)?"
   ◆ "what could they do differently to change the situation?"
   ◆ "what could John do to change things (and what impact would that have on Alan?)"
   ◆ "what could Alan do (and what impact would that have on John)?"
   ◆ "what options can you see for them that they have not thought of?"
   ◆ "what could they say to each other – (what could John say to Alan)?"
   ◆ "what advice would you give them?"
   ◆ "what advice would you give John?"

   Make notes of the answers that are relevant, for example options for John or things for him to do, or conversations for him to have.

NB. Although you as the mental skills coach need to be neutral in this exercise and particularly in position 3, clearly this exercise works best when 'John' realises that there are some things he can do differently. Therefore the coach would probably bias his questions towards what John could do differently. Keep in position 3 until there have been sufficient learnings for John, and sufficient new options or things for him to do that would move the situation forward.

9. Take John to position 1 (there is probably no need for a break state, as you would want John to retain this new mindset). Ask John, "how is this different now?" (Notice the physiology and voice tonality, compare it to how it was at step 4, the first time he was in position 1.) Ask for the 'scores on the doors'. Ask John what he will do, what actions he will take to move the situation forward.

   NB. If the desired score was, say two out of ten, and the score had reduced from, say 'nine' to a 'four, firstly acknowledge John (and yourself!) for the big movement. Seek incremental changes. Ask "what would it take to get to a 'three'?" Check the score – if it is a 'three', ask, "what would take it a 'two'?" It may also be useful to re-visit position 2 and/or 3 as necessary. Always end in position 1.

   It will normally be appropriate for the player to take some action - make sure that he commits to what he will do and by when.

10. Remind John of the actions he has committed to. Check how he is feeling about future situation(s) and interaction(s) with Alan compared to how it was 15 minutes or so ago (the exercise typically takes only 15 minutes).

Tip App 13.2

There are several things for the mental skills coach to do to help make the 'perceptual positions' exercise very effective.

1. Make sure that the player uses the appropriate language for the position he is in (e.g. 'he', 'she', 'they' when in position 3).

2. Avoid the temptation to make suggestions or offer advice. Be patient enough to allow the player to find his own answers. It is more empowering for him if he comes up with his own solutions, and he cannot resist or argue with his own advice, whereas he can argue with or resist yours!

3. Be next to the player in the three positions, standing if he stands, seated if he sits. Maintain rapport at all times.

4. Start and end in position 1.

5. Be creative if necessary – create a position 4 if the player is not sufficiently dissociated in position 3.

6. If it is not appropriate to take the player into position 2 after position 1, go to position 3 after position 1 and then to position 2. Always end in position 1.

7. If it is not appropriate to move around into three different physical positions, it is completely possibly and effective to use this technique whilst you and the player remain where you are. It becomes especially important to break state in this scenario.

Further Reference Material

Here is a list of further reference material and resources.

Books and handbooks:

Topic	Reference
Fundamental Filters and Values	Shelle Rose Charvet. *Words That Change Minds*. Kendall/Hunt Publishing
Personality Traits	David Keirsey and Marilyn Bates. *Please Understand Me – Character & Temperament Types*. Gnosology Books Ltd
Submodalities	Richard Bandler. *Using Your Brain For A Change*. Real People Press
Submodalities	Steve Andreas and Connirae Andreas. *Change Your Mind And Keep The Change*. Real People Press
General NLP	Romilla Ready and Kate Burton. *Neuro Linguistic Programming For Dummies*. Wiley
General NLP	Joseph O'Connor and Ian McDermott. *Principles of NLP*. Thorsons
General NLP	Joseph O'Connor. *NLP Workbook*. Element (HarperCollins)
General NLP	Gillian Burn. *NLP Pocketbook*. Management Pocketbooks Ltd
General NLP	The Lazarus Consultancy. *The NLP Pocket Handbook*. Available from The Lazarus Consultancy Ltd – www.thelazarus.com

Topic	Reference
Mind-Body Link	Deepak Chopra M.D. *Quantum Healing.* Bantam
Mind-Body Link	Robert Dilts, Tim Hallbom & Suzi Smith. *Beliefs – Pathways to Health & Well-Being.* Metamorphous Press
Mental Aspects of Sport	David Hemery. *Sporting Excellence – What Makes A Champion?* CollinsWillow
Mental Aspects of Sport	Kenneth Baum with Richard Trubo. *The Mental Edge – Maximise Your Sports Potential with the Mind-Body Connection.* The Berkley Publishing Group
Mental Aspects of Sport	Gary Mack with David Casstevens. *Mind Gym – An Athletes Guide To Inner Excellence.* Contemporary Books
Mental Aspects of Sport	Jeff Grout & Sarah Perrin. *Mind Games – Inspirational Lessons From The World's Biggest Sports Stars.* Capstone
Mental Aspects of Sport	W. Timothy Gallwey. *The Inner Game Of Tennis.* Pan Books
Sports Psychology	Lew Hardy, Graham Jones and Daniel Gould. *Understanding Psychological preparation For Sport – Theory and Practice of Elite Performers.* Wiley.

CDs

The following CDs are available from The Lazarus Consultancy, covering most of the topics contained in this book.

1. NLP Practitioner CD Series

A 16 CD set, lasting 12 hours, with a fully-referenced training manual. This comprises the pre-study material for The Lazarus Consultancy Fast-Track NLP Practitioner Course.

2. Understanding, Predicting and Influencing Behaviour - Four CD Series

A 4 CD set, lasting 4½ hours, covering the 'values' and 'fundamental filters' topics referred to in this book plus a lot more, with a fully-referenced manual.

3. Understanding, Predicting and Influencing Behaviour - Six CD NLP Series

A 6 CD set, lasting 6 hours, covering the 'values' and 'fundamental filters' referred to in this book, plus a fully-referenced manual. In addition, the CDs cover how to change 'values' and 'fundamental filters', and for that reason are of relevance mainly to NLP Practitioners and Master Practitioners.

It is the intention of the author to produce a set of CDs for mental skills coaches and sports coaches, and players/athletes. Contact the author or visit www.thelazarus.com for further details and updated information.

Training Courses

The Lazarus Consultancy Ltd offers several courses related to mental skills coaching and NLP, for example:

- ◆ Fast-Track Certified NLP Practitioner
- ◆ Fast-Track Certified NLP Master Practitioner
- ◆ Fast-Track Certified NLP Sports Practitioner
- ◆ Certified NLP Diploma
- ◆ Certified NLP Sports Diploma
- ◆ Understanding, Predicting & Influencing Behaviour (covering 'fundamental filters' and 'values')
- ◆ Introduction to NLP courses, for business, coaching and sport.

Contact the author or visit www.thelazarus.com for further details and updated information.

Glossary

Anchor: A stimulus that leads to a consistent or repeated emotional response.

Anchoring: The process by which any representation, internal or external (the stimulus), gets connected and linked to and triggers a subsequent emotional responses. Anchors can be naturally occurring or set up deliberately.

Associated: The relationship we have with an experience or a past event (memory) or future event. Experiencing a situation as if it were happening now, looking through our own eyes, hearing the sounds and feeling the feelings.

At Cause: Having the mindset of taking responsibility for the results of one's actions and one's results in life.

At Effect: Having the mindset that one's results and state of mind are dependent on others and external factors.

Beliefs: Generalisations we make about the world and our opinions about it. Those convictions we hold as being true. They often form the rules we have about what we can and cannot do.

Circle of Excellence: Using an imaginary circle on the floor as a 'spatial anchor' to install new or additional resources in a situation where different behaviour or thinking is wanted.

Collapsing Anchors: The process of replacing a negative anchor with a positive anchor, giving us more choice of behaviour in future similar situations.

Conscious Mind: The element of our mind that we are aware of, normally that which does, for example, logical thinking and planning.

Deletion: One of the three major filtering processes (including Distortion and Generalisation). Deletion occurs when we leave out a portion of our experience as we make our Internal Representations.

Dissociated: The relationship we have with an experience or a past event (memory) or future event. Experiencing the situation as if seeing or watching ourselves in a film.

Distortion: One of the three major processes (including Deletion and Generalisation). Distortion occurs when something is mistaken for that which it is not, when things are incorrectly included in our Internal Representations.

Ecology: The study of the consequences or results or impact of any change that occurs on the wider system. For example, what are the implications on the partner or family if the player becomes even more successful.

Fundamental Filters: These are unconscious, content-free programs and thinking patterns we run which filter our experiences.

Future Pace: Asking an athlete to imagine situations and scenarios in the future which they had been not looking forward to, or which if they had happened in the past would have caused them problems. This is done after the mental skills coach has 'tested' whether change work has been successful. A future pace has a similar affect to mentally rehearsing success.

Generalisation: One of the three major processes (including Distortion and Deletion). Generalisation occurs when one specific experience represents a whole class of experiences. Generalisation also occurs when one experience is generalised to the whole.

Internal Representations: The content of our thinking or the formation of information which includes pictures, sounds, feelings, tastes, smells, and self-talk.

Limiting Beliefs: Beliefs or decisions we make about ourselves, and/or the world, that limit the way we live or the results we achieve.

Logical Levels: A model by which we can structure our thinking. There are six levels – Purpose, Identity, Beliefs and Values, Capability, Behaviours and Environment. Generally, changing one of the 'higher' levels will impact on the levels below it.

Mapping Across: Mapping Across is the submodality process of actually changing the set of submodalities of a certain Internal Representation (food, drink, activity etc) into that of another Internal Representation (food, drink, activity etc) to change its meaning (for example, changing a food you like into a food you don't like).

Matching: See Rapport. Doing the same, copying or adopting the behaviour of the client or replicating some aspect of a person's physiology or voice tonality.

Mental Rehearsal: Preparing for an event or competition in our mind, by seeing, hearing and feeling (and possibly even tasting and smelling) what will be happening in that future event.

Meta Program: See Fundamental Filters.

Modality: Representational system.

Modelling: In Modelling we elicit the strategies, Beliefs, Values and Fundamental Filters, and the 'physiology' that allows someone to produce a certain behaviour. Then we codify these in a series of steps designed to make the behaviour easy to reproduce.

NLP: NLP is the study of excellence, which describes how the language of our mind produces our behaviour, and allows us to model excellence and to reproduce that excellent behaviour. There are a series of techniques which have been developed within NLP to help people make changes to have more of what they want and less of what they don't want.

NLP Qualifications: Within the NLP world there are three main levels of qualification – NLP Practitioner, NLP Master Practitioner and NLP Trainer. Certified Trainers are authorised not just to work with individual clients, but also to train and certify Practitioners and Master Practitioners.

Generally, NLP Practitioners are trained to be able to use NLP techniques effectively with 'clients'. NLP Master Practitioners receive further training and learn additional techniques, and are expected to demonstrate greater flexibility and fluidity with NLP techniques. Trainers take this level of knowledge even further, not just being required to be able to do the techniques but also to teach them.

PB (Personal Best): An individual athlete's best performance in their event.

Perceptual Positions: Describes the point of view in a specific situation. 'First position' or 'position 1' is our own point of view. 'Second position' or 'position 2' is usually someone else's point of view. 'Third position' or 'position 3' is the point of view of a dissociated, neutral observer.

Peripheral Vision: The area of vision which surrounds the main area of our focus. There is a technique to use Peripheral Vision which allows us to be in a calm, relaxed state.

NLP Presuppositions: A series of convenient beliefs that underpin much of the work done in NLP and, when we operate from those beliefs and as if those beliefs are true, we will normally get better results.

Rapport: The ability to relate to others in a way that creates a climate of trust and understanding. Rapport can be built by Matching.

Reframing: The process of making a shift in the nature of a problem or changing the structure or context of a statement to give it another meaning. Turning a negative into a positive.

Representational System: This is the way we code sensory information and experience our world. There is a representational system for each of our senses – visual, auditory, kinaesthetic, olfactory and gustatory.

Resource Anchor: An 'Anchor' with a series of positive states attached to it, so that we can have access to these states whenever we want or need to.

Ring of Power: See Circle of Excellence.

Secondary Gain: The reason someone has or reward someone receives for not changing from the current situation.

State: Our internal emotional condition at any given moment.

Submodalities: These are finer distinctions (or subsets) of the Modalities (Visual, Auditory, Kinaesthetic, Olfactory, Gustatory, and Auditory Digital) that are part of each Representational System that encode and give meaning to our experiences. Changing the submodalities of an experience will change its meaning.

Testing: Asking the athlete about the situation(s) which were 'problems' to check whether the 'change work' has been effective. See also Future Pacing.

Unconscious Mind: The part of your mind that you are not consciously aware of. The unconscious mind runs our body, including doing the sporting tasks that form part of our sport (throwing, jumping etc).

Values: What is important to us or what we want in a certain context. Values vary by context – what is important to us in sport may not be what is important to us in a job or a car. Values are a key to motivation.

Visualisation: See Mental Rehearsal. Some people refer to Mental Rehearsal as Visualisation. Strictly speaking, Visualisation only covers the visual Representational System, whereas Mental Rehearsal covers any or all of them.

Well-Formed Outcome: A goal that is stated in such a way that it is far more likely to be achieved, because the language and principles of the goal conforms to certain tried and tested concepts.

Index

Note: Glossary items are indicated by page numbers in *italic*.

Lightning Source UK Ltd.
Milton Keynes UK
26 February 2010

150648UK00001B/15/A